New Perspectives in German Studies

General Editors: Professor Michael Butler, Head of the Department of German Studies, University of Birmingham and Professor William Paterson, Director of the Institute of German Studies, University of Birmingham

Over the last twenty years the concept of German studies has undergone major transformation. The traditional mixture of language and literary studies, related very closely to the discipline as practised in German universities, has expanded to embrace history, politics, economics and cultural studies. The conventional boundaries between all these disciplines have become increasingly blurred, a process which has been accelerated markedly since German unification in 1989/90.

New Perspectives in German Studies, developed in conjunction with the Institute for German Studies at the University of Birmingham, has been designed to respond precisely to this trend of the interdisciplinary approach to the study of German and to cater to the growing interest in Germany in the context of European integration. The books in this series will focus on the modern period, from 1750 to the present day.

Titles include:

Peter Bleses and Martin Seeleib-Kaiser
THE DUAL TRANSFORMATION OF THE GERMAN WELFARE STATE

Michael Butler and Robert Evans (*editors*)
THE CHALLENGE OF GERMAN CULTURE
Essays Presented to Wilfried van der Will

Michael Butler, Malcolm Pender and Joy Charnley (*editors*)
THE MAKING OF MODERN SWITZERLAND 1848–1998

Paul Cooke and Andrew Plowman (*editors*)
GERMAN WRITERS AND THE POLITICS OF CULTURE
Dealing with the Stasi

Wolf-Dieter Eberwein and Karl Kaiser (*editors*)
GERMANY'S NEW FOREIGN POLICY
Decision-Making in an Interdependent World

Jonathan Grix
THE ROLE OF THE MASSES IN THE COLLAPSE OF THE GDR

Margarete Kohlenbach
WALTER BENJAMIN
Self-Reference and Religiosity

James Sloam
THE EUROPEAN POLICY OF THE GERMAN SOCIAL DEMOCRATS
Interpreting a Changing World

Henning Tewes
GERMANY, CIVILIAN POWER AND THE NEW EUROPE
Enlarging Nato and European Union

Maiken Umbach
GERMAN FEDERALISM
Past, Present, Future

New Perspectives in German Studies
Series Standing Order ISBN 0–333–92430–4 hardcover
Series Standing Order ISBN 0–333–92434–7 paperback
(*outside North America only*)

You can receive future titles in this series as they are published by placing a standing order. Please contact your bookseller or, in case of difficulty, write to us at the address below with your name and address, the title of the series and the ISBN quoted above.

Customer Services Department, Macmillan Distribution Ltd, Houndmills, Basingstoke, Hampshire RG21 6XS, England

The European Policy of the German Social Democrats

Interpreting a Changing World

James Sloam
Lecturer in European Studies,
King's College, London

First published 2005 by
PALGRAVE MACMILLAN
Houndmills, Basingstoke, Hampshire RG21 6XS and
175 Fifth Avenue, New York, N.Y. 10010
Companies and representatives throughout the world.

PALGRAVE MACMILLAN is the global academic imprint of the Palgrave Macmillan division of St. Martin's Press, LLC and of Palgrave Macmillan Ltd. Macmillan® is a registered trademark in the United States, United Kingdom and other countries. Palgrave is a registered trademark in the European Union and other countries.

ISBN 1–4039–3581–5

This book is printed on paper suitable for recycling and made from fully managed and sustained forest sources.

A catalogue record for this book is available from the British Library.

Library of Congress Cataloging-in-Publication Data

Sloam, James.
    The European policy of the German Social Democrats : interpreting a changing world / James Sloam.
        p. cm. — (New perspectives in German studies)
    Includes bibliographical references and index.
    ISBN 1–4039–3581–5
        1. Sozialdemokratische Partei Deutschlands – Platforms. 2. European Union – Germany. 3. Political planning – European Union countries. 4. Germany – History – Unification, 1990. I. Title. II. New perspectives in German studies (Palgrave Macmillan (Firm))

JN3971.A98S62453 2004
341.242′2—dc22   2004052592

10 9 8 7 6 5 4 3 2 1
14 13 12 11 10 09 08 07 06 05

Printed and bound in Great Britain by
Antony Rowe Ltd, Chippenham and Eastbourne.

To Debra, for her love and support

Contents

List of Tables and Figures

Tables

Figures

Acknowledgements

I am indebted to a large number of individuals and organisations, who/which have provided advice and support and have contributed to the analyses included in this study and have made the writing of the book a more rewarding experience than it would otherwise have been:

- The ESRC for the financial support it has provided for the writing of the book.
- Professor William Paterson, whose knowledge and expertise contributed immensely to this study (following on from his groundbreaking PhD 30 years earlier), and whose contacts proved invaluable during the research fieldwork.
- Professor Charlie Jeffery and Dr Jonathan Grix who at various times provided extremely important comments on my work.
- Debra Bolger, Peter Hill, Alister Miskimmon and Brian Sloam, for their comments and suggestions on the amendments to the chapters.
- The staff in the Archiv der Sozialen Demokratie for their friendly assistance and the Friedrich Ebert Stiftung in Bonn for giving me access to indispensable archive material and a place to work.
- The Deutsche Gesellschaft für Auswärtige Politik for the assistance of their staff, and for providing me with the resources with which to conduct my fieldwork in Berlin.
- The Archiv/Dokumentation Department of the SPD *Vorstand* in Berlin for allowing me to work in their offices and giving me access to their archives of SPD policy documents and press coverage of the party.
- All of the many interviewees, particularly the politicians and officials in the SPD, whose thoughts and guidance were an essential part of the work.
- To all the staff at the Institute for German Studies for their advice and guidance.
- To my mum and dad, without whom none of this would have been possible.

Introduction

The purpose of this study is to examine the course of European Union (EU) policy in the German Social Democratic Party (SPD) from 1990 up until the end of 2003. In the late 1980s and early 1990s the SPD was characterised by 'loosely coupled anarchy',[1] a term referring to its organisational, ideological and strategic pluralism. This anarchy also manifested itself in the party's EU policy in the mid 1990s, as illustrated by the fight for control of this policy area at the Mannheim party conference in November 1995 (Chapter 8). At this point, there was little evidence to suggest that the SPD would rise from inner-party conflict to form the next government of Germany. There was equally little sign of the party establishing the contours of a cohesive policy on Europe. The destination of EU policy was nevertheless a detailed, comprehensive and *pragmatic* 'vision' of the Union, which provided a synthesis of the views of key domestic and European actors and the different positions within the SPD, characterised by the European policy motion drafted for the party's 2001 conference, 'Responsibility for Europe'.[2]

The aim of the following work is to examine the European policy[3] of the SPD since reunification against the backdrop of significant geopolitical and socioeconomic change in Germany and a rapidly changing European environment. Recent academic literature has typically focused on the European policy of German governments under Kohl (1982–98) and Schröder (after coming to power in 1998). While the amount of literature dealing with the German Social Democrats has been small,[4] there have been no independent and comprehensive accounts of SPD European policy in the 1990s.[5] This study will investigate continuity and change in SPD policy through the 1990s and into the new millennium (in opposition and government) through the lens of the party on the 'federal' (national) plane.[6]

SPD European policy since reunification will be analysed through four broad periods of change: first, policy formation in opposition in the early 1990s which was characterised by strategic and programmatic pluralism; second, a period in the mid-1990s when raging battles within the party leadership were mirrored by a confused European policy; next, from 1996 to 1998, when the SPD European policy groups developed a more coherent policy *linked* to issues of domestic interest; and, finally, policy formation through a new, more structured framework of pressures and influences in government. The SPD offers an opportunity to examine EU policy from both an *outsider* (of government) and *insider* perspective with regard to the interpretation of 'national interests'. The party has been freer, during its years in opposition, to respond to dramatic changes in the context of German European policy, to construct new concepts for the pursuit of German interests. The introduction will, first, look at the 'background to change', the key events that have led to a reassessment of Germany's objectives in Europe since unification. It will, then, set out the role of the different chapters in the book, highlighting the central hypotheses of the study captured in Figure I.1, which explain the European policy of the German Social Democrats as the party has tried to interpret a changing world.

Political Climate: main issues – the regeneration of eastern Germany/ the state of the German economy, the *proximity* of eastern Europe, and the implictions of EU and global integation.

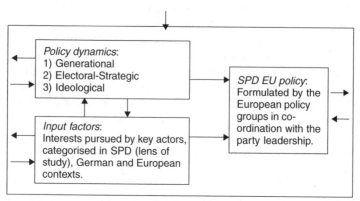

Figure I.1 Model for SPD EU policy since reunification

Background of change

In drawing a distinction between the EU policy of the SPD and German policy in general, this study will demonstrate that a more confident Germany has emerged from its Cold War divisions, overcoming the institutionalised practice of self-restraint depicted by Peter Katzenstein.[7] Unity nevertheless placed pressure on Germany's commitment to European integration. By the mid-1990s, the country was struggling to cope with decreasing economic growth rates, increasing unemployment and a burgeoning national debt incurred by the cost of renewing the economy in the new 'Bundesländer' (federal states) amid a global recession (see Chapter 2). Helmut Kohl's drive towards embedding Germany in a European economic-monetary and political union gradually came to undermine his domestic position, since it was supposed that he was neglecting a faltering domestic economy while pursuing Monetary Union at an overly rapid pace. Kohl's *euro-idealism* was not shared by the German public. In the year the Maastricht Treaty came into force (1993), only 32 per cent of Germans supported a Single Currency.[8]

The geopolitical location of Germany, furthermore, was radically altered (Chapter 2). The fall of the Iron Curtain relocated the Federal Republic from the eastern end of a highly integrated Western Europe, to the centre of a Europe open to the possibilities of economic and political integration. This resulted in the need to establish new relationships with both Russia and the former Soviet-bloc countries of Eastern Europe, which was reinforced – in both a psychological and a physical sense – by the move of government from Bonn to Berlin. The focus of EU policy for Germany became blurred between a *deepening* of the existing European Community (EC), and the need to politically stabilise and economically energise Central and Eastern Europe – to draw it into an expanded European Union. German politicians in all mainstream parties at that time claimed that deeper integration and enlargement could be achieved simultaneously, though popular feeling remained sceptical, deeming it to be an 'either ... or ...' scenario.

While the post-unity SPD tended to favour a broad cross-party consensus on EC affairs, it nevertheless concentrated more than its Christian Democrat (CDU/CSU) rivals on domestic issues (e.g. unemployment). The new generation of SPD leaders (not alive or very young during the last World War) that emerged in the 1990s felt freer than their predecessors to address EU politics with a greater emphasis on *domestic demands* or what were considered to be 'German interests' (see Chapter 5). The furtherance of European integration for its own sake was no longer good enough. They advocated a return to 'normality' in German foreign policy, which would bind the details of EU policy more closely to tangible benefits for the country. By normality they meant the wish to behave, within the European Union, like other large Member States. This development was not unique to the SPD, since these views were gathering pace in the country as a whole. Some in the Government coalition parties also wished for a return to this kind of normality. The presence of Helmut Kohl and his dominance of European policy, however, kept these ideas corked in the bottle, for a time at least.

The wish for a less restrained approach was backed by public opinion: '62% of those polled by *Emnid* believed that Germany's past should no longer play such an important role in relations with other countries ... 65% also stated that Germany should assume a leading role in Europe'.[9] One concrete example of the change in *style* since the election of the SPD in 1998 has been the way in which the new German Government has pursued a symbolic reduction in the country's contribution to the EU budget. Although not a vast amount compared with departmental expenditure in the domestic budget, Germany's *net contribution* set it out as the undisputed *paymaster* of the Union.[10] Yet when push came to shove, the German EU Council Presidency in the first half of 1999, emphasised the country's *softer* interests in multilateral negotiations rather than *narrower* materialistic goals that might scupper the chances of an agreement.[11] The new EU budget was agreed upon at the Berlin European Council (March 1999), when the SPD-led Government admitted that they had put the health of the EU as a whole before more short-term material considerations. Chancellor Schröder (SPD) underlined that, in the shadow of the Kosovo crisis and the resignation of the EU Commission a few weeks earlier, it was equally important that 'Europe speaks with one voice'.[12]

This work will contribute to the understanding of how European policy is formed and executed, with specific relevance to Germany and the SPD but also to the study of European policy in political parties as a whole. Work will centre on the perception of German *interests* in the SPD, and their pursuit of these interests. During the period studied, Germany was at an important juncture in its relationship with Europe, given the need for reassessment brought about by reunification, the end of the Cold War and the challenges faced with regard to European Economic and Monetary Union and the eastern enlargement of the EU. The SPD, in opposition at the federal level through the 1990s until its election in 1998, was in a position of relative freedom to respond to these changes, given the tighter constraints incumbent upon the government parties. In the past, Germany has worked in the engine room of European integration, but with the fading historical resonance of the War and the relative malaise of the domestic economy, the SPD-led German Government has stated that it is no longer satisfactory for policy to be based on what the country *should do*, but on what it *wants to do* in the reality of a deeply integrated EU. In his inauguration speech in November 1998, Chancellor Schröder called for

> a self-confidence of a grown-up nation that doesn't have to feel superior or inferior to anyone, that accepts its history and responsibility – but is forward looking.[13]

While most other literature has concentrated on European policy in Germany as a governmental or interest group tool, this study will provide an analysis of the mechanisms of policy formation and its expression in an individual political party through opposition into government within the broader context of multifarious policy pressures. Viewed through the lens of the SPD, this book will provide an important insight into the factors that influence EU policy, and the manner in which it is prioritised in both Germany and the European Union today. It will therefore provide important empirical data on European policy formation in an era of *Europeanisation*[14] for the governing party in the largest EU Member State.

Interpreting a changing world

The book begins with an exploration of the theoretical framework for SPD European policy (Chapter 1). Here, three factors are key to defining the strategic alternatives for policy-making. First, the established patterns of German and SPD European policy prior to 1990 set the scene, and are used as a base for the examination of policy after German unification. Next, German and SPD European policy is placed within the context of the pressures and constraints of German policy at the EU level (as viewed from *realist* and *multilateralist* perspectives), and the channels of power through which policy goals have been pursued. Third, Chapter 1 investigates the changing function of political parties in general and the SPD in particular with respect to party organisation (structures), ideology, and (electoral) strategy. This presents a general framework for policy formation in the party (Figure 1.2). Finally, the chapter defines SPD European policy in the twenty-first century as 'pragmatic multilateralism', a term used to describe the adaptability of the party leadership to the changing nature of the environment for European policy.This concept is utilised in the study of SPD European policy, focusing on Economic and Monetary Union (EMU) (Chapters 8 and 9) and the eastern enlargement of the EU (Chapters 10 and 11).

Chapter 2 examines the altered socioeconomic and geopolitical climate since 1990 that has created a new environment for the formation of European policy (Figure I.1). Three changes have led to a substantive alteration of the constellation of German interests in the EU. First, the regeneration of the East German economy has not yet provided the 'blühende Landschaften' (flourishing landscapes) Chancellor Kohl had foreseen. The cost of integrating East Germany added to the effects of a worldwide economic recession in the early 1990s, placing a heavy burden on the German economy. This led to questions being raised about the large German payments to the EU budget. The pressure increased on German governments to prioritise domestic economic issues more highly relative to their European policy goals. The psychological impact of full sovereignty, in addition, challenged German perceptions of the EU and other Member States' perceptions of Germany (e.g. the UK and France). Simultaneously, Germany was also relocated in its 'Mittellage' (central position) in Europe, which gave the country strong interests in securing the stability of and trade with the former Eastern Block states, and opened up the prospect of an eastern enlargement of the EU. The acceleration of European integration in the late 1980s and early 1990s further impacted upon the policy environment. On the one hand, greater interdependency led to the *Europeanisation* of German interests. On the other hand, European policy came into contact (and into conflict with) key areas of domestic policy, which altered the *rules of the game* for national governments and office-seeking political parties. Finally, 'globalisation', as perceived by politicians and parties, influenced the development of EU policy, as politicians increasingly saw the European Union as a battleground for the promotion of their favoured socioeconomic models.

Chapters 3 and 4 deal with the mechanics of policy formation in the SPD and the main actors and structures that together constitute the 'policy context'. On the *input* side of the equation (Figure I.1) a number of actors emerge as influential. The party does not behave as a homogenous actor in the formulation of its European policy and must, therefore, be examined as a context in itself. In the institutional context, the party leadership, in combination with the SPD's European policy groups, has dominated EU policy (Chapter 3). The number of elite level politicians interested in European affairs has nevertheless increased with the growing penetration of EU politics into areas previously reserved for domestic policy (*Europeanisation*). National political and socioeconomic structures are crucial for contextualising SPD policy. In terms of the national context, the SPD is a relatively open institution. The party has favoured certain groups (e.g. the unions), but these ties are flexible, and may vary according to the *opposition–government paradigm* (Chapter 4). The European context is also crucial, though the difference on this plane between opposition and government is especially great. With the advances in European integration, for instance, the importance of the SPD's social democratic sister parties, the EU Commission and member-state governments, in the formulation of policy has grown rapidly. Alistair Cole has written in his analysis of the French Socialist Party that 'party acts as a filter' (termed a 'lens' in this study – Figure I.1), through which policy can be examined.[15] The SPD is the central focus of this study, which formulates its policy within the *structured context*[16] of actors and structures within the institutional, national and European policy contexts.

Three *dynamics* have particular weight in an analysis of SPD EU policy, defining continuity and change in party policy (Figure I.1). There was a definite attempt after the Second World War to submerge German identity in a European identity as payment for past sins and to ensure a peaceful future. Although the SPD under the leadership of Kurt Schumacher (1949–53) did not share these submissive views about national identity, the party soon accepted the de-emphasis of national policy as a practical necessity for German foreign policy. By the 1990s, *exaggerated multilateralism* had become an institutionalised feature of German policy, which had succeeded in integrating Germany into the international community. The first internal dynamic, addressed in Chapter 5, is the emergence of a new *generation* of SPD leaders born during or after the War, many of who were involved in the radical student movement of the late 1960s.[17] After the resignation of Hans-Jochen Vogel in 1991, Björn Engholm became the first SPD chairman from a younger generation.[18] The rise of the 'Enkel'[19] (grandchildren) was in marked contrast to the domination of the Christian Democrat-led coalition by older politicians. It allowed the party greater freedom to consider the implications of German unification, the end of the Cold War and a more fundamentally integrated EU. The new generation acted as *political entrepreneurs* who could effect change at this window of opportunity or 'critical juncture' in German history.[20] The SPD-Green Government has been, thus, more willing than its predecessors to question the need to accommodate its EU partners' fears of domination, whilst aiming to achieve a more *normal* foreign policy (similar to other Members States).[21] Commitment to European integration is now seen in a more 'pragmatic' light, in terms of German interests. This is not to say that the emergence of the *generation of '68* led to a smooth break with the past. Criticism of Germany's high levels of payments to the EU budget, for example, was generally frowned upon by the party at the federal level in the early 1990s, but – by the time the SPD came to power in 1998 – the issue of 'budgetary justice' was almost unanimously seen as a cornerstone of European policy. The new generation, while in favour of European integration in general, felt less bound by the traditional patterns of post-war German European policy: 'We Germans ought to be backing full integration because we want it and believe in it, not because people must fear otherwise. We must not have a bad conscience about Europe. To say we want it because we don't trust ourselves unsettles people.'[22]

Chapter 6 analyses a second dynamic concerned with *electoral-strategic change* (Figure I.1). The SPD became more *responsive* to public opinion through the 1990s as part of an overall strategy to interact with the various domestic actors outlined in Chapter 3. This was a transition led by the party's leaders, and lay in stark contrast to the CDU in the late 1990s, which appeared to be much more old-fashioned in its campaigning and out of touch with the public mood. Electoral-strategic change was largely a product of the SPD leadership's increasingly urgent quest for power and a broad electoral coalition in the context of *voter dealignment* and a more heterogeneous electorate. It was also the result of the comprehensive penetration of the media into politics in recent years. In this respect, the SPD resembles the centre-left Democratic and Labour parties in the US and the UK respectively.[23] The media-friendly approach pioneered by the Clinton election team in the early 1990s took great pains, through focus groups and surveys, to keep abreast of public opinion, and to respond to this opinion.[24] The impact of this on European policy was to encourage the SPD leadership to respond to the concerns of domestic actors over such issues as the EU budget and Monetary Union (often resisted by the party's European policy groups), occasionally spilling over into the populist outbursts described in Chapter 6. As the SPD became a more effective opposition party the range of 'social participants' that they 'listened to' gradually broadened. This meant both interest groups and the public, though – in opposition – the electorate was the particular focus for the party machine. Here the abrasive tone of SPD policy was softened as the party sought to portray itself as a credible party of government. In power, even the most domestic-oriented members of the party leadership came to recognise the importance of EU-level actors (something the party's European experts had always factored into the European policy equation), so that policy was seen more in terms of Germany's *Europeanised* interests. Finally, the SPD's EU policy has been defined by the party's *ideology* (Chapter 7). It is evident that SPD ideology is not one simple, coherent strand. The length of time needed to agree to the Berlin Programme of 1989 (five years), demonstrated the difficulty of producing a synthesis between the traditional left-right paradigm and the emergent *postmodern* and *ecological* ('New Left') dimension in the party. The SPD most often sought to emphasise employment and workers' rights during the 1990s. After the resignation of Oskar Lafontaine as party chairman and Finance Minister (March 1999), the party at the federal level became increasingly dominated by the *Neue Mitte* group headed by Chancellor Schröder. The *Neue Mitte* has a more *centrist* ideology, focused on 'equality of opportunity' rather than 'equality of outcomes', embodied in the party's 'Agenda 2010' reforms developed in 2002 and 2003. In European policy terms, it is necessary to emphasise that the rapid pace of European integration, and the penetration of European politics into domestic politics, has meant that the SPD's domestic policy programme has had to be transposed onto the EU stage. This culminated in the synthesis of differing positions within the party and of domestic and European policy programmes in its 2001 Responsibility for Europe paper, which became the lead issue in the SPD's 2002 *programme for government*.

The arguments contained in this book can be summarised by four central hypotheses:

1. The dynamism in SPD European policy since 1990 has been characterised by a new generation of party leaders more willing to assert what they see as German interests; a party strategy that has become more 'responsive' to a widening range of 'domestic actors' and, particularly in government, 'European actors'; and, an ideology increasingly adapted to an EU polity that has deeply penetrated into erstwhile domestic policy fields.
2. The changes in SPD European policy since 1990 have reflected the changing views of actors within the institutional (SPD), national and EU contexts. Their modified positions have been conditioned by 'climatic changes' in the policy environment (e.g. German unification, European integration).
3. The EU policy of the SPD leadership at the beginning of the twenty-first century is defined by 'pragmatic multilateralism' (see Chapter 1) in

three respects: with regard to its keenness to pursue 'German interests' ('generational change'), to engage with actors on the institutional, domestic and European planes ('electoral-strategic change'), and to adapt its policies to increasingly Europeanised German interests ('ideological change').

4. A synthesis of the views of different European policy actors and of EU and domestic policy was achieved within the SPD in the form of an overarching European policy strategy in the party's most recent European policy review (2000–01).

The study, in short, investigates whether a new generation of leaders in government in Germany have managed to free themselves from the constraints of German *semi-sovereignty*, given the effects of *strategic* and *ideological* change. SPD European policy has shown a great degree of continuity, and is determined to seek German interests through further integration and enlargement of the EU. The party has nevertheless pursued objectives tailored to an altered domestic policy environment, and aimed to achieve them in a more strident manner (similar to other large countries): a policy that was not afraid to see German participation in NATO operations in Kosovo or risk antagonising Germany's closest partners in pursuit of a smaller contribution to the EU budget.

Part I

European Policy in a Changing World

1

Grounding European Policy: Policy, Power and Parties

The first chapter performs the important task of grounding SPD European policy in theory, locating the study within existing bodies of literature. This is achieved through an examination of three dimensions that together help us to understand the strategic alternatives for the party within the context of *established patterns* of European policy, the pursuit of German policy in Europe (*channels of power*), and the changing nature of political parties. The chapter starts by examining the policy framework for (West) Germany and the SPD since the establishment of the Federal Republic, illustrating the established patterns of European policy in place prior to reunification. It argues that German policy at the point of unification was identified by *exaggerated multilateralism* and an associated tendency to solve problems by donating extra funds to the EC coffers in deference to partner states (especially France). SPD policy at this time was firmly embedded in a cross-party consensus on European policy. This state of affairs was called into question by the *climatic changes* described in Chapter 2. Second, the chapter investigates the nature of German policy-making and the exercise of German power in Europe. It contends that the *exaggerated multilateralism* practised under the Kohl Chancellorship (and characteristic of post-war patterns of German diplomacy) oriented towards *agenda-setting* and *milieu-shaping*, but that this style of European policy was challenged by *climatic change* after unification. Political parties theory is used to explain the internal dynamics of the SPD examined in Chapters 5–7, and the strategic choices made by the party, by explaining the changing mechanics of party politics. While establishing more party discipline in the late 1990s, the SPD has sought to become a more efficient electoral machine, to resonate policy competence and win elections at the federal level. These three dimensions are central to understanding the development of SPD policy after 1990. The chapter finally sets out how a changing political environment has ultimately resulted in an SPD European policy characterised by pragmatic multilateralism – a commitment to represent (*Europeanised*) German interests more forcefully, but within the multilateral setting of the European Union.

European policy in Germany and the SPD

From 1949 onwards, West Germany began to build up a network of co-operative relationships with its western neighbours, helping to create an environment of multilateral structures for political and economic rehabilitation. Peace and stability were of prime importance with respect to the division of Europe between the West and the East, which placed the Federal Republic at the front line of the Cold War. The regeneration of the West German economy was also a top priority for the first post-war administration. In terms of foreign affairs, policy centred on re-establishing German diplomatic credibility (after the experiences of the Second World War) through partnership with its West European neighbours (in particular, France) and strong ties with the United States. This was put into concrete form through the establishment of the European Coal and Steel Community (ECSC) in 1951, and afterwards the Treaty of Rome (1957) which established the European Community. In security matters, affairs were soon conducted through the North Atlantic Treaty Organisation (NATO), joined by Germany in 1955. As these policies were customised, a West-oriented multilateral political strategy was reinforced by a booming economy with a heavy export bias,[1] heavily concentrated in Western Europe. Greater political co-operation was a logical by-product of greater economic interdependence. All these factors drew German leaders towards a European policy that was, by the late 1950s, unquestionably committed to co-operation, integration and multilateralism, in stark contrast to the 'Realpolitik' of the Wilhemine and National Socialist eras.

West Germany was, furthermore, mindful of the restraints placed upon her in the post-war period. In the domestic context, these restraints included: the constitution with its 'Basic Law'; co-operative federalism within the republic; the existence of powerful *parapublic*[2] institutions (e.g. the *Bundesbank*); the lack of a nuclear arsenal; the presence of Allied troops on German soil; and, the guilt and moral reparations that resulted from the War. They acted to mould West German power and policy towards reconciliation and multilateral co-operation with its Western neighbours. External pressures came from US policy within the context of the Cold War and the suspicious reaction of West Germany's partners to any slight sign of assertiveness. These internal and external restraints manifested themselves in a 'semi-sovereignty' that left little scope for unilateral action.[3] Seeking interests through multilateral institutions nevertheless empowered West German politicians with the ability to pursue policy objectives that they were restricted from aspiring to go it alone. The Bonn–Paris axis was central to this: Germany would typically dress up its policies in Franco-German clothing, as demonstrated by the governments' frequent joint declarations (e.g. the Schimdt–D'Éstaing proposals for a European Monetary System), and the extensive bilateral contacts between the two countries at all levels of government.

The West German 'Wirtschaftswunder' (economic miracle) calmed any domestic doubts about West European integration, and West European integration in turn calmed doubts about Germany. As West Germany grew in economic might, the picture of self-restraint became an established feature of its international relations. Hans Peter Schwarz claimed that the pre-war 'Machtbessesenheit' (obsession with power) was replaced by a post-war 'Machtvergessenheit' (neglect of power).[4] This description, however, underplays the more subtle usage of power employed in West German European policy, which Jeffrey Anderson fittingly describes as 'übertriebene Multilateralismus' (exaggerated multilateralism).[5] West Germany acted in an over-conciliatory manner in its European policy, to promote long-term integration and to allay the suspicions of its EU partners. Chancellor Kohl, for example, to prevent the UK from stalling over economic integration, agreed to grant Mrs. Thatcher a huge rebate in 1984 that, up until the Berlin Summit in March 1999, was reckoned to cost the German taxpayer £9 per head each year. This is not to say that West Germany was neglecting its key interests and allowing other countries to walk all over it, but rather that it was projecting power in a 'soft' manner,[6] concentrating on *setting the agenda* and developing a favourable environment in which policies could be pursued. In a review of West German European policy, Paterson has concluded that 'there is little doubt that it was successful in helping create a framework in which German exports could flourish and to reduce the diplomatic disadvantages that were associated with the external aspects of semi-sovereignty'.[7]

Within the SPD, other patterns of European policy emerged (Table 1.1). First, there was an antagonism between the ideas of European integration and German unity. In the early years of the Federal Republic, the SPD, under the leadership of Kurt Schumacher, was

Table 1.1   Features of SPD European policy in the Bundesrepublik

Issue	SPD positions
Basic cross-party consensus over European integration	The 'basic consensus' in favour of European integration dominated SPD European policy from the 1960s to the 1990s. Although, the consensus was increasingly disrupted through the 1990s, and after the party came to power in 1998, the spirit of consensus remained strong across the German political elites.
Tension between European Integration and German unification	Unification was the top issue under Schumacher: West European integration was seen as contradictory to this goal. Under *Ostpolitik*, rapprochement with the East became the priority: *widening* rather than *deepening* of EC was stressed.
Doubts over a 'narrow' European economic integration with a small membership.	The Left or Centre-Left credentials of SPD leaders made the party initially sceptical about what they saw as a *narrow* and *conservative*-led integration policy. Brandt championed UK membership of the EU.Lafontaine questioned a *one-dimensional* Monetary Union. Schröder challenged a Single Currency without Italy or the UK.
Concern for the material aspects of integration	Schmidt and Schröder regretted French financial gains from the EC/EU, calling for reductions in German payments to the budget.
Divisive nature of defence/ security issues in European policy	The Left balked first at the idea of rearmament (1950s); then at nuclear armament (1980s/1990s); and, finally, the use of German units in *out of area* situations.

openly hostile towards West European integration, since they felt it would hinder any possibility of unification with East Germany and were suspicious about what they saw as a conservative and market-led integration process. By the mid- to late-1950s, the success of the West German economy and West European integration[8] and the increasing unlikelihood of German unification amid the Cold War persuaded the SPD (under Ollenhauer) to lift its scepticism and hostility, and move towards a consensus with the Christian Democrat Parties on the virtues of European integration. This went hand in hand with the party dumping its Marxist ideological baggage, confirmed at the watershed Bad Godesberg Conference (1959). During the 1960s, Willy Brandt developed and implemented what became known as 'Ostpolitik'.[9] This involved peace treaties and mutual recognition agreements with (among others) the Soviet Union and East Germany, and a general *rapprochement* with the Eastern Bloc. With respect to West European integration, Brandt (while committed to existing levels of ties) appeared to prioritise the *widening* and *democratisation* of the EC during his Chancellorship over further steps towards European integration.[10]

Progress was made towards a deepening of the EC under Helmut Schmidt, with the proposal of a European Monetary System for Member States. This marked a practical response to the oil crises: Europe could protect itself from the vagaries of the world market through a common monetary and social system. He also argued the case for a smaller contribution to the Community budget. The second phase of *Ostpolitik* in the 1980s expanded ties with the ruling party to the East. Separate recognition of the GDR was seen as the way forward. The SPD leadership (and, in particular, Oskar Lafontaine) were subsequently wrong-footed by the rapid chain of events leading to reunification in 1990. The difference in SPD attitudes to Europe depended upon who was in power in the party. The Left or *traditionalists* often followed a different course to the Right or *party establishment*. This was particularly clear over the issue of economic integration, because the Left were sceptical about the market-oriented basis of the EC. It is the Right of the party, however, who have tended to be in control when the SPD has been in power, because the party has necessarily moved to the centre of politics to become electable.[11] Finally, the party has been bitterly divided over defence policy: in the 1950s, the SPD opposed German rearmament; the emergence of the New Left led to fierce disputes over the stationing of US nuclear missiles in Germany in the 1980s, and over German participation in UN peace-keeping operations in the early 1990s (Table 1.1).

Reunification in 1990 had a profound effect on the geopolitical and socioeconomic foundations upon which European policy was based, with the economic burden of regenerating the East German economy and the new interests in economic and political integration with the new regimes in East Central Europe (Chapter 2). The immediate (negative) reaction of Germany's partners in Europe (most notably Britain and France) to the prospect of unification was to express fears that a united Germany would begin to dominate the EU as a consequence of its increased size and central position in an *opened* European continent. Since Monetary Union was decided upon among the existing members in 1991, however, it appeared that deeper Western integration was still the Government priority. The Kohl governments continued to exercise practised patterns of German foreign policy, taking care not to arouse the suspicions of their partners, with little account for public opinion and the dawning realities of a new Europe.

In the ten years since the fall of the Berlin wall, much has been written on the development of new German national interests and a new style of pursuing those interests within the EU. Some domestic observers called upon Germany to build a new *grand strategy* for European policy, pointing to the breakdown in consensus since 1989 on foreign policy goals and means.[12] Christian Hacke quotes the former British foreign secretary, Douglas Hurd, saying that British foreign policy protects and pursues British interests as defined by each new generation.[13] Hacke continues that it would be better for Germany if it clearly defined its national interest, dampening the suspicions of partners, which grow when German politicians pretend to be altruistic.[14] German policy under Kohl stressed further EU integration and was prepared to foot a great part of the bill for Monetary Union. At the Edinburgh Summit (1992), 'it was Mr. Kohl who reached into a deep pocket' to underwrite payments for the Cohesion Fund.[15] The Government also failed to directly answer the question of how eastern enlargement of the EU would be paid for, so people were suspicious of the costs it would involve (Chapters 10 and 11). The new environment led many Germans to question the advantages of what has become seen as a financially costly commitment to European integration. With Germany's budgetary contribution in mind, Chancellor Kohl's EU policy was viewed as *unpragmatic*. According to polls in 1998, only 36 per cent of Germans believed they had 'benefited' from EU membership, compared to 61 per cent in 1993 (Chapter 4).[16] With such a discrepancy between elite and public opinion, the Government avoided representing – or *being seen* to represent – *harder*, more material German interests at its own peril.

German policy in Europe

German EU policy is inextricably linked to perceptions of Germany's *national interest* and *leadership role* in Europe. The SPD's policy in government has been founded on what it considers to be in the national interest, weighing up of the pros and cons of European integration in combination with domestic issues that are important to the party. The question of Germany's *leadership role* also translates into more specific questions about the way German governments pursue what they see as German interests in Europe. SPD perceptions of Germany's interests and role in the EU were defined by the party's changing policy context. For instance, the party's approach, as it finally gained power at the federal level, was to contextualise domestic demands into the more constrictive framework of European politics (Chapter 6).

In aiming to explain and interpret SPD European policy, the book tries to fathom out the reasons why the party has perceived a particular formulation of EU policy as being in German interests.[17] This study recognises the *intersubjective* nature of interests, but argues that they do exist, and are a product of actors' perceptions or knowledge of their political environment (*structured context*). In short, interests exist, even if they are subjective. Different ontological positions regarding the nature of states and their interests in the international system have informed the quite different interpretations of German European policy after 1990. Some from the *realist* school put forward a simple *zero sum* analysis, suggesting that Germany, united and free from external sovereignty, internal division and the imperatives of the Cold War, would adopt a strategy that pursues or rejects each policy on a win–lose basis.[18] This, so it has been claimed, would lead to Germany asserting its hegemony over both the EU and the former Eastern Bloc countries. Markovits and Reich argued that, because of its economic muscle, increased by unification, Germany would inevitably dominate Europe and European institutions.[19] They singled out the growing predominance of German as the second language in much of Eastern Europe as evidence of increasing German hegemony.[20] The realist view of foreign policy is also based on an innate belief in the *anarchy of international relations*. In this world, countries behave like Hobbes' pre-social man: their interests based purely on self-aggrandisement and self-interest. However, under 'complex interdependence, this conventional wisdom begs two important questions: which self and which interest?'[21]

The realist school was perceived to lose much of its potency in the 1970s through the work of Keohane and Nye (among others) from the *neo-liberal* school,[22] who emphasised the interdependent nature of international relations in the modern world (Chapter 2). This included complex relationships between the state and domestic actors, and the state and international organisations. They pointed to the existence of *issue linkage* as proof that interests were, in reality, divisible. Interests are reconciled through negotiated policy objectives and issues will vary in importance with no set hierarchy. International organisations, what is more, have the capacity to 'set agendas' and to 'induce coalition-building'.[23] In essence, there is a time dynamic at work here. Increasing economic integration and technological advances have led to a smaller world – one in which foreign policy is more market-oriented. Countries have become more reliant upon each other in terms of import, export and economic infrastructure. William Wallace states that, 'to a remarkable degree, the processes of government in Europe overlap and interlock among different states, between different levels of government below and above the old locus of sovereignty in the nation state'.[24] The realist view of power is not redundant, but is merely one part of the whole picture, incomplete and less important in defining countries' objectives in a highly integrated Western Europe. Germany's economic success, avoiding the realist aspects of power, has demonstrated the potential effectiveness of a co-operative and multilateral foreign policy.[25]

The *multilateralist* paradigm stresses the *positive-sum* aspects of integration – that Germany has profited greatly, both economically and politically, from a long-term and multilateral European policy, and is unlikely to diverge too far from this course in the future.[26] German interests have been *softened* by a *Europeanisation* of identity through the Community institutions, which set the framework for the reconciliation of interests.[27] German policy has been characterised by a *legitimised leadership role*[28] or even *exaggerated multilateralism*. These perspectives add to the realist approach (anchored in the inter-governmental paradigm) two further dimensions, those of domestic politics and international or supranational organisations (i.e. the EU), in the examination of German European policy. They also emphasise the importance of history and institutions in addition to geopolitical and economic factors (stressed by *neo-realists* and *neo-liberals*, respectively). This study rejects the idea that there is some kind of natural hierarchy between these four factors. For instance, the powerful historical influences relating to Germany's responsibility for the Second World War, have without doubt receded *vis-à-vis* new geopolitical and economic realities in recent decades (e.g. unification and the end of the Cold War). The key to the multilateralist approach is the idea of *central* or *merged* interests – the common *interests of a positive-sum game*. While this approach is broadly accepted, this study will temper its view of the world as 'socially constructed' with an emphasis on the privileged role of certain actors (such as state governments and even the SPD itself), which act as 'gatekeepers' for different interests (Chapters 3 and 4).[29]

The general perception of German interests by the country's political elites has been based on a multitude of factors outlined in this chapter and in the introduction: these include geopolitical reasoning (e.g. the *Mittellage*); the interests of the national economy (e.g. Germany's export-oriented industry); historical factors (e.g. the success of post-war institutionalised patterns of multilateral policy); and, institutional logic (e.g. the centripetal force of European integration in the 1980s and early 1990s). The examples selected here capture the fact that German policy is conducted within a changing policy environment. Just as important as the changing perception of German interests, is the changing view of how those interests should be pursued. This latter point, given Germany's economic might within the EU, has been strongly debated with regard to *how* and *to what extent* politicians should project German power within the European Union. The question of the use of power, or what Bulmer, Jeffery and Paterson prefer to call 'diplomacy', is therefore of key importance.[30]

The analysis of the pursuit of German goals in Europe will be adapted from the three dimensions of power set out in Stephen Lukes' 'Power: a radical view'.[31] These dimensions of power provide a simplified account of the different ways policy goals can be achieved. The first dimension is the orthodox pluralist approach, advocated by Robert Dahl, which suggests that power is exercised where determined views prevail in a case of *observable conflict*.[32] Much like the realist conception of international relations, this approach is *one-dimensional*, neglecting the unseen and latent aspects of power at work. While this dimension is very important, and certainly cannot be ignored, it is but one component of power – an actor-centred approach – which lies inside two more structural dimensions (Figure 1.1). Bulmer, Jeffery and Paterson explicitly term this dimension 'realist' power and equate it to 'tactics', which usually involve decisions over material issues (e.g. money for the EU budget).[33] It would be right to add that these *tactics* are often aimed at solving problems in the short-term. The second dimension represents the views of Bachrach and Baratz who write about 'potential issues' and decisions that are prevented from even coming under discussion.[34] They also write of the need to distinguish between the way power is distributed in different policy areas[35] – a further necessary revision of the first dimension of power. In sum, this dimension represents the ability to *set the agenda*, which has been a particularly effective means of exercising power in the multilateral institutional setting of the EU. *Agenda-setting* is a more strategic approach to power than the first dimension, in that it seeks to achieve longer-term and more substantive policy goals (Figure 1.1).

Finally, Lukes' own third dimension attempts to take power out of its *individualistic framework*. He writes of 'manipulation' and 'authority' as forms of power, and the existence of a *dominant ideology*.[36] The problem with the concept of a dominant ideology is that it presumes that individual actors within the domain of this ideology have 'genuine'

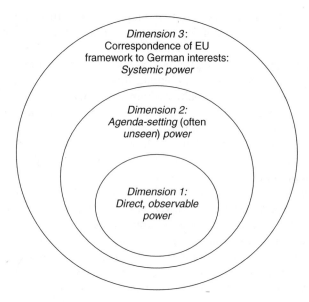

Figure 1.1   The nature of German power in the EU

interests of which they are not 'conscious'.[37] Yet Lukes' idea of creating a less actor-centred account of power is very important, and can be modified to make an important contribution to the concept of power. For instance, A might see something as in his or her interest if B successfully influences the ideational and institutional structures upon which A's initial position is based. This is the basis of a third dimension of power – 'systemic power' (Figure 1.1).[38] It is similar both to Hay's concept of 'context-shaping', and – in direct reference to German European policy – Bulmer, Jeffery and Paterson's concept of 'milieu goals', which both deal with the idea of shaping the conditions in which politics takes place.[39] *Systemic power* is an indirect form of power with two main aspects: first, the shaping of the political environment in an ideational sense (through the success of ideas); second, the shaping of the political environment through an alteration of the structures of institutions (modifying the *rules of the game*). Both the ideational and the institutional aspects of systemic power came into play for Germany in the creation of the European Central Bank (ECB), which was modelled on the German Central Bank, the *Bundesbank*. One of the main reasons that other Member States accepted a central bank with entrenched rules on independence and a stability-oriented monetary policy, was their common respect for the success of Bundesbank in steering German economic policy (see Chapter 8). The ECB, in turn, has begun to shape economic policy in the Euro-zone. *Systemic power* may not be intentional, but it is the most structural dimension of power used in this analysis, and therefore contains the first two dimensions (Figure 1.1). Multilateralists propose a similar take on power and the pursuit of interests, as set out in Bulmer's succinct categorisation of 'four faces of power' with respect to German foreign policy.[40] The Federal Republic of Germany, due largely to its post-war circumstances, has most frequently rejected a direct approach in relations with its EU partners. Given past German military aggression and sensitivity to the country's dominant economic position, such a show of naked assertiveness would – it was suspected – result in negative reaction and suspicion of German attempts to dominate. Within its European policy, a German desire to *go it alone* would backfire. This view appeared to be confirmed by the backlash following Germany's unilateral decision to recognise Croatian independence in December 1991. Tempered by the important effects of deeper EU integration, the field of *observable* or *direct power* represents one face (the first dimension) of German power in Europe (Figure 1.1).[41] Bulmer, Jeffery and Paterson point out that whereas Germany has generally followed the path of agenda-setting, other countries like the UK have pursued their policy objectives with greater use of *direct power.*[42]

Agenda-setting in the European Union formed the backbone of post-war (West) German European policy (the second dimension of power – Figure 1.1), based as it is on the *positive-sum* assessment of European integration, and was clearly evident under the Kohl Chancellorship. The focus on multilateral agenda-setting in the was especially well suited to the use of *soft power* characteristic of Germany's post-war European policy. The agenda for EC politics was often constructed within the Franco-German alliance. After unification, there was more pressure on Kohl to use direct power, but his personal authority in the Government and his own party and the strength of his strategic vision for Europe (shared by the German Foreign Office), meant that he could effectively isolate Germany from these forces for the best part of a decade.

Finally, the success of German policy in the highly strategic and structural third dimension of power has led to the shaping of the EU (intentional or unintentional) to a structure that both suits and resembles German federalism, benefiting Germany and giving it an advantage in negotiations (the third dimension of power – Figure 0.1).[43] One of the end goals of systemic power is to create what Bulmer sees as a high degree of 'institutional fit' between German and EU institutions.[44]

The European Union is a quasi-federal structure based on a bargaining culture that is similar to the German political system. What is more, the necessity for the German government to pass major European legislation through the 'Bundesrat',[45] and to abide by the decisions of the 'Bundesverfassungsgericht' (Federal Constitutional Court), has helped mould the European Union to complement these features of the German system. The EU, for instance, took on board the idea of a *Europe of the regions* and the principle of *subsidiarity* to pacify the German *Länder*.[46] The correspondence of Germany to the EU gives it an 'institutional advantage', which is a consequence of *systemic power*. Chapter 11 shows how the Red-Green Government's plans for a constitutional settlement were based on the promotion of a distinctly German model of governance.

The changing role of political parties

After examining the pursuit of German policy goals in the European Union, it is now necessary to look at power structures within the confines of the political system and the political party, to examine in closer detail the SPD as a political party formulating European policy within its institutional and national contexts. In terms of political parties theory, a broad range of analyses have been presented since the Second World War. They have frequently concentrated on change within national systems outlining models for West European politics. Maurice Duverger first made the distinction between *cadre* and *mass parties*, the latter originating from the introduction of universal suffrage, which required them to be more inclusive in order to appeal to a larger electorate.[47] Other important contributions included Kirchheimer's work on the emergence of the 'Volkspartei' (catch-all party) and Pizzorno's analysis of the role of the political party in pluralist democracies. Kirchheimer claimed that the Duverger model was undergoing change. He illustrated that process by pointing to 'shifting and less obtrusive class lines ... the former class–mass parties and denominational mass parties are both under increasing pressure to become catch-all people's parties'.[48] This implied that political parties were aggregating opinion to a greater degree and becoming more instrumental in policy-formation as pressure groups and public opinion became more important. Kirchheimer stated that the development of catch-all parties involved several important changes: including a 'drastic reduction of the party's ideological baggage ... further strengthening of top leadership groups ... downgrading of the role of the individual party member ... de-emphasis of the *classe gardé*'.[49]

For the SPD, the reduction of ideological baggage and de-emphasis of the *classe gardé* began at Bad Godesberg in 1959 where clear commitments were made to dropping the remnants of its Marxist ideology and appealing to the electorate beyond the traditional working class. Organisational changes were more difficult to achieve, but came about de facto as the need for a strong centralised leadership became greater. This was the subject of Panebianco's model of an 'electoral-professional' party, whose professionalism – with regard to vote maximisation – was further accelerated by the scrutiny of political parties under the microscope of the modern mass media.[50] A party must adapt to the realities of the modern world or face extinction. These changes are of particular relevance to social democratic parties, whose journey from their original electoral base (the working class) – enforced by the shrinkage of their core electorate – has not been easy. It has been all the more important, therefore, 'to distinguish between two key characteristics ... the historic political identity, on the one hand, and the contemporary appeals of parties, on the other ... between *what parties are* and *what parties do*.'[51] Sani and Sartori differentiate between 'domains of identification' and 'dimensions of competition',[52] to which a third aspect, that of party structure or organisation should be added. In sum, it is necessary to examine ideology, organisation and strategy within the context of the indigenous political system (see Figure 1.2) in an analysis of policy-making in political parties (see Chapter 3).

German Political System: e.g. federalism, politics of the middle way, consensus/ multiparty system

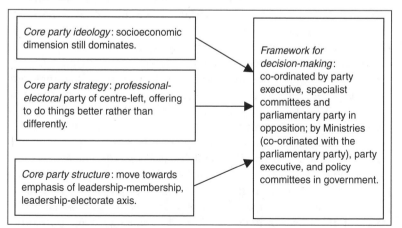

Figure 1.2 General framework for policy formation in the SPD

The nature of the German political system is, of course, fundamental in shaping political parties in that country (see Chapter 4). The German system is characterised by 'the dispersion of state power among competing institutions'.[53] First, government powers are split between the federal and regional level. One anomaly of this structural fact was that the SPD in the 1990s, though not in power at a federal level, always maintained a strong representation at *Länder* (regional) level, achieving a *blocking majority* in the *Bundesrat* chamber of parliament. Although it has often been difficult to co-ordinate the *Länder* for the purposes of the party at the federal level, the SPD's influence on German European policy as an opposition party has nevertheless been significant when compared, for instance, to the Labour Party in the UK between 1979 and 1997. Because of the dispersion of power, consensual politics has become the norm in Germany, and this has been especially true with regard to European affairs.

Power has been further delegated to a number of *parapublic* institutions for example the *Bundesbank*, and centralised associations. In other words, the concentration of power in the state is paradoxically offset by the dispersion of power across the federal planes and parapublic organisations in a system of power structures designed to avoid extremes (Chapter 4).[54] Parties and interest groups are involved directly in government through institutionalised patterns of consultation. Saalfeld adds that, 'In many sectors, therefore, co-operation between government and socioeconomic interests is relatively formalised',[55] in what one might call a *neo-corporatist* model. The formalisation of governmental relationships, including the need for a written coalition agreement, means that policy is tightly structured when in office but has a greater chance of successful implementation. The set-up of the 'Bundestag' (the lower chamber) allows for formal contacts between MPs and these various interests. While each party has certain groups to which it is particularly drawn, the German system remains a relatively pluralist model. Party financing in Germany has, what is more, helped create a situation where political parties have been, to a large extent, absorbed into the state apparatus. The architecture of the German political system thus provides the main environment within which political parties formulate policy, the national policy context (Figure 1.2).

Although social change will inevitably lead to party change, as mentioned above in connection with the SPD, 'no institution, however, can entirely escape from its past. No matter how extensive the renewal of leadership, change in organization or *succession of ends* may be, many traces of the organization's *genetic model* remain visible.'[56] In other words, however much parties may appear to differ between what they *are* and what they *do*, there are always some issues that overlap, and these often represent the party's core values (Figure 1.2). Within a party's ideology, Lijphart outlines seven dimensions, the most important of which he considered to be the socioeconomic one.[57] This is especially so for social democratic parties whose genetic model was rooted in ensuring the material well-being of the working class. Remembering Kirchheimer, it is nevertheless important to recognise that the major issues of conflict in this dimension will change as the electorate changes, and political parties attempt to aggregate their opinion. Some issues put forward by Lijphart, for example, have become outdated or less controversial (e.g. *government versus private ownership of the means of production*), while new conflicts, such as *stakeholder value versus shareholder value*, have emerged.

The role of organisation and structure in political parties has been the focus of a number of works in recent years.[58] It has been emphasised that to study parties, one must look closely at the 'internal structural and decision-making processes'.[59] This is not, of course, to make the assumption that the political party is a unitary actor, but rather to state the importance of a closer examination of the party's inner workings with regard to European policy (Chapter 3). As mentioned above, the political party has greatly changed in the last century since the introduction of universal suffrage: from the *mass party* envisaged by Michels through Lipset and Rokkan's *freezing theory* to Kirchheimer's *catch-all parties*. Panebianco later attributed the 'emergence of the electoral-professional party ... [to] modernization, increase in education, increase in the living conditions of certain groups, classes and segments that were previously socially and politically under-privileged.'[60] He added that this results in an electorate that is far less 'subordinate to political elites' but also undermines a sense of 'collective identity'.[61] Once again, this has been particularly significant in social democratic parties, who were founded to deepen the collective identity of the working class.[62] Put simply, party identification has declined, so parties must offer something different to a more educated electorate under the scrutiny of the media.

One result has been that the party leadership appeals more directly to the public and the pressure for party discipline has increased (Chapter 6). For party leaders in modern politics there is no need, however, to downgrade the role of the party member (as Kirchheimer had suggested). In fact, a strengthening of member-based democracy has been seen as a good means to circumvent local delegates (Figure 1.2). In terms of the SPD, a strengthening of the leadership has occurred, accompanied by a strengthening of the party's *regional princes* or minister-presidents of the *Länder*. The distribution of power within the SPD is of great consequence and will be further analysed in Chapter 3. This study will concentrate on policy formation at the elite level, which dominates the policy formation of political parties, particularly in the area of EU policy. It will analyse the role of the SPD elite in policy formation – operating around the locus of the party executive,[63] specialist European groups (Chapter 3) and the parliamentary party.[64] The Länder elites are also represented in the party's top decision-making bodies, and the SPD Minister-Presidents constitute a core part of the party leadership. Although it will be remembered that organisation within a party is 'an order depending on the equilibrium reached between varied pressures and demands',[65] the party leadership is the defining lens through which all opinion must pass before it becomes policy (Figure 1.2).

The strategy of a political party is very closely linked to its ideology and structure, and is often overshadowed by the other two. It merits separate recognition because strategy or *dimensions of competition* are central to the choice of policies adopted if a party is to have a realistic chance of gaining power. Mair underlines the point that 'the policies which parties pursue will also inevitably be restrained by the strategic imperatives imposed by the system of competition in which they operate'.[66] In order to achieve the necessary level of electoral appeal, a party must adapt both to social change and an ever more crowded *political space*. The SPD's electoral space has been compromised by the success of the Green Party and, more recently, the Party of Democratic Socialism (PDS) (in the new *Länder*).[67] The addition of the Greens, in particular, to the political equation, caused the SPD great problems. According to Panebianco, 'Political socialisation no longer depends upon party organization, but rather upon mass media and interpersonal contact facilitated by horizontal mobility.'[68] The waning of direct political socialisation impacted strongly on party strategy: as Kirchheimer observed in the 1960s, the political party was 'turning more fully to the electoral scene, trying to exchange effectiveness in depth for a wider audience and more immediate electoral success'.[69] The SPD moved in this direction – where the votes were thickest – post-Godesberg in the late 1960s and early 1970s much as it did in the late 1990s. The nomination of Gerhard Schröder (popular in the country rather than the party) to fight the 1998 federal elections demonstrated the power that core strategic concerns can have over a political party (Figure 1.2). The programmatic debates in the SPD in the 1950s, and the 1990s and 2000s, have therefore sought to resolve a 'dualism' between how the party acts in the reality of government and its ideological identity.[70]

SPD European policy in the twenty-first century: 'pragmatic multilateralism'

The sections above explored the frameworks for SPD policy formation within the context of established patterns of policy, power relations on the international stage, and political parties and party systems. The book argues that SPD European policy in the twenty-first century, borne out of the experience of government, has been marked by *pragmatic multilateralism*. According to the 'strategic-relational' approach,[71] the interaction of actors with structures forms a 'structured context', within which actors must operate. Following this logic, this study takes the view that people and even countries act 'rationally', but only based upon their perceptions of complex and changing *structured contexts* (such as those described in Chapters 3 and 4).[72] The SPD's pragmatism or flexibility is an expression of responsiveness to its policy environment and the *climatic changes* set out in Chapter 2. Actors behave 'pragmatically' when they draw implications from the *strategic learning* about their external environment. In sum, *pragmatism* implies a *flexible* approach to strategic learning, observable in the SPD's *flexibility* towards *strategic learning* with regard to Germany's past (*generational change* – Chapter 5), the views of actors and structures on the institutional, national and European planes (*electoral-strategic change* – Chapter 6), and the gradual adaptation of its political positions to Germany's *Europeanised* interests (*ideological change* – Chapter 7). This study is not, therefore, using pragmatism as a normative concept to endorse SPD policy. It agrees with John Dewey, who argued that pragmatism means thought for the purpose of action and the resolution of a problematic situation.[73] In these terms, one of the main problems for the SPD in the late 1990s was to construct a coherent European policy which voters would see as competent, and also to offer solutions to pressing domestic problems (e.g. unemployment), to enable electoral victory. After the party came to power in 1998, it therefore sought to construct a more comprehensive set of policy goals to cope with the reality of government.

This study will examine the EU policy of the SPD with reference to the interpretations of German policy mentioned above, asserting the importance of the *multilateral* approach for the content of SPD policy (Table 1.2). The smooth running of the Single European Market and, since January 1999, the *Euro-zone*, is crucial to Germany, given its export-oriented economy heavily concentrated in the EU (the destination in 1999 for 56.4 per cent of German exports).[74] While *realists* have neglected the diversity of actors and structures behind a differentiated policy formation process, multilateralists have tended to underplay the development of a new assertiveness in the style of German diplomacy (Table 1.2).

SPD EU policy in practice has fallen in between these two interpretations, as it has increasingly recognised the need to pursue both short-term, material (*realist*-type) goals and long-term, strategic (*multilateralist*-type) objectives. Through the 1990s and into the twenty-first century the party has been increasingly characterised by pragmatic multilateralism. Put simply, the SPD continues to see Germany's European interests in terms of EU *multilateral* arenas, but the party has become more *pragmatic* in terms of its *responsiveness* to domestic interests in the selection of its policy goals (Table 1.2). The pursuit of a smaller contribution to the EU budget provides a prime example of where SPD leaders have sought to 'represent Germany's interests more plainly',[75] illustrated in the run up to the 1998 federal elections and in its early months of government (Chapter 11). This was indicative of a growing emphasis on *direct power*. Yet the conclusion of *an* agreement on spending at the Berlin European Council (1999), proving the EU's ability to do

Table 1.2 Main characteristics of pragmatic multilateralism

Style of policy	What may appear to be *national interests* seem clearer: material interests are spoken of with greater frequency, and policy goals are generally pursued with more vigour.
Content of policy	Germany's interests remain tied to the EU. Through economic and political interdependence, a co-operative, multilateral policy is central to *Europeanised* German interests.
Responsiveness to key actors in domestic and European contexts	The SPD's European policy was increasingly influenced by domestic actors when in opposition (e.g. public opinion) and, then, European actors in government (e.g. EU partner states).
German leadership role/ continuing multilateralism	Germany may appear assertive (and even dominating) to others, but is behaving less assertively than its economic clout might allow and is prepared to compromise for the common good.

business, was of key significance to the new SPD-led government. This was shown by the fact that Germany was not prepared to push to the wire reforms that would have saved them a lot of money,[76] if it meant that no budgetary agreement at all would be reached for an enlarged European Union. Here, the SPD adapted to its new *structured context* in government – behaving less assertively than Germany's economic clout would allow and prepared to compromise for the common good (Table 1.2).

The SPD in government has attempted to influence the *detail* of EU polity more than had been the case under Kohl, but the reality of a more interdependent EU has ensured that key issues such as European Economic and Monetary Union and eastern enlargement continue to be central themes in the governance of Germany (Table 1.2). The SPD focus on the *plains of European integration* was largely a response to the *electoral-strategic change* explained in Chapter 6, through which the party's leaders became more *responsive* to public opinion and domestic actors in general, even if these views were softened under the influence of EU-level actors and structures and the mediating influence of government ministries when in power (Chapters 3 and 4). The intention of the SPD leadership has been to create a Germany more willing to play a leading role in international affairs, and more apt to represent her material interests when necessary (Table 1.2). With regard to tactics, leading SPD politicians in Government have sought a *normalisation* of German EU policy, but with a strong emphasis on Germany's *Europeanised* interests (Chapter 7).

2
A New Policy Environment

Chapter two examines the development of a new environment for European policy that led to the redefinition of national interests in Germany and the SPD. Here, we investigate the dramatic changes to the environment for European policy-making in Germany after 1990. Foreign Minister Fischer, for example, cited 'the rapid pace of European integration' and 'globalisation of the economy' as a major cause for the 'urgent need ... for a recalibration of our foreign policy'.[1] 'Climatic change' has altered the foundations for European policy both in Germany and the SPD – the framework within which political parties and politicians formulate European policy – providing a *critical juncture* in German European policy. *Climatic change* has created what Marsh and Smith call 'strong external uncertainties', which 'affect network structures, network interactions and policy outcomes'.[2] In all the four instances listed below, it has served either to question or reinforce established patterns of European policy in Germany, whose previous success provided much of the rationale for continuity. To emphasise the importance of *climatic change*, is not – of course – to negate the fact that German policy may influence the policy context. The Federal Government, for instance, insisted on the creation of the EMU Convergence Criteria at Maastricht and the independence and stability-oriented ethos of the European Central Bank, which has been fundamental in shaping the Euro-zone. Due to Germany's political and economic strength in Europe, the relationship is, therefore, a dialectic one.

The 'climatic factors' that explain the changing environment are highly interrelated, but can be divided into four areas. The first is 'German unification' (Table 2.1) – the economic and psychological changes that came with the incorporation of the former GDR into the Federal Republic. A second factor is the geopolitical impact of the end

Table 2.1   The development of SPD European policy since 1990 – 'climatic change'

Climatic factors	Impact
German unification	The cost of German unity challenged the country's position as *paymaster* of the European Union, and the attainment of full political sovereignty also contributed to a more assertive style of multilateralism.
The *Mittellage*	The end of the Cold War repositioned Germany in the centre of a new Europe, and altered the country's geopolitical priorities, opening up the perspective of a more pan-European approach.
European integration	European integration, particularly the Single Market and EMU, has increased the penetration of EU politics into domestic politics, while at the same time increasing interdependency within the Union.
Globalisation	The pressures of global markets have increasingly been a factor in political governance, promoting a broadening of EU-level policy responses in areas where individual states feel they are losing control.

of the Cold War for German European policy. In particular, the relocation of a united Germany in the *Mittellage* of an opened-up European continent (Table 2.1). A further dynamic is European integration itself (Table 2.1). The extension of EU policy competences through the 1990s – most evident in the EMU project – has developed its own momentum, pressurising member states to 'download' policies from the EU.[3] Finally, the increasing prevalence of a globalised economy, the increased speed of cross-border financial transactions and global communications, have made countries view international co-operation at a regional level in a different way, as 'globalisation' has challenged the incongruity of national socioeconomic models (Table 2.1). *Climatic change* has, thus, provided the impetus for developments in the positions of major domestic and European actors, and consequently in SPD policy itself, and it is the objective of this chapter to look more closely at these phenomena.

Germany unification

On 3 October 1990, Germany was reunited, and the event was greeted with much euphoria in both halves of the new state. Unity affected the rationale behind German European policy, as the country's key priority became the economic regeneration of the new *Länder*. Chancellor Kohl, in foretelling of *flourishing landscapes*, had, however, glossed over the costs of this regeneration, both understating and underestimating the hardships entailed in modernising the economic infrastructure of eastern Germany. German Economic and Monetary Union placed a heavy economic burden on the economy of Eastern Germany through the adoption of a 1 : 1 parity between the two German currencies. Deeper difficulties were created by the trade union-led drive for an equalisation of wages between the old and the new *Länder* despite large differences in levels of productivity. Anderson emphasises that this 'produced severe hardship in eastern Germany, which eventually resulted in a significant political challenge to the passive consensus in Germany about the domestic model of political economy and the larger goals of European integration'.[4] The net transfer of public funds from East to West ten years after unity was estimated at over €600 billion, 'more than double this year's [2000] entire federal budget'.[5] These economic difficulties were further worsened by the fact that they had come on the brink of a global recession.

The economic burden of unification led to spiralling government debt – from 42 per cent of GDP in 1991 to 57 per cent in 1995 and 63 per cent in 1998,[6] which was highlighted by the EMU convergence criteria that limited debt to 60 per cent of GDP. The amounts spent on the former GDR were so great that ten years on, according to Finance Minister Eichel, every fourth Mark of government spending went on debt repayment: 'Interest repayments now account for 22 per cent of government spending, compared with 12 per cent in 1982', much of this 'debt mountain' is due to the increase in spending after unification.[7] Large transfer payments are set to continue in the medium term given the SPD-led Government's agreement of a new 'solidarity pact' in 2001, costing about €100 billion and lasting till 2019. Unemployment rates, in addition, increased rapidly in the 1990s, reaching a peak of over 9 per cent (and almost double that in the East),[8] which narrowed the SPD's focus onto domestic economic problems. The sharp downturn in the economy in the mid- to late-1990s impacted strongly on German perceptions of the EC/EU, leading many to question their large budgetary commitment to the Community. German policy under Kohl, however, stressed further integration, and was prepared to foot a great part of the bill. At the Edinburgh summit (1992), 'it was Mr. Kohl who reached into a deep pocket' to secure payments for the Cohesion Fund.[9] Through the 1990s, objections to what some saw as Germany's 'Zahlmeister' (paymaster) role in the EU became increasingly vocal.

According to Schröder in 1995, 'We can not afford an additional engagement in Europe in the face of the burdens coming from German unity.'[10] Or, as one government official recently put it: 'the German budgetary contribution simply cannot be shaped how it was when there was just Western integration'.[11]

Germany's economic problems did not, furthermore, start and end with unification. The country also faced a number of pressing structural problems. Besides the mountain of debt, public spending was further pressurised by slow economic growth (which brought about falling tax receipts) and the demographic challenge of ageing populations with regard both to pensions and healthcare. After a brief period of growth in the late 1990s and 2000 under the Red–Green government, the economic situation deteriorated again. Aside from the problems that this caused for Germany to keep within the limits of the EMU Growth and Stability Pact (Chapter 11), this also led to increased pressure on the domestic scene to focus political energies on domestic economic affairs rather than European policy. This was evidenced by the centrality of the Red–Green Government's *Agenda 2010* package of national tax, labour market and welfare reforms accompanied by austerity measures.

In political and psychological terms, reunification allowed politicians to consider a new role for Germany in Europe. Should Germany act more confidently in line with its greater population, economy and full political sovereignty, or should it keep more strictly to the successful style of foreign policy practised since the War? Should it concentrate more on resolving its new domestic problems as the interests of the new *Länder* might suggest? To what extent should it seek to engage with its eastern neighbours whilst keeping Western Europe at the core of European policy? Should Germany pursue its own interests more actively like other states such as France or the UK? For Helmut Kohl at least, German unification and European integration were *two sides of the same coin*.[12] After 1990, however, public opinion became increasingly sceptical of the EU: the percentage of Germans who believed they had 'benefited' from membership halved between 1993 and 1998 (Chapter 6).[13] The up-and-coming leaders of the SPD were more prepared than Kohl to explicitly assert material German interests such as the reduction of German contributions to the EU budget (Chapter 5).

The reaction of Germany's main EC partners to unification (with the exception of the UK) was to seek to restrain the centrifugal forces which they thought would result from a united Germany in a post-Cold War Europe. The increased size (both in population terms and in levels of production) of a unified Germany, raised fears (especially in

France – Germany's key partner – and the UK) that the country would begin to dominate Europe by virtue of its new found strength and central location. The French President, Francois Mitterrand, for example, expressed concern at the pace of unification, and sought concrete commitments from Germany that it would embed itself more deeply in the European Community. This took the form of Economic and Monetary Union, which would at least see the communitisation of Germany's already dominant monetary policy (Chapter 8). The immediate consequences of unification were, therefore, at first, to strengthen the institutions of the Community and further bind Germany to the EC. Though enlargement was to become increasingly important, deeper integration in the form of Monetary Union was to be the immediate priority. In this, the Kohl governments kept with practised patterns of German policy, taking care not to arouse the suspicions of their partners, but with little account of any changes in public opinion.

In sum, unification provided Germany with a whole raft of new interests to consider, but none more so than the economic problems at home, which – set against the backdrop of global recession, the strict EMU debt criteria and an oversized contribution to the EC budget – contributed to a growing public resentment towards the Community. This allowed Eurosceptic voices to emerge (particularly in the *Länder*) even among the overwhelmingly pro-EU political elites. Such scepticism was, however, somewhat superficial in its nature, since anyone with a grasp of European integration could see that it was in Germany's economic interests to maintain its high level of commitment (even if integration seemed to be moving too fast for some). The doubts raised by the SPD over Monetary Union thus originated from its regional premiers rather than the party's European policy community, which had a greater understanding of politics on the EU plane (though less appreciation of public feeling). Concerns about particular aspects of European policy could not, on the other hand, be easily expressed by the CDU (or the CSU at the federal level), whose Chancellor was deeply committed to European integration, and had to operate within the context of the tighter framework of pressures and influences at the EU level.

The German '*Mittellage*'

The end of the Cold War and the fall of the Iron Curtain left the Federal Republic of Germany in a vastly different geopolitical location. While West Germany had formerly been located at the eastern end of a highly integrated Western Europe, the unified state found itself occupying the

Mittellage in an unlocked continent. Though steps had been taken under the policy of *Ostpolitik* to hold a hand out to the Central and East European (CEE) states, West Germany's relations with these countries, as with East Germany, were always clouded by the reality of Soviet domination. The question presented itself: how would the new situation affect German policy in Europe? While there was concern amongst Germany's partners about a German 'mission' in central and eastern Europe,[14] there was no real danger of a return to the adventurism of pre-1945. The Federal Republic had learnt too much from the positive experience of West European integration for this to be a possibility. For Germany, the priority was to become a force for stability in the fledgling democracies, through financial investment and the promotion of its eastern neighbours' interests in Western Europe, whilst utilising the opportunity of central and eastern Europe for the benefit of its own economy (Chapter 10).

After the Russian withdrawal from the former Soviet satellite states, these countries needed German political and economic support to help secure their emerging systems. Germany saw itself as the 'advocate' of these countries, helping them integrate into existing multilateral structures. Paterson explained that: 'the ending of bipolarity' meant that Germany became 'singularly vulnerable to breakdown and collapse in the east. This gives it a particular interest in the dual enlargement of NATO and the EU'.[15] German governments also encouraged enterprises to invest in these states, and direct investment in, for instance, Poland, began to increase, growing by over 400 per cent to DM 1.8 bn (€920 m.)[16] between 1994 and 1996.[17] More important was trade with these countries, which, by 1997, 'already exceeds trade with the United States' (Chapter 10).[18] Germany's eastern neighbours likewise depended upon their rich and powerful western neighbour to act as a bridge for their political and economic integration into Western Europe. Germany, on the other hand, rather than deliberately seeking hegemony in central and eastern Europe as some have suggested,[19] pursued its interests through increased economic and political integration, so that the *Mittellage* in many respects provided for a continuation of West German policy in the EC. By these means, Germany overcame much of the historically based suspicions of its intentions that lingered in these countries. Polish writer, Andrzej Szczypiorski, commented that: 'Germany has done more for Poland in recent years than France, traditionally favourably inclined towards us, or the US, so beloved of the Poles.'[20]

In addition to the new resources of a unified Germany, the country's West European partners were also concerned about the geopolitical implications of unity for the European Community. This was a further reason behind the French insistence on a swift decision on EMU, to bind Germany to the West above and beyond any commitment to the East. The German political elites, on the other hand, saw no contradiction between a deepening and a widening of European integration, which could provide a synthesis of its new interests. The 'Weimar triangle', which arranges the meeting of politicians and businessmen from Germany, France and Poland, is an example of how Germany has at least tried to achieve these new goals while retaining old alliance structures. There was certainly no return to a crude notion of 'Geopolitik', where 'geographical features determine the interests and fate of a state's foreign policy'.[21] Zimmer makes the point that 'geographical location is *one* [author's italics] major element that conditions, modifies or restrains national interests'.[22] Other key factors are described elsewhere in this chapter.

Germany was still to some extent diverted from its eastern policy by the hugely significant EMU project and the reticence of France towards eastern enlargement of the EU. The Kohl governments, unlike their successors, were not prepared to jeopardise the closeness of the Franco-German relationship by an assertive articulation of German interests. The grim reality of the conflicts in the former Yugoslavia, and the influx of hundreds and thousands of refugees into Germany, nevertheless ensured that the East was not forgotten. While continuing to advocate enlargement in the EU, Germany went down the route of encouraging trade and bilateral contacts with these states. For the Red–Green Government, the necessity of enlargement was further brought home by the Kosovo conflict in 1999, and the symbolic move of the German capital from Bonn to Berlin served as a daily reminder to German politicians of the proximity of Eastern Europe. There can be no doubt that the opening up of Europe altered the shape of German interests, but it is equally clear that Germany has sought political integration through the existing multilateral institutions of the EU and NATO, a policy characteristic of post-war German foreign policy and strongly supported by the German political elites. With the enlargement of the EU in May 2004, it will be interesting to observe the extent to which Germany can maintain such close relations with the diverse political and economic systems of the East when involved in the day-to-day detail of European governance.

European integration

European integration has developed in two main ways: first, in terms of institutional or formal policy developments in the EC/EU; second, in terms of economic integration or 'trade' between Member States. Both forms of integration drive each other on. While increased trade has encouraged common rules, increased mutual access to national markets has led to more trade. In this way, European integration contains its own self-perpetuating dynamic that encourages domestic systems to integrate further where there is 'fungibility' in terms of their 'administrative fit', 'domestic institutional setting' and 'agents within these settings'.[23] Cole explains that in 'an increasingly Europeanized policy space ... path-dependent processes can escape from the control of national or party actors'.[24] This can be observed in the case of the Single Market: greater trade between member states has bolstered support for common rules on, for instance, security markets (as set out in the 'Lamfalussy report'[25]). Eyre and Lodge explain that, as a result of integration, it is logical for officials to 'desire a reduction in policy incongruence'.[26] Therefore, to formulate a realistic European policy, German policy has had to take account of the increasing penetration of the EU polity and to *download* policy from this plane in a number of key areas. While the SPD could ignore these pressures for a long time in the relative freedom of opposition, they became ever more influential as the party became a *government in waiting* (Chapter 3) and, then, finally gained power.

In the years leading up to German unity significant advances were made in European Community integration. The Single European Act (SEA) of 1987 greatly increased the potential for economic integration, though many were unaware of its political ramifications at the time.[27] In the 1990s, the pace of integration increased yet further as significant steps were taken in the key fields of economic and monetary policy (i.e. EMU), foreign and security policy (e.g. the creation of a Council 'high representative' in this area), and justice and home affairs (e.g. the 'Schengen agreement' on open borders). Manfred Schmidt has identified ten policy areas where the European Union extended its influence over policies between 1992 and 2000: changes have been particularly great in the areas of economic and labour market policy where the EU now predominates in 'the free movement of people', 'debt policy', 'fiscal policy' and 'monetary policy'.[28] Trade between Member States has increased, furthermore, producing an even greater interdependence in the sense of market integration. Take-over deals within the EU reached $1500bn in 2000, 'a higher volume of deals than the US'.[29] Trade of manufactured goods has been estimated to have risen by 20–30 per cent as a result of the Single Market.[30]

According to Hanns Maull, 'The borders between domestic and foreign policy have fallen away with important results not only for contents (policies), but also for political processes (politics).'[31] In other words, European integration has highly significant consequences both for specific areas of European policy, and for the way in which European politics is formulated in Member States (as it covers more and more areas of erstwhile domestic policy), greatly modifying the context of policy-making. The growing influence of EU policies has challenged both 'national traditions of policy making' (structure), and also 'the freedom of manoeuvre for national decision-makers' (agency).[32] In policy terms, greater interdependence in the EU has created more pressure to secure, for example, low inflation and economic growth for national economies in the Euro-zone, while meeting the goals of the EMU stability pact. Although the imposition of fines for countries transgressing these limits is open to interpretation – as shown by the decision in the Council to let France and Germany off the hook in 2003 – Commission warnings and even ultimatums to reign back public spending have encouraged governments not to transgress too far.

The pressures within the EU to enhance economic co-ordination, with the development of the Single Market and a Single Currency, have therefore been great. Even countries outside the new Monetary Union are committed to the EMU Stability and Growth Pact. What is more, the Lisbon Summit in 1999 established a system of economic co-ordination between Member States, where countries are judged by the Commission on their progress towards economic reform with regard to the completion of a Single Market (e.g. liberalisation of state-run utilities) and the maintenance of EMU Convergence or Stability Criteria. This has been used in combination with a 'peer pressure' exercise established in 1997, to 'out' poor performing states. 'Best-practice' is praised and promoted as a model of success, while unwillingness to reform is singled out, which can prove a major embarrassment to Member State governments. In September 2000, for example, the Commission called on Germany to 'cut taxes on labour further ... do more to encourage older workers into employment and to tackle labour market skills gaps'.[33] This was a particularly stinging critique for the SPD, as employment was their top-ranking electoral issue.

Common interests promote common solutions, and the Single Market and the Single Currency increased the logic of a common EU foreign policy in areas of economic interest. Improvements have, therefore, been made in the co-ordination of trade policy, which is now negotiated by an EU Commissioner for Trade on behalf of the Member States both bilaterally with trading partners and multilaterally through the World Trade Organisation (WTO). This, of course, affects the way in which EU members can conduct their own foreign policies, leaving less scope for unilateral action in this area. For Germany, however, it has come as less of a change, since its foreign policy has largely operated on a multilateral basis since the Second World War, through the EC/EU and NATO. Common problems, furthermore, encourage common policy, and the instability in the Balkans and the changes to the whole security climate after *September 11* acted as a spur to the development of the security pillar of the EU's Common Foreign and Security Policy.

The significant steps taken in EU integration since 1990 have also affected political processes in national settings by causing greater differentiation within European policy itself. In short, as EU policies have penetrated into domestic policy domains, it has become more difficult to pursue an overarching strategy for European policy, and more necessary to set out goals according to the individual policy area. It has also had implications for the formulation of European policy within national governments. The role of the German chancellor *vis-à-vis* the foreign minister has, for instance, clearly been strengthened as the EU has permeated into the affairs of the whole range of government ministries (Chapter 4). The Chancellor's responsibility for departmental co-ordination means more control over an increasingly departmentalised European policy. The national context of governmental policy-making is, therefore, in a state of flux, with the influence of finance ministries also growing as a result of the economic nature of the Single Market and EMU projects.

In terms of European integration, while German institutions have profited from a good 'administrative fit' with the institutions of the European Union,[34] Germany's social market principles do not necessarily fit well with policies directed from the EU level by the Commission, with particular regard to issues surrounding the completion of the Single Market. For the SPD, as most interviewees pointed out, the issue of state provision is a key one.[35] EU Competition Policy was pursued with particular vigour by Commissioner Monti after 1999. State support was questioned in the form of guarantees (and in some cases 'aid') to German state banks ('Landesbanken'),[36] and over the operation of local transport monopolies, which will eventually have to be altered in some way. One SPD politician revealed: 'we have had talks with Mr. Monti, and made it clear that it can in no way be a question of competition policy if you, for example, are talking about *Landesbanks* giving credit which private banks would never give in structurally weak areas'.[37] The questioning of state aid attacks a tenet of social democratic policy, which has given the more domestic-oriented of SPD politicians a reason to enter the European debate. The greater emphasis placed by the party on European policy (explained in later chapters) reflects the second dimension of *Europeanisation*.[38] In addition to *downloading* from the EU plane, the SPD had increasingly sought to *upload* its own policies to the EU level, to shape the *rules of the game*.

The domestic setting enjoys a two-way relationship with the EU polity, as member states can try to modify or limit integration. This is particularly important for the SPD in government as it has had a powerful voice in shaping the structures in which it operates: the 2003–04 Intergovernmental Conference (IGC) on institutional reform was, for instance, established at the insistence of the German Government, to – principally – resolve the division of competences between the EU institutions and the member states. Despite competition policy, furthermore, state subsidies still have a large part to play within the EU framework. This has been shown by the continued acceptance of subsidies for Eastern Germany and the Federal Government's victory on the subsidisation of renewable energy in March 2001.[39] European integration nevertheless provides a tight framework for European policy – especially at governmental level – which encourages congruence that is often supported by the international trends discussed in the next section.

Globalisation

The concept of 'globalisation' has been utilised to explain a whole range of international trends since the 1970s. The term is, therefore, 'multi-faceted' as well as 'amorphous' in the way it has been used.[40] International interdependency has increased both inside and outside the European Union through the integration of financial markets, markets for goods and services, the increased strength of multinational companies in the production process (*global sourcing*), a growth in the volume of global trade and the speed of capital movement, and the major advances in communications technologies characterised by the rise of the internet. What is clear, is that governments have become more aware of these global tendencies in calculating both their foreign and domestic policy. A set of global norms have been promoted, which represent a framework of pressures (real or perceived) in which EU politics takes place. While it is certainly contestable that *globalisation* offers a unipolar set of norms, governments undoubtedly came under pressure from financial markets to move towards free market goals. In formulating policy, therefore, political parties have tried to respond in some way to these trends, which begs three questions: what is the nature of *globalisation?* What effect is it having on Germany? How have policy-makers in the SPD sought to respond to these challenges? Economic globalisation is underpinned by interdependency, and this can be demonstrated by the growth in international trade. Between 1965 and 1980, world exports as a proportion of GDP jumped from 9.1 per cent to 11.5 per cent, increasing further to 15 per cent by 1995,[41] while external trade for the EU 15 grew by almost 2 per cent per year on average (as a proportion of world GDP) through the 1990s.[42] In terms of the German economy, the export quota increased from 18 per cent to 28 per cent of GDP between 1970 and 1989. While this had dropped down to 20 per cent by the mid-1990s as a result of the concentration of resources on eastern Germany, it increased steadily thereafter,[43] totalling over $1000 bn for the first time in 1999.[44] This illustrates the fact that Germany is an export-oriented economy and more susceptible to global trends than most. As 'one of the world's most open economies',[45] it is also one of the most sensitive to influence from external economies, both in the EU and in the outside world. According to Fritz Scharpf in 1998, '36 per cent of the working population are employed in the internationally "exposed" part of the economy' (compared with 32 per cent in the US and 27 per cent in the Netherlands), so this same proportion of German workers is dependent upon international competitiveness in 'a sector which must continually drive down costs and increase flexibility'.[46]

Pressure has been exerted on Germany by the markets and the dominant discourse of economic liberalism to reform in the direction of the US model, which enjoyed so much growth in the 1990s. For greater competitivity within the global system, it is argued that America's 'equity culture and flexible labour markets are better suited to technological and structural trends'.[47] In other words, an equity culture allows the quick movement of capital needed to utilise the new information technology, the deregulation of state-run industries produces greater competitivity, while flexible labour markets may be needed to aid rapid restructuring of service industries. Since unification, Germany has pursued the liberalisation or partial liberalisation of several industries (e.g. telecommunications) for these reasons and to reduce pressure on growing government debt. These dominant economic values have attacked state aid, but without the sophistication of the EU approach which allows structural aid for social cohesion. In 2001, for instance, the OECD accused Germany of 'squandering billions of D-Marks in aid to the economically depressed east'.[48] In line with current wisdom, the SPD-led Federal Government has sought to encourage growth and trade through major reforms which have lowered direct taxation significantly for individuals and companies.

The German *stakeholder* model operated in the past has come under threat. Large German companies, exposed to the Anglo-Saxon equity culture in the New York and London stock markets, have been increasingly working under the *shareholder* principle. Legislation passed by the Red–Green Government in 2000 to abolish Capital Gains Tax on the sale of cross-shareholdings is likely to accelerate this process. Given the principle of free trade, the deregulation of state-owned companies can be a precondition for striking international deals. In September 2000, for instance, the German Government had to assure US officials that it would reduce its stake in Deutsche Telekom to enable a take-over of the American company Voicestream.[49] The increasing penetration of *shareholder value* into the German economy has led to pressure on companies to restructure in line with this principle, that is, to take steps that the markets see as improving efficiency. It has also resulted in calls for Germany to restructure its labour market. The OECD, in its review of Germany in 1999, focused on 'the urgency of labour market reform'.[50]

While markets are undoubtedly becoming more integrated, it is a mistake to see economic globalisation as a unipolar force. The popularity of US-inspired economic theory, which John Gray has termed 'the Dow Jones interpretation of history', has been very much based on the short-term success of the US economy in the 1990s, and Gray rightly predicted that the US itself would become more protectionist with the 'pricking of the Wall Street bubble'.[51] Some have seen the EU as an opportunity for a political response to economic globalisation, which – according to Trade Commissioner Lamy – 'essentially amplifies and reinforces the strengths, but also the contradictions, of market capitalism'.[52] Despite Germany's high volume of foreign trade, however, the vast majority of its exports go to the EU market, so EU-level policy is actually 'as sovereign against external shocks as the USA'.[53] The SPD recognised in its major European policy paper in 2001 that 'individual Member States are less and less in the position to bring their interests to fruition internationally'.[54] The desire to 'tame' the excesses of the markets was a major part of the reasoning behind this European policy concept, which aimed to offer *security in change*.[55] The keystone of the SPD's policy review was to support deeper European integration in a number of areas as a response to *globalisation*,[56] extending central aspects of the social market model such as the right to 'co-determination' in the workplace onto the EU plane (Chapter 7). At the same time, *globalisation* prompted the party in government to engage in its *Agenda 2010* programme of welfare, labour market and tax reforms (or was, at least, *instrumentalised* to show that reform was necessary). In his efforts to convince the party and the country of these proposals, Chancellor Schröder argued: 'Either we modernise as a social market economy or we will be modernised by the untamed forces of the market that will force the social element to one side.'[57]

A final aspect of globalisation that cannot be ignored has been the globalisation of security risks after the events of 11 September 2001. Just as economic globalisation has increased the desire for an EU-level economic and social policy in the SPD, the War on Terror and the conflict in Iraq illustrated the importance of a European Common Foreign and Security Policy. The SPD has sought to integrate the wide array of security challenges within an integrated foreign policy, to be pursued by the European Union (including so-called 'soft security' areas like development aid).[58] Chancellor Schröder stated at the Progressive Governance Summit in London in 2003 that 'Globalisation and the changes it engenders do not wash over us in the way natural phenomena do. It is up to us to address the risks of insecurity, inequality and unfair access to opportunities, and to promote social democratic answers.'[59] The party's commitment to EU-level solutions to foreign policy problems external to the Union has been illustrated by the SPD's position on the communitisation of foreign policy (Chapter 11). The SPD's 2002 *programme for government* therefore argued that: 'Globalisation is a reality. To want to stop it is an illusion. Its free course is dangerous ... The European ideal has its own value, but it is also the indisputable answer to globalisation.'[60]

Part II
The Formation of Policy

3
European Policy-making in the SPD

Part II looks into the mechanics of policy-making in the SPD in the light of the political parties' literature tackled in Chapter 1. The examination of 'policy contexts' is an especially helpful way of looking at policy formation, as it maps out the central actors and structures that have impacted upon SPD EU policy since 1990. The purpose of the section is to lay out the context for EU policy formation within the SPD, and the pursuit of its policy objectives both in opposition and in government since 1990. The *climatic changes* described in Chapter 2 demonstrate the transient nature of the policy contexts, and the chapters in this part will seek to bring out this dynamism (Figure 3.1).

Before looking at the *policy contexts* and the structures and the actors operating within them, it is necessary to explore two vital factors outside the model for European policy depicted in the introduction. Chapter 3 will therefore start by examining at the organisational framework for European policy within the SPD and the key transition from opposition to government. The party organisation must be defined as it represents the institutional framework of the SPD (Figure 3.1) and is, thus, essential in determining the opportunity structures for European policy-making. Second, it is acknowledged here that the process of policy formation is to a large extent based upon the anticipated reaction to policy proposals and/or upon their chances for implementation. SPD European policy has, for this reason, been critically dependent upon whether the party has been in opposition or in government (Figure 3.1) as several interviewees have pointed out.[1] Here, the shifting relationships between policy formation and policy implementation are captured in the *opposition–government paradigm*.

In the *institutional* (party) *context*, the key to understanding SPD policy is to realise that there has been more than one stream of thought – the

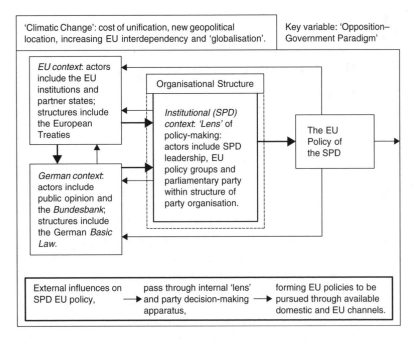

Figure 3.1 Policy context – the formation of EU policy through the lens of the SPD*

Note: * The arrows with thick stems indicate a strong link between the boxes, a thin stem denotes a moderate to low linkage.

views of the party's leadership *Troika* of Gerhard Schröder, Oskar Lafontaine and Rudolf Scharping in the mid-1990s on European Monetary Union were, for example, very far detached from those of the party's specialist European policy groups.[2] This underlines the need for a detailed examination of the interplay between the federal leadership, the parliamentary party, the SPD's European Policy groups, and – in brief – the party in the *Länder* and at grass-roots level. The SPD is a prism for the aggregation of a wide multiplicity of interests, the most important of which will be addressed in this section. The *institutional context* explores the nature of this prism, which is crucial to the SPD's role as the 'lens' of this study (Figure 3.1), concentrating on the locus of policy-making at the *federal* level, within the broader German and EU contexts explored in Chapter 4.

Party organisation

Social democratic parties across Europe have sought to emphasise their democratic credentials, to show that they are working for the people.

Their organisations have, therefore, been based on a *bottom-up* structure for which the chief organ has been the party conference.[3] This was traditionally true of the Labour Party in Britain and the *Parti Socialiste* in France as it was of the SPD in Germany. The SPD has been termed a *delegate democracy*, since the party delegates, elected through a bottom-up representational system are dominant in terms of voting power at the party conference. The realities of decision-making in the modern world nevertheless require a much more *top-down* approach, essential for a political party to work efficiently in the electoral marketplace. Only the central leadership has the ability and resources to act quickly and effectively enough in the age of the *24-hour media*. While party delegates may not be ignored all the time, the federal leadership, when it remains cohesive, has very great advantages. The 'Jusos' (Young Socialists) group within the SPD has lamented this situation after the party came to power in the late 1990s: 'the classical party structure is scarcely the place where plans for the future are discussed and opinions are formed ... Even party conferences only relate to what is being developed in the federal SPD or the Government, the administration and ... the parliamentary group'.[4] This is especially the case in European policy where issues are often highly specialised and only of a limited interest to the majority of delegates from regional, district and local associations.

The organisational structure of the SPD can be classified along two lines: the federal structure moving outwards from the centre to the regional parties in the *Länder*, to the local associations within the *Länder*; and, the many associations, commissions and working groups at the federal level all under the roof of the SPD 'Vorstand' (executive), which is elected by delegates from the regions and districts at the federal 'Parteitag' (party conference). The individual parts of the SPD, along the federal axis, have a high degree of autonomy, and the party *Vorstand* is largely utilised to find internal compromises between the different planes and ideological wings. Disinterest and particularism over European policy in the SPD in the regional and local associations is high, however, and EU policy as such is given far less attention than more local issues. Roth agrees that at the regional and local levels 'the relevance of structures and their contribution to policy formation [in the area of European policy] bears no relation to the [party's] programmatic output'.[5] For this reason, the study will concentrate on the party leadership, European policy groups and the parliamentary party at the *federal* (national) level, which represent the core of European policy-making in the SPD.

In his definition of 'loosely coupled anarchy' in the early 1990s, Peter Lösche stated that the SPD was 'strongly decentralised, fragmented and flexible ... The three party planes, local, regional and federal, are almost not bound to each other'.[6] This was the result of organisational pluralism, and the political autonomy at the regional and local levels was aided by relative independence in terms of financial resources. The difficulties caused by these decentralised power structures were clear to see in the early 1990s when the regional leaders of the party jockeyed for power in the federal leadership structures. From the use of German peace-keeping troops in *out-of-area* activities to disagreements over strategies of co-operation or non-cooperation with the Government parties, the *Länder* Minister-Presidents, imbued with a sense of personal rivalry and a lack of party discipline, did not allow the party to settle for a consistent political strategy at the national level. Rudolf Scharping, party chairman from 1993 to 1995 attempted to draw in the other key figures from the *Länder*, Lafontaine (Saarland) and Schröder (Lower Saxony), into a leadership 'Troika', but this only led to further internal friction. One party analyst argued at the time that it was inappropriate for Scharping to surround himself 'with ambitious *Länder* princes like Schröder and Lafontaine, who must always represent their own regional interests'.[7]

Changes in the social composition of the party greatly contributed to its ideological pluralism,[8] and this was not easily contained by the organisational structures of a *weakly institutionalized* party.[9] Lösche has described this diversity: 'The social composition of voters, members and functionaries of the current SPD is extremely heterogeneous in contrast to the solidarity community ... workers with blue, white and grey collars, academics, small business people, some managers of transnational concerns, (some) students, housewives and (many) pensioners.'[10] A new generation of leaders, more individualistic and ecologically minded, were furthermore beginning to permeate the upper echelons of the party in the *Länder* and on the federal plane, so that social and ideological heterogeneity now existed at the highest level. The emergence of the Greens as a major political force, in addition, turned ideological uncertainty into a strategic dilemma which exacerbated the divisions: should the SPD move to the *centre* to gain votes from the Christian Democrat parties or to the ecological Left to gain votes from the Greens? Worse still, these problems had come at a time of *climatic change* in Germany, and the SPD was without a strong and charismatic leader to unite the party as Willy Brandt had done in the late 1960s and early 1970s. The drafting of the Berlin Programme between 1984 and 1989 was a case in point, as the main wings of the party – *traditional Left, New Left* and *centre-establishment* – all attempted to exert their influence.

In the end, a programme was produced that was vague and quickly outdated. It was not just the lack of leadership autonomy that challenged the SPD, but also the party's declining and ageing membership. Common to most other parties in the Western world, *voter dealignment* was increasing and *party identification* was decreasing, and the party's ties with its core electorate were weakening.[11] The SPD leadership was not ignorant of these organisational weaknesses, and after the crushing defeat at the federal elections in 1990, there was a common feeling among the party elite that organisational change was required to compete effectively with Chancellor Kohl's Christian Democratic Union. A new reform agenda, 'SPD 2000', was published in 1991 under the chairmanship of Björn Engholm and his new party manager, Karlheinz Blessing. It aimed to strengthen internal democracy within the party and, by establishing a stronger axis between the leadership and members and opening the SPD up to non-members, to strengthen the authority of the leadership and the party's appeal to the electorate.[12] Party analyst, Uwe Jun has argued that 'Direct democracy is more easily instrumentalised in support of the power centres than a delegate democracy ... In the same vein the targeted opening of the party means a greater degree of heterogeneity in the decision-making process, giving the party leadership a greater degree of autonomy.'[13] Engholm phrased it succinctly: 'We want to remain the party with the largest membership ... and win people to social democracy who do not yet belong to us. We want to enable our members to play an even greater role in the political decision-making process in the SPD ... We want to organise an electoral majority and win the elections.'[14] The measures included the introduction of primary elections for the party chairman and the opening up of SPD local associations, 'working communities' (like the Young Socialists) and thematic groups to non-members.[15] Further proposals were made to modernise and professionalise the party through communications training for its activists and the introduction of quotas for 'Under 30s' at communal elections.[16] After Engholm's resignation in 1993, his successor as party chairman, Rudolf Scharping, shied away from taking these changes to their logical conclusion.

Under the chairmanship of Oskar Lafontaine (1995–99), the party leaders nevertheless began to put aside their differences (despite tensions between two key figures, Lafontaine and Schröder) in a final push to remove Chancellor Kohl from office. Less than five months after coming to power at the federal level, however, Lafontaine resigned, sparking a change in political direction and a summer of internal party squabbles in 1999. The new SPD leadership, recognising the party's organisational deficiencies, embarked on a reform initiative. Franz Müntefering was elected as the first General Secretary of the party in December that year with a mission to reorganise the SPD. Müntefering, with the assistance of party manager, Matthias Machnig, set out a list of proposals most of which reflected the recommendations of *SPD 2000* to assist the transition from a 'membership party' to a 'network party'.[17] Though initially successful in effecting greater co-ordination and harmony on the federal plane, his attempts to streamline the party through the creation of general secretaries and presidiums at the regional level (with autonomy over regional and local finances) proved more difficult to achieve.[18] The current leadership nevertheless remains determined to move towards a more centralised system with a stronger federal leadership–membership axis and a more 'flexible' or 'hierarchical' party structure. Aside from these formal changes, party leaders have used the media more and more to get their message across not only to the electorate in general, but also to their own members, to make the party more cohesive and manoeuvrable in an age where campaigning has rapidly been moving away from the streets and onto the television screens. These organisational changes, if not formalised, have yet taken place in practice.

The opposition–government paradigm

Paterson has stated that: 'Perhaps the most popular approach to the study of parties and foreign policy in West Germany has been to see the main determinant of party policy being whether it is performing a government or opposition role.'[19] While agreeing that this determinant is very important, the book argues that it is by no means the sole causal factor behind change: of the three major dynamics in SPD EU policy set out in this study, only one – the *electoral-strategic* dynamic (Chapter 6) – is directly related to the opposition – government axis. Paterson, developing the work of Joseph Frankel, implies three stages of development along this line: the pure opposition party; the 'government party in waiting' (as perceived by the electorate), which is 'no longer a *de facto* opposition party whatever may have been its *de jure* status'; and, finally, the party in government.[20] Though the lines dividing these phases are somewhat blurred, it is nevertheless essential to examine the opposition–government paradigm *vis-à-vis* the SPD's access to the levers of power on the federal plane.

The phases mentioned above are particularly important in terms of characterising the coherence, consistency and 'pragmatism' (in terms of implementation) of SPD European policy. The quest for regional and national votes when in opposition allowed SPD politicians to give European policy a lower priority than would have been possible in power at the federal level. They could also afford to be more populist (though this was not necessarily a good thing in electoral terms) because, unlike the Government, they did not have to negotiate deals at the EU level. Policy in opposition was also divorced from the interdependent reality of the EU by the opaque, intergovernmental nature of decision-making in the Union. This is no more evident than in the debate over European Monetary Union in the mid-1990s (Chapter 8). Chancellor Schröder explained the difference between formulating European policy in opposition and government in an interview with 'Die Zeit' a few months after coming to power: 'In opposition, one can comment in a different manner on Brussels decisions. As head of government, however, one must participate in organising the difficult process of European integration. Of course, the view of Europe as a concept changes as well as the reality if one holds the office of head of government.'[21] The federal leadership's focus on winning elections meant that it was easy to lose sight of the realities of policy-making at a governmental level. Maull has argued that this resulted in a steep learning curve for the SPD-led government in 1998: 'The real problem of German foreign policy lies not in the "what" of policy but in the "how". It centres less on which priorities and goals the Red–Green government pursues, than on the fact that they are learning to come to terms with different structures in foreign policy.'[22] It is interesting to note that the EU policy of the party's European experts remained relatively constant during this period.

In the first phase of opposition, party policy was less under the control of the chairman, as the power struggles and disparate discourse of the SPD minister-presidents from the *Länder* demonstrated. As party discipline increased under the chairmanship of Lafontaine in the late 1990s, the formulation and presentation of its policies became more coherent and thus more credible in the eyes of the electorate – more like a *government in waiting*. Former party manager, Matthias Machnig has argued that 'central changes of position were achieved between 1996 and 1998: demonstrating a decisive and governable party; organising the co-operation of leading personnel and coming to a clear decision on the [Chancellor] candidate; developing a new face for the SPD in a programmatic and communicative form ... and constructing an effective campaigning organisation for polling day'.[23] Policy for the party in government had to be fitted to a new, even tighter set of constraints.

With particular regard to European policy, the general consensus between the major parties in the German system meant that the SPD – in opposition – could only produce a clear counter-position to the Government by taking what could be considered an extreme position in the context of German European policy (e.g. support for a postponement of Monetary Union). Such a position was unlikely to bear any fruit with the electorate, because – given the known commitment of the SPD to European integration – it was viewed as opportunistic.[24] The problem of Europe as an election issue for the federal party was that the overarching consensus 'made it difficult for the opposition to gain a profile in this area',[25] forcing the party to concentrate its energies elsewhere.

One crucial aspect of this three-phase process for the SPD was the effect that being in opposition had on the relative influence of the federal leadership in the party. Without the independent apparatus of government, the SPD was far more a prey to particularist fiefdoms within the party organisation. The office of party chairman, for instance, was constantly in the grip of *Länder* Minister-Presidents from 1991 up until 1998.[26] Each of these chairmen had to put up with implicit or explicit opposition and rivalry from other regional leaders. The SPD elite, in addition, had to pay attention to the delegates elected to the party conference from the regional and sub-regional level. The move to a *government in waiting* meant the solidifying of this loose party discipline in the years leading up to the 1998 elections. Continual defeats at the polls pushed the party towards a stronger, more co-ordinated leadership. According to Franz Walter: 'For the first time in years, the SPD in 1996 acted in a disciplined and decisive manner.'[27] The drive towards the *centre* in search of votes to gain power, led to an emphasis on the domestic weaknesses of the Kohl Government (e.g. high unemployment, low growth), while stressing continuity in European policy. The increasing effectiveness of the SPD electoral machine also made the party more *responsive* to the *climatic changes* that were taking place in Germany during the same period (Chapter 6).

Another important distinction is the one between party and Government. In the study of SPD EU policy beyond 1998, the two must where possible be disentangled. In government, European policy has been highly co-ordinated both between government and party at the federal level and within the party at the federal level: according to one European policy expert attached to the SPD 'Bundestagsfraktion' (parliamentary group), 'party policy is government policy and vice-versa'.[28] Furthermore, as Gerhard Schröder was both Chancellor and party chairman between 1999 and 2003, commonality of personnel existed at the highest level. Six of the party's thirteen-strong presidium were government ministers in December 2003 (Table 3.1), including most of the senior SPD ministers in the Red–Green coalition. Problems in the co-ordination of European policy have, therefore, been just as often questions of governmental co-ordination as differences between government and party.[29] European policy groups within the party and parliamentary party thus co-operate intensively with each other (Table 3.2) and the relevant government ministries, especially if they are led by an SPD Minister.[30] Another factor supporting the dominance of the Government over the party in the issue of European policy is the question of resources. Peter Glotz, one of the party's foremost strategists, has argued that the SPD must be less 'reactive' in the area of European policy: 'If the party only discusses ... what the Government has already done, it will be impotent.'[31] This situation was somewhat remedied by the launch of the party's European policy review in 2000, which resulted

Table 3.1 Federal government offices of SPD presidium members, December 2003

Presidium member (party office)	Government office
Gerhard Schröder	*Chancellor* (chair)
Kurt Beck (Minister-President of Rheinland-Pfalz)	—
Wolfgang Clement	*Economics and Employment Minister* (deputy chair)
Wolfgang Thierse (*Bundestag* President)	(deputy chair)
Ute Vogt	*Parliamentary State Secretary in Ministry for Internal Affairs* (deputy chair)
Heidemarie Wieczorek-Zeul	*Minister for Economic Co-operation and Development* (deputy chair)
Edelgard Buhlmahn	*Minister for Education and Research*
Bärbel Dieckmann (Mayor of Bonn)	—
Hans Eichel	*Finance Minister*
Andrea Nahles (chair of *Democratic Left 21* group)	—
Harald Schartau (chair of regional association, North Rhine-Westphalia)	—
Olaf Scholz (General Secretary)	—
Inge Wettig-Danielmeier (SPD treasurer)	

Table 3.2   SPD European policy groups as of October 2001: functions and key personnel

Group	Function	Chairman	Key members
Kommission Europa: operating at party HQ (Willy-Brandt-Haus) under the *Vorstand*.	'to critically assist the policy of the Federal Government ... to prepare strategically and anticipate possible discussions at home. It will draft the European policy chapter for forthcoming Basic Programme.'[1]	Norbert Wieczorek	Kristian Gaiser (head of West European section of *Internationale Abteilung*), other EU experts.
Arbeitsgruppe Angelegenheiten der Europäischen Union (in SPD parliamentary group).	'to co-ordinate European policy tasks inside the SPD *Bundestags-fraktion* and, in particular, to prepare for key SPD *Fraktion* European policy decisions ... [to provide] a cross-cutting function within the SPD *Fraktion*.'[2]	Günter Gloser	Norbert Wieczorek, Jürgen Meyer (including all SPD members of the *Bundestag* European Affairs Committee.

Notes
[1] SPD Bundestagsfraktion, *Arbeitsgruppe Angelegenheiten der Europäischen Union* (June 2000).
[2] www.spdfraktion.de.
Source: SPD *Arbeitsplaning 2000/2001, Kommissionen: Europa* (June 2000), www.spd.de.

in an important contribution to the European policy debate through its 'Responsibility for Europe' paper.

Paterson argues that it 'is rare for political parties in government to bring pressure to bear on the government in matters of foreign policy. Parties in opposition attempt to bring pressure to bear but, given a government enjoying a majority they are normally condemned to failure.'[32] At surface level, there is 'a virtual osmosis between political party and government',[33] and it is impossible to say with any great certainty where one begins and the other ends because of the need for unity in government. The influence of the party is nevertheless exerted through behind-the-scenes activity in the *Vorstand* and Presidium, while key figures in the party hold key ministerial posts (Table 3.1). The party can, therefore, effect government policy at the 'agenda-setting' stage: a government may abstain from a certain course of action to prevent a detrimental reaction from one of its composite parties. An SPD-led government must equally interact with or within the SPD institutional context. Though party policy-makers must operate under tighter strictures, the government still has the capacity to interpret their policy preferences.

The institutional context

An investigation of the institutional context of European policy-making in the SPD, must study the relationship between actors within the party. Cole confirms that, 'We can understand parties as diffuse power networks.'[34] Indeed, the purpose of an exploration of the institutional context is designed to shed greater light on the nature of the internal machinery. It should be re-emphasised that the party cannot be viewed as a single entity in policy terms (even at the federal level). The SPD at the federal level, which is the focus of the book, has the job of balancing internal interests with external interests, to produce policies that are acceptable to the party as a whole, that will appeal to the electorate and other important actors, and that will achieve the ideological or political goals of the party. As a 'government spin doctor' admitted after the Government had conceded extra income tax cuts for the worse-off in their 1999 programme of tax reform: 'We had to think of how to package it for our own people ... The SPD can be very tricky sometimes.'[35]

Jürgen Bellers, in his extensive examination of SPD European policy in the 1950s and 60s stated that: 'As for decision-making committees relevant to European policy in the party, the following stand out: (1) Party executive and Presidium with their affiliated committees; (2) The executive of the parliamentary grouping and the *Arbeitskreise* [working groups] assigned to it (whereby a high personal continuity exists between the executive of the party and the parliamentary grouping) ... and, (3) the SPD representatives of the European Parliament who are organised within the European policy working group.'[36] This study broadly agrees with the assessment of Bellers, underlining – in particular – the role of the leadership and the European policy groups. The examination of the SPD's EU policy network will seek to establish the importance of the actors involved at the federal level. Since the lower levels of the SPD tend, quite naturally, to occupy themselves with issues closer to home, EU policy – more than any other area – is the preserve of the federal level of the party with its greater resources and inclination to look into these matters. It is essential, however, to go beyond the federal plane, if only to show that this assertion has, by and large, proved correct. The chapter will therefore provide a brief overview of the SPD at *Länder* level, and the party 'Basis'(grass roots) at local and district level. Because pressures for electoral efficiency and *climatic change* have ensured that the context for policy has been in a state of flux, all these areas will be analysed with reference to the changing nature of European policy-making in the SPD.

The federal leadership

Political parties in Germany have three distinct leadership roles: party chairman, Chancellor (or 'Chancellor Candidate') and chairman of the parliamentary group. Although these offices do not have to be mutually exclusive – as Chancellor Schröder's election to the chairmanship of the party (April 1999) showed – they have tended to be separated in the SPD. The most famous example of tripartite leadership occurred under the Chancellorship of Helmut Schmidt (1974–82). Schmidt, who was not overly popular in the party, led the government, Willy Brandt led the party, and Herbert Wehner marshalled the parliamentary group. The chairman of the parliamentary party is normally subordinate to (but not directly responsible to) the party leader, and they co-ordinate high-level policy decisions together in the party presidium or in smaller unofficial meetings. Though it is common for the party chairman to become the Chancellor Candidate (e.g. Scharping in 1994), this is not necessarily the case (e.g. Lafontaine in 1998). This separation of powers has caused problems for the SPD. In the early-and mid-1990s, the parliamentary party was regularly producing policies at odds with the party executive. The post of General Secretary was established in 1999 partly in recognition of this problem, to maintain a high level of co-ordination between the upper echelons of the party.

The hand of the party leadership is greatly strengthened when in power at the federal level, as party policy and parliamentary party policy must be co-ordinated with government policy. The leadership may not, however, move too far from the main body of party opinion for long, even in the relative autonomy of government. Gerhard Schröder's SPD-led Government was seen by the party (particularly at grass-roots level) to have made too many concessions to industry in 1999 and again in 2002–03, and was forced to make serious amendments in the reform proposals to pacify the party. Heidi Simonis, minister-president of Schleswig-Holstein was quoted as saying: 'Many consider Gerd to be an egotist, but he too wants to be loved ... He has grasped that one can not govern on an enduring basis against the party.'[37] The relative dominance of the party leadership in EU policy is heightened by the 'responsibility of the Chancellor in setting the guidelines of governmental policy [as stipulated in Article 65 of the Basic Law] ... [and] The principle of ministerial autonomy [which] allows ministers considerable discretion in their particular area of responsibility.'[38]

The SPD *Vorstand* is elected by the delegates at the party conference, and is thereby a broad representation of the different groups and wings of the party. The executive elects the members of a thirteen-member presidium, which is usually biased towards politicians close to the party chairman or Chancellor (Table 3.1). Lösche states that 'the presidium is naturally the power centre, supported by the party bureaucracy in the presidium, the *Vorstand* however is more a centre of integration for the party, including different associations, wings and working communities, than a centre of power'.[39] In terms of European policy, issues are co-ordinated and formulated by the European policy groups under the *Vorstand* at party headquarters when the party is in opposition, where most internal compromises will be made. Major decisions on policy guidelines are, however, often taken in the presidium, which comprises leading figures from the federal party and the *Länder* (Table 3.1), on the ideas drafted in the policy groups. In government, policy is often formulated in the relevant ministries, most commonly the Chancellor's Office, the Foreign Office and the Finance Ministry in co-ordination with the European groups in the party, before being agreed upon in the Cabinet and the Presidium (several politicians will be present in both). The views of the party and the parliamentary party are sounded out beforehand, so that their opinions are usually factored into the policy equation before they are formally launched.

A further development in recent years common to most political parties in Western Europe, is the growth in importance of advisors, hastened by the arrival of a new, professional and media-friendly generation of party leaders. The growth in stature of these advisors in the party's policy formulation from opposition to government can be very great. Chancellor Schröder epitomised this change – several close advisors from his time as Minister-President of Lower Saxony followed him to the Chancellor's Office. Together with the other leaders of the party, they form a so-called 'Kanzlerlager' (Chancellor's camp), that has been called 'the true centre of power in Berlin'.[40] In August 2000, this group was reported to include the then SPD General Secretary, Franz Müntefering ('with his intimate knowledge of the SPD's soul'); chairman of the parliamentary grouping, Peter Struck; government spokesman, Uwe-Karsten Heye; minister of state at the Chancellor's Office, Hans Martin Bury; the Chancellor's personal advisor, Franz-Walter Steinmeier; and, Schröder himself.[41] The Chancellor also has special advisors for particular policy areas. His foreign policy advisor up until November 2001, Michael Steiner, had direct access to Schröder and travelled with him on political trips abroad, and became an increasingly central player with the growing involvement of the Chancellor in German foreign policy.[42]

In terms of European policy the federal leadership, while having the say on major policy decisions, has often – in practice – left the details of policy to experts in the party's EU policy groups. As one party official, deeply involved in SPD European policy through the 1990s, explained: 'European policy was not made by these people, and they were little interested in it. This theme is not something one can use in an election or when talking to people on the street ... European policy was focused in a relatively small group.'[43] This was especially the case in opposition when electoral gain was key: the party concentrated on domestic issues, perceived of as more important by the voters. In government, however, the party leaders holding ministerial posts have been required to concern themselves with the details of European policy as a fact of life in – for instance – the Council of Ministers.

European policy groups and European policy

There are several groups at the federal level that provide expertise and help in drafting EU policies to be decided upon by the Presidium, *Vorstand* and parliamentary party, and – if it is a major policy programme – by the party conference. The high level of co-ordination between these groups must be stressed, as must the number of key personnel common to them (Table 3.2). First of all, under the international section (Section III), which operates under the SPD *Vorstand* at party headquarters, is the 'Kommission Europa'(Commission on Europe – Table 3.2 and Figure 3.2).[44] The Commission complements the work of the 'Arbeitsgruppe Angelegenheiten der Europäischen Union' (Working Group for European Union Affairs) in the parliamentary party, launched in the early 1990s in parallel to the *Bundestag* European Affairs Committee (Table 3.2 and Figure 3.2). The politicians in direct charge of the drafting and formulation of European policy are the SPD European spokesperson in the *Bundestag* (the head of the European policy *Arbeitsgruppe*) and the head of the *Kommission Europa*. The two European policy groups examine current European issues (Table 3.2). The tasks of the *Kommission Europa* for 2000–01, for instance, were to 'steer and co-ordinate [policy] on Europe, EU enlargement, the European defence identity, the Turkey question and likewise Bundeswehr reform'.[45]

Like other policy groups within the party, the European groups have a larger role to play in policy formation in opposition than in government.

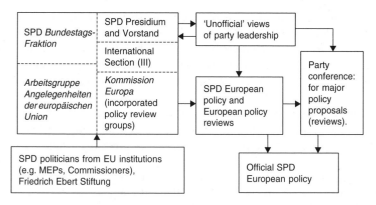

Figure 3.2 The structure of European policy-making in the SPD

When in power, the party leaders in government have far greater resources in the ministries than the party's EU policy groups. European policy between the Government and party at the federal level has proved quite coherent since 1998. The European policy groups have tended to play a 'reactive' role in policy after the SPD came to power, analysing the details and political and strategic implications of Government policy (Table 3.2). In opposition, the European groups under the *Vorstand* were responsible for developing the contours of policy, while the role of the parliamentary working group was to prepare the work of the SPD *Fraktion* in the *Bundestag* through a constructive engagement with government policy in the *Bundestag* committees. In power, both groups have played a complementary role to the Federal Government – though the *Kommission* has been more pro-active in the development of party policy with regard to the 2000–01 review process (Table 3.1).

The European groups were brought together – in opposition – under the umbrella of the '*Koordinierungsstelle*' (co-ordination point) for European policy, headed by Heidemarie Wieczorek-Zeul.[46] The role of the *Koordinierungsstelle* and other European groups at this time was described in an internal paper, circulated in 1995, on the preparations for the 1996 IGC on the 'Maastricht leftovers': 'In our given timetable, our reform schedule should be agreed in the SPD committees in the Spring of 1995, and in its most important elements it will be permeated by the work of the SPD parliamentary grouping in the German *Bundestag*. The entire reform concept should be agreed upon at the SPD party conference in Mannheim in November 1995' (Figure 3.2).[47] Wieczorek-Zeul then asked for questions about the development of the EU to be resolved in the party's European committees.[48]

In opposition, from the early 1990s onwards, SPD European policy was formulated by a small group around Wieczorek-Zeul in close co-ordination with Norbert Wieczorek, chairman of the *Bundestag* European Affairs Committee. Policy was co-ordinated across all policy areas in the *Bundestagsfraktion* by the European policy 'Querschnittgruppe' (cross-cutting group). A special *'Schwerpunktkommission'* (literally, 'focussed commission') for EU affairs was launched at the Mannheim party conference in 1995 to accompany a general policy review, producing an interim report in 1997. The *Schwerpunktkommission* was formed with Wieczorek-Zeul as chair and involved such influential figures as Rudolf Scharping (chairman of the parliamentary party after Mannheim) and Norbert Wieczorek, to draft a report which could form the basis of European policy for the 1998 federal elections (Figure 3.2). The policy review nevertheless involved, for the large part, a group of European policy experts in Wieczorek-Zeul's home district of South Hessen in conjunction with local Members of the European Parliament (MEPs) Will Görlach (head of the SPD group in the European Parliament) and Barbara Schmidbauer.[49] The *Schwerpunktkommission* was later followed, in government, by the major European policy review launched in 2000, which is examined in detail in the following chapters. The SPD at the federal level has heavily utilised the specialist knowledge of its MEPs and other contacts in Brussels such as Klaus Hänsch (former President of the European Parliament), Monika Wulff-Mathies (Commissioner for Regional Development before 1999) and Günter Verheugen (Commissioner for Enlargement after 1999 – Figure 3.2). The MEPs, in addition, proved a useful point of contact with other EU social democratic parties, providing channels of information and influence, which were particularly useful in opposition (Figure 3.2).

European policy nevertheless occupied a low status in the party for many years. It could be argued that the apparently low rank of EU policy in SPD policy programmes or statements, and in elite party activity merely reflected electoral strategy, since public opinion has not rated Europe highly in its list of priorities.[50] Several interviewees likewise emphasised the point that it has often been quite difficult to convince their colleagues of the importance of EU affairs.[51] European policy experts were sometimes irritated by the way party leaders used European policy for populist gain, or diverted attention away from official SPD European policy. Wieczorek-Zeul complained, for example, that 'the *Vorstand* had published tax proposals on the same day' as the SPD's new European policy programme was launched in 1997, 'thereby taking media attention away from the [SPD European] Conference' where it was being set out.[52] The growing importance of European policy within the SPD described in Chapter 7 can, therefore, only be viewed in relative terms to its large-scale neglect in previous years.

Paterson has made the point that: 'The much larger research staffs available to German political parties create the preconditions for influencing through discussion.'[53] The SPD has had access to the vast resources of its own academic institution, the Friedrich Ebert Foundation, which receives huge financial support from the state equal to approximately €110 m in 2002.[54] As a semi-autonomous institution, the Foundation has been free to explore European policy issues in great detail. This expertise has been utilised by the federal party through regular consultations and participation in SPD European committees (Figure 3.2). This has been vital in policy areas like EU enlargement, which have been largely ignored (and therefore under-researched) by the party. At the federal level, as we have seen above, SPD European policy has tended to be the preserve of the European experts with deference to the party leadership. The fact that, 'neither the parliamentary group as a whole, nor the party conferences or other committees have the necessary sources of information at their disposal',[55] only serves to reinforce the dominance of the party leadership over European policy.

The SPD in the *Bundestag*

The parliamentary party has been part of the integrated federal policy team illustrated above. As Bellers noted in the 1970s: 'The executives of the parliamentary grouping and the party are crystallised in the "core leadership" of the SPD, which presently agrees the foreign policy and European policy course of the party.'[56] This statement is equally true today. Policies that are formulated in the European policy groups must be agreed by the Presidium and/or *Vorstand* in which the leaders of the parliamentary party are also present. The European Union Affairs Working Group is headed by the *Bundestagsfraktion*'s European spokesperson and comprises all the SPD members of the *Bundestag* Committee for European Affairs (Table 3.2).[57] In an assessment of the European policy work of the parliamentary party between 1998 and 2002, the *Fraktion* reported: 'The SPD parliamentary group supported and helped shape the European policy of the Red Green Government ... the European Union Affairs Working Group supported and promoted the work of the Government with initiatives, meetings, debates and discussions position papers etc ... It has argued for and promoted the European policy positions of the Government and [of] the coalition parties against the opposition groups in the European Committee.'[58] In this period, work concentrated on the German EU presidency, the Lisbon process, and EU institutional reform.[59] The European Affairs Working Group has the additional function of co-ordinating work across the various other policy committees in the SPD parliamentary group – 'e.g. on foreign policy or the environment'.[60]

Social Democratic MPs also participate in the *Bundestag* Committee for European Union Affairs. The Committee was set up in the wake of the Maastricht Treaty on European Union. Originally an SPD proposal, it began work on 15 December 1994 (under the chairmanship of Norbert Wieczorek) in accordance with the amended Article 23 (3) of the Basic Law (Chapter 4).[61] Although the establishment of the Committee did not mean that the SPD increased its influence substantially over Government policy, it did afford the party the right (in theory at least) to be informed 'comprehensively and as quickly as possible of all [Government] initiatives within the framework of the Union which could be of interest to the Federal Republic of Germany'.[62] This gave the SPD at least some insight into the intergovernmental negotiations taking place in the EU. Co-operation in the *Bundestag* committees with the CDU-led Government before October 1998 and the CDU-led opposition afterwards has also contributed to the general feeling of consensus over European policy between the major parties (Chapter 4).

One could argue that Europe has had a greater significance for SPD members of the *Bundestag* than for the non-*Bundestag* leaders of the party in the 1990s, because of their day-to-day involvement with European affairs, 'through the necessary engagement with EEC guidelines and directives and alike in the *Bundestag* committees'.[63] The SPD's European group nevertheless mainly fulfils a technical role in the *Bundestag*, focusing on the details of German EU legislation and fine-tuning the details of SPD policy – essentially a *reactive* exercise. Lindner has argued that the 'SPD parliamentary group differentiates itself from the consensus and the resulting European policy programme of the Government groups only through a somewhat differently weighted ordering of priorities.'[64] The result has been general disinterest over EU affairs within the *Fraktion* where 'European policy ... plays a subordinate role.'[65] European policy has, however, been made a higher priority in recent years, especially in organisational terms where European policy 'emancipated' itself from foreign policy, under which it was previously subordinated.[66] This development was (significantly) supported by the creation of a new deputy chair of the *Fraktion* responsible for European policy after the 2002 elections.[67]

The European policy of the SPD in the *Bundestag* has changed since unification, from opposition to government, but its views – unlike those of the party leadership – have been greatly moderated by its consensual, institutional setting (Chapter 4). The make-up of the parliamentary party, in addition, is less heterogeneous than other parts of the SPD, so has oscillated less than the federal party as a whole in its policy positions and electoral strategies. This was particularly true in the early and mid-1990s when control of the party leadership swung between the feuding regional premiers.

The SPD at *Länder* level

The German *Länder* play an important role in the federal structure of the country. In the 1990s, before the SPD came to power at the federal level, they were the power bases from which most of the party's heavyweights operated. The office of minister-president in the *Länder* administrations allowed these regional leaders a large degree of independence from the party structures, which was a major source of the *loosely coupled anarchy* inside the SPD. SPD leaders mostly originated from *Länder* politics, and – even in government – regional party leaders are strongly represented in the SPD presidium (Table 3.1) and *Vorstand*. The existence of extensive governmental powers at the regional level lessened the imperative of party discipline that might have bound these leaders to the federal level more strongly. Party analyst, Joachim Raschke, compared Germany to the UK: 'Election defeats in England are always total, there is no comfort on the regional plane ... This strengthens the will to win. The SPD participates in governing Germany even when it loses. Perhaps this suffices for them. The power to reform is given up, however, by making do with the *Bundesrat* corrective powers.'[68] Rudolf Scharping, prior to his tenure as party chairman, admitted that: 'It is not acceptable that the Bonn SPD is one thing and the *Länder* are another', but his attempts to 'dovetail' the two met with failure.[69]

The SPD already possessed a majority in the *Bundesrat* in 1991, when they were in coalition in eleven of the sixteen *Länder*, with SPD politicians leading the governments in nine of these regions. This gave the party, in theory, a great deal of leverage over the Government's European policy, since European Treaties had to be passed through the *Bundesrat*. Because of the basic consensus on the merits of European integration, however, the Kohl governments could relativise SPD influence in the upper chamber, because they supposed that they could always rely on the party in the end to support European Treaties. The

SPD, furthermore, was not cohesive enough across the regions in the early 1990s to block Government measures: thus 'Kohl was able to counter the SPD's hold on the *Bundesrat* by offering incentives for Social Democrat *Länder* to break ranks and vote with the government.'[70] The views of the SPD *Länder* on EU policy have commonly had more to do with regional politics and regional interests than with party politics. This was not helped by the added factor that the new German *Länder* had different interests to the old *Länder* in the West, as they profited significantly from EU Structural Funds.

The impact of the SPD's strong regional identity on its EU policy in the early and mid-1990s was characterised by two further traits – particularism and populism – which was not aided by the fact that the regional leaders had little expertise in this area. The *Länder* were largely uninterested in European affairs: SPD regions only became excited over issues relating to *Länder* competences[71] and EU funding. This apathy was accompanied by the opportunist use of European policy for electoral advantage, as illustrated by the scepticism of *Länder*-based politicians towards Monetary Union in the mid-1990s (Chapter 8). Once in government, former minister-presidents such as Schröder had to find out through experience about the necessity of the EU and the interdependent nature of European Union politics. SPD *Länder* have not, however, been *Eurosceptic* in the UK sense. While seeking to stop the EU from encroaching on their competences, they still desire 'EU competences to be extended in areas of grand politics ... foreign and security policy, for example, or tax policy.'[72] The party leadership in government nevertheless found itself performing a bridging role between these regional interests and the realities of the EU polity as during the 2000 IGC on institutional reform (Chapter 11).

Delegate democracy and the party grass roots

The de jure organisational structure of the SPD, centres on the party conference (see above). The party conference consists of 400 delegates comprised mainly of those elected from party conferences at district or regional level, the members of the party *Vorstand* and one tenth of the parliamentary party. The main tasks of the party conference are: 'The acceptance of reports on the activity of the party *Vorstand*'; 'the election of the party *Vorstand*, [and] the control commission';[73] 'the passing of a resolution on the reports ... about the party organisation': and, 'the passing of a resolution on the agreed motions'.[74] For local and regional delegates, who tend to represent *traditional* positions in the party (e.g. for workers' rights, greater redistribution through taxation), the conference is their main means of exerting influence on the leadership.

In the SPD, the 'local party organisations have a high degree of autonomy' from both the regional and federal party,[75] and quite naturally have more interests in common with the regional organisation. Aiding the overall autonomy of the local associations is their relative financial independence. Lösche has pointed out that the '*Ortsvereine* and *Unterbezirke* are not only financially independent, but also do quite well out of it.'[76] While the federal party may pursue its own course to a certain extent, the autonomy of the local associations means that the federal leadership cannot stray too far from the party's *genetic model*. Delegates can embarrass the federal leadership at the conference by, for instance, denying members of the national executive adequate votes for their election at the first ballot and abstaining or voting against the re-election of the General Secretary (after 1999) and party chairman (Chapter 7). General Secretary, Olaf Scholz, was fatally wounded in 2003 for his part in the SPD leadership's plans for programmatic renewal, when he received only 53 per cent in a conference vote. In this way, the party *Basis* necessitates the development of party policies that are able to bridge the gap between electoral strategy (moving to the Centre where the votes are thickest – see Chapter 6) and ideological identity (the party's *core support*).

While EU policy is often subordinated to domestic policy at the federal level, and very often subordinated to regional and national policy at the *Länder* level, it is almost buried without trace beneath more immediate local, regional and national policy at the local level. The lower levels of the SPD are uninvolved in the European policy of the party to any meaningful extent, due to a lack of expertise and a lack of interest in EU politics – local associations wish to concentrate on local issues. While the salience of European issues may grow as the EU penetrates increasingly into citizens' everyday lives, the interest of local associations is likely to remain low and external to a policy formation process that is de facto dominated by the federal party.

4
Policy-making in a Wider Context

The *national context* has provided a crucial external framework for SPD European policy. As a relatively pluralistic *Volkspartei* (catch-all party), the party is an intricate network in terms of its organisation and the various groups that influence its European policy, and is relatively porous to a wide spread of interests within Germany and, to a lesser degree, Europe.[1] Chapter 4 will, thus, concentrate on central actors and structures that have influenced the development of SPD European policy. It comprises an analysis of the political, constitutional, institutional and federal structures in Germany, along with public opinion, the media and the 'social partners' (trade unions and big business), examining the key actors to be considered in European policy formation in Germany. The growing scepticism of public opinion on the benefits of the EU and its policies (e.g. German payments to the budget, EMU and Eastern enlargement), for instance, provided a clear lead for an SPD leadership eager to improve its poor electoral performance on the national stage. The *European context* will briefly look at SPD policy within the EU framework, studying the central actors and structures on this plane and highlighting the very different opportunities for achieving policy objectives between opposition and government. Hanns Maull has written of the complex nature of interest aggregation with regard to the Red–Green government in Berlin: 'German policy has ... to register the demands of other governments as well as the opposition, of international institutions as well as the social actors and private companies, and must appeal for support and mobilise coalitions.'[2] It is their role in the aggregation of interests that places political parties at the centre of the process, the *lens* through which those interests are processed (Figure 3.1, in the previous chapter).

The national context

In any study of European policy within a political party, the national context for policy-making is central. With regard to the European policy of the SPD, the influence of various domestic actors has been particularly great given the general lack of importance attributed to this policy area inside the party itself (Table 4.1). It is, therefore, necessary to investigate the party's changing relationships to key German actors and structures. The pluralism found within the SPD's institutional context (Chapter 3), is a reflection of the pluralism found in the German political system, designed to include all the large societal groups within the political structures of the country. According to orthodox pluralist

Table 4.1 Groups contacted for consultation, July 1993

Main themes	Groups to be contacted for consultation
Delors initiative for a new European economic model	partners to be contacted – for research and development, Rolf Linkohr [MEP]; for training systems, the labour research institutes through the DGB[1] [German Trade Unions' Federation].
The fight against unemployment	possible partners to be contacted – trade unions, churches, workers.
Debt, inflation, loss of the Deutschmark	partners to be contacted – institutes like the DIW[2] [German Institute for Economic Research].
Internal security	partners to be contacted – police unions, police representatives at the regional level, graduates from policy schools.
Environmental politics	partners to be contacted – environmental institutes in Wuppertal and Bonn.
Centralisation in Europe	arrangements to be made with the Socialist Parliamentary Group [in the European Parliament] on the establishment of The Committee for the Regions.
Co-operation with CEE[3] states	meetings with representatives of the parties closest to us in the CEE states, organised by the FES [Friedrich Ebert Foundation] bureaux in these countries.

Notes
[1] DGB stands for Deutscher Gewerkschaftsland.
[2] DIW stands for Deutsches Institut für Wirtschaftsforschung.
[3] CEE stands for Central and East European.

Source: SPD Bundestagsfraktion, *Vermerk für Heidemarie Wieczorek-Zeul MdB: Europapolitische Themen* (Bonn: Koordinierungsstelle für Europafragen, 14/07/1993), pp. 2–3.

theory, a state is made up of competing interests, each attempting to put its own views across to effect government policy and the policy of political parties.[3] It is duly noted, however, that despite the institutionalised nature of pluralism in Germany, politics is not a level playing field for the competition of interests, so that the relative influence of domestic actors is essentially uneven. Table 4.1, taken from an internal party document, shows the actors from the institutional, national and European policy contexts which the SPD European policy groups wished to consult in the second half of 1993, giving a snapshot of potential influences on party policy.

German EU Policy has followed certain established patterns, embodied in the basic consensus over support for multilateralism and European integration. The belief in the good of European integration was a mindset that extended beyond the political elites to other major organised interests in Germany. The groundbreaking events surrounding re-unification (described in Chapter 2) nevertheless brought this consensus into question, creating dynamics in the EU policy of the SPD that continued into government. With these grand alterations to the policy *climate*, it is doubly important to study the changing domestic context that has defined SPD European policy, and to examine how the party has interpreted these *domestic demands*.

Political context

As described in Chapter 1, European policy has been an area of consensus for mainstream political parties in Germany. Since the late 1950s, no major party has opposed European integration for any sustained period of time. SPD doubts over Monetary Union in the mid-1990s only related to the timetable, and never in any case became official policy. It is therefore possible to speak of a 'cartelisation' of European policy by the political elites in Germany in which European policy has usually been left to the European policy experts, and differences between the parties have not been great enough to turn them into major election issues. Foreign Minister Kinkel (Free Democratic Party – FDP), for example, praised the level of cross-party co-operation for the 1996 IGC as 'a good example of the agreement of the Federal Government, the *Bundestag* and the *Bundesrat* on basic questions of European policy. Our co-operation before and during the Conference was good ... The joint recommendations of the CDU/CSU, FDP and SPD point in the right direction.'[4] This high level of political consensus nevertheless concealed changes to SPD policy in opposition and neglected the fact that many of the most important elements of European politics lay in the details of integration.

The European policy consensus was nowhere more evident than in the *Bundestag*. The SPD's role in the parliamentary committees, when in opposition, was constructive yet *reactive*. The Committee for European Union Affairs was influential in amending and checking government policy, but played little part in policy formation. In support of co-decision in the *Bundestag* over EU affairs, the SPD was behind the establishment of this committee, which, theoretically at least, gave the party knowledge of the Government's basic strategy for intergovern-mental negotiations. Those SPD politicians closest to this process have been the most adamant – in interviews with the author – about the lack of difference between SPD and Christian Democrat EU policy.[5] The SPD European policy groups in the *Bundestag* were nevertheless compelled to compromise with those party leaders more *responsive* to public opinion and Germany's altered interests, which eventually led to a less elitist approach (Chapters 5 to 7).

In terms of German EU policy, the intra-governmental development of ministerial influence over European policy is of great importance to this study, as the Red–Green Government has had an SPD Chancellor and an SPD Finance Minister, but a Green Party Foreign Minister. Relative influence over European policy in Germany has alternated between four key ministries: the Chancellor's Office, the Foreign Office, the Economics Ministry and the Finance Ministry. Under the early Kohl governments, the guidelines of European policy were very much formulated by the foreign minister, Hans-Dietrich Genscher (FDP), co-ordinated in the Economics Ministry, with only a small level of input from Chancellor Kohl. With the negotiations for the Maastricht Treaty and the departure of Genscher in 1992, Kohl became much more dom-inant. More influence was also moving into the hands of the Finance Ministry at this time. EU politics focused on Economic and Monetary Union after the signing of the Maastricht Treaty (1991). Finance ministers now attend summits and are a central component in the governmental decision-making process. Theo Waigel (CSU), Finance Minister from 1989 to 1998, noted that 'Before his era ... European foreign ministers made a lot of agreements among themselves', but that the negotiations over EMU leading to the Maastricht Treaty showed that foreign ministers 'no longer had the authority to represent that new dimension of foreign policy'.[6] The Finance Ministry's powers were further enhanced after it took over many of the organisational powers for European policy from the Economics Ministry with the formation of Lafontaine's new 'Superministry' in October 1999 (see Chapter 9). While the foreign minister and the Chancellor continue to set the programmatic agenda for European policy, it is the Finance Minister who increasingly deals with the nuts and bolts of EU affairs in the 'Euro-zone'.

The key functions for European policy are now held by the Foreign Office, the Chancellery and the Finance Ministry – the European under-secretaries in these departments thrash out policy between themselves and any other directly affected ministries.[7] These meetings are chaired by the Minister for Europe in the Foreign Office.[8] Thereafter, 'the intentions of the German states' are 'sounded out' in the Bundesrat Working Group for European Union Affairs ('Ausschuß für Fragen der Europäischen Union').[9] In the case of broad strategic aims for the EU, all the most important ministers expect a say, given the penetration of the Union into all their domestic portfolios. In March 2001, for example, it was reported that the Chancellor, his key foreign policy advisor Steiner, Foreign Minister Fischer, Defence Minister Scharping, Development Minister Wieczorek-Zeul and Finance Minister Eichel, were all present to agree on 'a new strategic concept for ... foreign and security policy'.[10]

This brings us to another part of the German political system that defines governmental policy on Europe, namely the nature of coalition government. The Greens became more pro-European than the SPD in the 1990s (having previously been more sceptical), with their focus on environmental issues – an area with a much clearer EU dimension than, say, employment. Two factors characterise the nature of the coalition government: first, personal and power relationships between the key ministers; and, second, the policy programme set out in the *coalition agreement*. The post of foreign minister has traditionally gone to the junior partner in the coalition in Germany. In this respect, the relationship between the foreign minister and the Chancellor is crucial. While Genscher (foreign minister from 1974 to 1992) had a relatively free reign in European affairs due to his personal qualities and long tenure in the office, Kinkel (1992 to 1998) was seen to be under the thumb of Chancellor Kohl. The interplay between Schröder and Fischer after 1998 is, therefore, very meaningful to this study. While Schröder has taken a more assertive approach to German policy in the EU (Chapter 5), attaching conditions to German support for key EU policies (Chapters 8 to 11), Fischer has 'set out a modernised version of Kohl's narrative' and has been a clearer advocate of European integration.[11] The first coalition agreement, while not a cast iron guarantee of Government action, committed SPD members of the Government to pursue 'ecological and social reforms on the national and European planes' to accompany Monetary Union.[12] It is nevertheless the Chancellor who has the final say when he wishes to, as exemplified by the bizarre spectacle of Jürgen

Trittin, the Green Party Environment Minister, being forced to oppose a European directive on car recycling he had initially strongly supported in June 1999, because it placed too much financial burden on manufacturers.

One final nuance of the German political context is the fact that top civil servants do not have to be neutral in terms of political allegiance and 'Beamten' (officials) may become junior ministers. The implication of this for the incoming SPD-led Government in 1998 was that, after a long period in opposition the new Government wanted to replace many of the officials with its own people, including various specialist advisors (as discussed in Chapter 3). Though departmental officials may well be drawn from the diplomatic service for key jobs in European and foreign policy,[13] the consequence of the change in government was the appointment of a number of advisors, officials and politicians that were inexperienced at the federal level when the SPD came to power. This helped lend the new Government's European policy a chaotic appearance during its first months in office. While Chancellor Schröder made unrealistic demands for the reduction of Germany's contribution to the EU budget, Finance Minister Lafontaine banged the drum for tax harmonisation and a growth-oriented European Central Bank in a naively optimistic manner. Government departments and the civil servants manning them have nevertheless shown more continuity, tending to support established German policy positions. The Foreign Ministry, in particular, remains a firm advocate of the pro-integration European policy consensus and the Franco-German partnership. Departmental influences, thus, encouraged the SPD and its party leaders to adopt a less *tactical* and more *strategic* approach in the recent tradition of German European policy.

Constitutional and institutional markers

The *Basic Law* of the German constitution, as interpreted by the Federal Constitutional Court, offers comprehensive guidance on political affairs, setting specific parameters for German European policy. A two-thirds majority is required in the *Bundestag* and the *Bundesrat* to ratify the handing over of sovereignty through international treaties or for amendments to the *Basic Law*.[14] One might have supposed that this would have made the Kohl governments dependent upon the SPD to ratify international treaties. As parliament was only ever faced with a 'Yes–No' choice on European integration, however, and given the cross-party consensus, the SPD was highly unlikely to reject any such agreement. Parliamentary influence on German European policy could only be utilised successfully in combination with pressure applied by other Member States – as seen with the Federal Government's eventual acceptance of an EU employment policy in 1997 (Chapter 8).

In order to ratify the Treaty on European Union, changes to the Basic Law were required to integrate Economic and Monetary Union into the German constitutional structure. (1) Article 23 was amended in December 1992 to expressly include the *Bundestag* and the *Bundesrat* in European Affairs. (2) The *Bundestag* and the *Länder* through the *Bundesrat* are to co-operate in European Union affairs. The Federal Government has to report to the *Bundestag* and the *Bundesrat* at the earliest possible opportunity. (3) The Federal Government is to give the *Bundestag* the opportunity to form an opinion before its co-operation on European Union acts of law.[15] Against the backdrop of rapidly progressing European integration in an overwhelmingly intergovernmental form, these measures formally strengthened the powers of the *Bundestag* and the *Bundesrat* in relation to the executive.[16] The *Bundestag* Committee for European Affairs was established as a consequence of these constitutional amendments.[17] The work of the Committee became important in supervising the technical details of Germany's European policy for the SPD. It provided an important forum for discussion of key issues with the government parties and a good source of information on the course of policy in the Federal Government and the EU institutions.[18] The second consequence of the constitutional amendments was the establishment of formal *Länder* participation in European policy: in areas in which the *Bundesrat* would normally have 'the right to legislate, the Federal Government must take account of the position of the *Bundesrat*', and in areas where the *Länder* have the right to legislate internally or in issues affecting their 'administrative procedures' the views of the *Bundesrat* 'should take precedence over those of the Government'.[19] These rights have been actualised through the participation of two *Länder* representatives on German delegations to the EU, who participate in negotiations involving areas of *Länder* interest.[20] Parliament was nevertheless usually faced with a *fait a compli* in EU affairs, because intergovernmental policy-making often fell outside the scope of formal negotiations (e.g. the Franco-German summits).

The German Constitution is watched over by the Constitutional Court based in Karlsruhe. Its judgement on the Brunner case (October 1993),[21] in particular, established guidelines for German policy with respect to two areas: the input of Germany's democratic institutions into the executive's policy-formation process; and, the need for an *enduring* EMU stability zone. Brunner had challenged the validity of the Maastricht

Treaty with respect to Article 38 of the Basic Law, which cited the inviolability of the democratic principle.[22] He claimed that it implied that parliament should have a 'substantial' role in the decision-making process. The ruling put further pressure on the Government to accept the steps to ensure the inclusion of parliament referred to above. The judgement concluded that the Federal Government was required to seek parliamentary approval for the decision to embark on Stage III of Monetary Union in accordance with the stability criteria, and that Germany could remove itself from EMU in the future should the conditions for a 'stability zone' not be met.

In the German political system, many semi-autonomous bodies exist underneath the political structures. The prime example of this is the German Central Bank, the *Bundesbank*. In an analysis of European Economic and Monetary Union, it is difficult to underestimate the importance of this institution (see Chapter 8): the *Bundesbank* was prominent in establishing convergence criteria for EMU and the stability-based ethos of the European Central Bank, and after the conclusion of the Maastricht negotiations 'made it clear that the criteria had to be applied to the assessment of the level of convergence in order to make Monetary Union viable'.[23] Due to the unblemished reputation of the *Bundesbank* in the eyes of the German public, it would have been difficult for the Government to ignore its views. These events came at a time when the SPD was trying to present itself as trustworthy in running the economy, to improve their electoral prospects. It made good sense, therefore, to use the *Bundesbank* policy of supporting 'hard' convergence criteria as the basis of SPD policy on EMU from the early 1990s onwards (Chapter 8). While the impact of the Constitutional Court may not have been as great as some have suggested,[24] given the room for political interpretation of the criteria set out in the Maastricht Treaty and the Growth and Stability Pact (Chapters 8 and 9) and the political consensus behind European integration, the Constitutional Court ruling on the Brunner case and the *Bundesbank* stance on EMU gave the SPD 'institutional markers' within which to frame its policy on Monetary Union. It also gave the party a sound base from which to attack the Government on the *democratic deficit* in its European policy and its *softening* of the Convergence Criteria.

Federal structures

The German federal system is a defining characteristic of the country's polity. The relationship between the federal and *Länder* levels is a power relationship that impacts heavily on decision-making in both government and political parties. Most important legislation requires the consent of the *Bundesrat*, and the Federal Government requires the help of the *Länder* to implement their policies. The regions, on the other hand, are dependent on the Federal Government for their revenue through tax legislation. The pressure for both sides to co-operate and seek consensus is, therefore, high. This means that political parties at the federal level, in opposition or government, must negotiate with the *Länder* if they wish to push through or block government programmes.[25]

One anomaly of the German federal system in recent years is the fact that the Federal Government has rarely possessed a majority in the *Bundesrat*, as a result of *Länder* elections falling between federal elections and increased levels of voter volatility (especially after unification). Despite opposition blocking majorities in the *Bundesrat*, however, their capacity to influence policy has been limited. This was certainly the case with the SPD majority in the *Bundesrat* in the early and mid-1990s. For example, it was reported in 'Der Spiegel' that 'the Brandenburg Minister President, Manfred Stolpe helped the wily Kohl Government to raise VAT, so that his poor eastern province thereby profited with added income'.[26] As this extract goes on to suggest, the SPD was not yet disciplined or coherent enough to stick together, to block or force the government to amend its legislation.[27] The Federal Government could often push through legislation against a disunited opposition with the offer of *incentives* to individual *Länder*. The Red–Green Government managed to push through Finance Minister Eichel's tax reforms in July 2000 in just such a manner. The SPD only became a coherent force in the late 1990s, when 'different from before, there was an uncompromising *Bundesrat* policy with which Lafontaine smashed the tax reforms of the Christian Democrat–Liberal coalition'.[28]

The examination of the institutional network above (Chapter 3) showed how important the regions were to the SPD during their years in opposition. This was less the case in the area of European policy, which – with a few exceptions (e.g. Monetary Union) – did not capture the imagination of the *Länder* chiefs or governments. The reason for the lack of regional influence in European policy is that the *Länder* work primarily in the interests of their own political constituencies. As a consequence they are often particularist in their policy objectives, and only interested in a narrow range of European issues relating to EU subsidies or their own political and administrative competences. The *Länder* have nevertheless impacted on German European policy and, indeed, EU politics in general, in the area of competences. They helped ensure that the principle of 'subsidiarity' was enshrined in the Maastricht Treaty and pressed the Red–Green Government strongly to gain agreement at the Nice European Council (December 2000) on a further IGC, they hoped, to rule on the division of competences between the EU and its Member States (Chapter 11). With the progress of EU integration, it seems likely that the controversy over competences will – with regard to issues like the state-funding of public provision (Chapter 9) – continue until a clear constitutional settlement is reached. It should, however, be re-emphasised that the *Länder* remain firmly behind European integration in *grander* issues like the extension of EU foreign policy.

The media and public opinion

Public opinion on European policy in Germany carried surprisingly little weight after 1990. Due to the overwhelming consensus among the political elites, European integration proceeded 'despite' rather than 'because of' public feeling. German opinion, for instance, was consistently opposed to the introduction of the Single Currency throughout the 1990s. Only 32 per cent of Germans expressing an opinion supported Monetary Union in 1993, the year the Treaty on European Union came into force, and support for the European currency remained well below 50 per cent in the period leading up to the introduction of the Euro.[29] The scepticism towards the Single Currency filtered through into German perceptions of the EU as a whole: the percentage of Germans who thought that the country had 'benefited' from EU membership dropped significantly from the early to the late 1990s (Chapter 6). European policy formation in Germany since 1990 can therefore be seen as an elite-led process.

It proved difficult to incorporate the views of the public and SPD voters into the European policy of the party because of the policy elite's vehement belief in the good of European integration. The sceptical comments of Schröder, Lafontaine and Scharping on Monetary Union in the early to mid-1990s examined in Chapter 8 did, however, mark the beginning of a change in the party's attitude to European affairs, a consequence of a more *responsive* attitude to public opinion (see Chapter 6) and the confidence of a new generation of SPD leaders brought up on the regional stage (see Chapter 5). Although party policy remained pro-integration, these trends in public opinion encouraged the SPD (both in opposition and in government), to pursue a more assertive style of EU policy.

The media has played an increasingly influential role in German politics in recent years. As in most other Western democracies, leaders of political parties utilise it as a resource with which to appeal directly to the party membership and the electorate. The SPD leadership increasingly focused on the media as it moved towards power, to communicate its goals more effectively to these groups and to turn the party into something resembling an electoral machine. Lösche explains, in relation to the party membership, that using the media is 'no conscious autocratic decision of the party leader, but a necessity in the age of the electronic media'.[30] The SPD chose Schröder instead of Lafontaine to stand against Kohl in 1998 largely because of his superior media skills. The nature of media coverage, furthermore, made it hard for the party in opposition to profile itself against the Government by offering realistic European policy alternatives, because – unless they were very radical – they were unlikely to reach the electorate. While the media was always keen to report SPD statements against the introduction of the Euro that broke with German policy tradition, this was still nothing like the level of media interest it attracted once the party was in government.

The media is, of course, extremely responsive to public opinion. Therefore, in terms of European policy, despite its broadly pro-integrationist leanings and general support both for EMU and eastern enlargement, the German media also reflected some of the growing public concerns over the EU. The more central position of the media (in particular, the broadcast media) in politics allied with the developments in public opinion on the EC/EU have – together – affected German policy in the sense that the Federal Government must now be seen to be fighting Germany's corner, especially in Summit situations, where all Member State leaders are expected to come home with a *prize*.[31] This was clearly demonstrated in the run-up to the European Councils in Berlin (1999) and Nice (2000).[32] Yet German governments have recognised better than most that the advantages derived from the EU are too great to push these *hard interests* too far.

The social partners

The German trade unions have always maintained a strong relationship with the SPD. The German Social Democrats, unlike their UK counterparts, however, are not a direct offshoot of the labour movement, and the trade unions are obliged to remain organisationally independent from political parties. The unions have nevertheless had many interests in common with the SPD, since they have sought to serve similar constituencies. They also permeate the party both through ideas and personnel and provide a useful source of information on industrial affairs (Table 4.1). Former Employment Minister, Walter Riester, for instance, was a former 'Second Chair' of the powerful IG Metall union, Ursula

Engelen-Kefer, deputy chair of the German Unions' Federation, was on the SPD *Vorstand* throughout the 1990s, and many SPD politicians have union affiliations.[33] Oskar Lafontaine, as party chairman, had a close personal relationship with Klaus Zwickel, chair of IG Metall, and the unions publicly supported the SPD in the 1998 and 2002 election campaigns.

The SPD has been less partisan in its support of the unions (as opposed to business interests) when in government – since it has to run the economy with the co-operation of both – forming a triangular, broadly corporatist arrangement, as typified by the Chancellor Schröder's 'Bündnis für Arbeit' (Alliance for Jobs), set up after the 1998 elections. The SPD increasingly courted big business both to establish the credibility of its economic policy in opposition, and to manage the country when in government. Schröder, the embodiment of the business-friendly approach, was on the board of directors for Volkswagen when Minister-President of Lower Saxony. After the Red–Green Government embarked on its *Agenda 2010* reform package in 2002 (see Chapter 7), relations with the unions somewhat soured. Although trade union action failed to prevent the progress of these measures – here, the failure of an IG Metall strike in Eastern Germany in summer 2003 was especially important – there may be a bumpy road ahead.

The unions have proved influential in specific areas of European policy. Since the policies of the SPD and unions have been relatively close, this has tended to reinforce policy rather than change its direction. The unions tried to keep the SPD-led Government to its *worker-friendly* policies formulated in opposition. Their efforts were largely focused on improving levels of employment and workers' rights. IG Metall clarified its views in January 1999: 'IG Metall expect the initiatives of the Federal Government to lead to a change of course to an active employment policy and social regulation.'[34] Although, the unions would undoubtedly have wanted a greater emphasis in the EU on employment and social regulation, this was unlikely given the free-market stance of other EU governments (e.g. the UK and Spain) and out of question once Lafontaine had departed from the scene. The German Government nevertheless concluded an Employment Pact at the Cologne Summit (June 1999), and pushed for social regulations to be incorporated within the European Charter of Fundamental Rights and a European constitution. The Government, furthermore, was happy to see the establishment of EU-wide quantitative goals for employment in Lisbon in 2000 (see Chapter 9).

The European policy goals of big business have been fairly consistent. In general, they have supported financial discipline (with regard to the

German state and the EU), free markets (fettered by a minimum of social regulation) and economic stability (in terms of low inflation and a stable exchange rate). Big business has, therefore, been interested in securing a broad-based EMU under the stability criteria to create the largest possible Single Market in which to conduct their affairs. Though the SPD leadership must take greater account of business interests in government, the ideology of the *Neue Mitte* is also sympathetic to many of their aims (Chapter 7). An EU directive on car recycling, for instance, was blocked by the Government in June 1999 after intervention from the Chancellor (allegedly spurred into action by a telephone call from Ferdinand Piëch, head of Volkswagen). The differences between business and trade unions in EU policy should not, however, be over-exaggerated. Both are generally in favour of European integration, and many business interests support the export of the German social market model to the EU level both in terms of societal values and comparative advantage for Germany in the EU.

The European context

The importance of the European context in shaping both EU policy formation and the pursuit of policy goals on the EU level is self-evident. The European context for the SPD can be split into three domains: relations with the EU institutions; with EU Member States; and, with other social democratic parties in the EU. Given the intergovernmental nature of the European Union, the influence of these actors and structures on SPD policy (*downloading*) and on the effectiveness of that policy at EU-level (*uploading*) has been extremely dependent upon the *opposition–government paradigm* (Chapter 3). In opposition, the SPD played no real part in the EU intergovernmental fora in which many of the most important decisions were made. In government, the party benefited from the influence of its leaders with the EU institutions and other Member States through their ministerial roles, which – conversely – placed pressure on the SPD to moderate its policy to the *European context*.

Non-governmental contacts were crucial in opposition. Lindner stated with regard to the SPD in parliament that: 'contacts to persons and institutions outside the *Bundestag* play a great role for the *Bundestag* opposition, which is not involved in negotiations at the European level. It offers the possibility to agree to positions and exchange information.'[35] The key SPD contacts on the European plane were: the party's Commissioner in Brussels; SPD MEPs in the European Parliament (also influential in the party's European policy groups – Chapter 3) and their contacts in the Socialist Group; social democratic Commissioners from other Member States; and, social democratic contacts from other Member States' governments. The SPD's European Congress in Bonn in 1997 characterised this network of actors well. Among the participants and speakers were Jacques Santer (Commission President), Monika Wulff-Mathies (SPD, Commissioner for Regional Affairs), and all of the SPD members of the European Parliament. At the Conference, Art Melkert, the Dutch Labour Minister, spoke explicitly of his frustration at the Federal Government's reluctance to accept a Dutch draft for an EU employment Policy at the IGC.[36]

The Party of European Socialists (PES) has provided a good opportunity for the SPD to exchange ideas and information with major figures in European politics. The PES holds a congress every two years when the president is elected. The President from 1994 to 2001 was Rudolf Scharping, a central figure in the SPD through this period,[37] so the party was involved at the heart of this network. While its importance should not be overstated given the fact that EU negotiations are still largely an intergovernmental affair, its significance is increasing. The leaders of the member parties now 'meet on a regular basis, often on the eve of a European Summit, to discuss the broad framework of EU policy',[38] to outline a common agenda for the most important questions of EU governance. As more and more EU states became governed by social democratic parties in the mid-to-late 1990s, the SPD's access as an opposition party to EU politics grew through its PES contacts. In May 1997, for instance, Oskar Lafontaine, SPD chairman and Lionel Jospin, First Secretary of the French Socialist party produced a joint European policy declaration against what they saw as a one-sided Monetary Union just a month before Jospin became Prime Minister: 'The Euro will only have the approval of the citizens if Monetary Union advances growth, employment and stability in all participating states ... [which is] only attainable if Member States come to a close understanding over economic and financial policy.'[39] The SPD's bilateral relations with its sister parties were intensified during the late 1990s and extended to sister parties in the EU applicant states through the work of the party's International Section.

The SPD gained greater levels of information, and – to a lesser extent – influence on EU politics through domestic channels. As mentioned above, the amendments to the constitution in 1992 'theoretically' obliged the Federal Government to inform parliament of their bargaining positions at the earliest possible opportunity – even if it was hard to know for certain what the German Government's negotiating stance would be without access to the vast majority of intergovernmental meetings and other informal dialogues. In government, on the other hand, the party has had access to all the inside information it needs through formal and informal channels to the EU institutions, Member State governments, council meetings and the German EU representation in Brussels. Informal and formal summit meetings can be used to decide issues of fundamental importance. In government, real influence is exerted through the party's key ministries, where the relationship between the SPD leadership and EU-level actors and structures is a two-way interactive process. The Red–Green Government, for example, has influenced the parameters of EU policy in the institutional reform debate (Chapter 11).

Apart from governmental participation in the EU's multilateral institutions, Germany utilises bilateral relations with other Member States. The long-standing partnership with France had been termed the *motor of European integration*. The two countries have regular summit meetings at which they can resolve their differences and agree on joint statements for the key issues. Relations with France have been deeply institutionalised through regular meetings at the highest level. After the SPD came to power, the relationship became somewhat strained, as the Government has begun to assert new German interests, divergent from those central to France. Schröder, in particular, was in favour of a more fluid alliance structure, as illustrated by his keenness to intensify bilateral ties beyond the Franco-German partnership (e.g. the Blair–Schröder paper, 1999). While some differences remain, contacts were intensified further after a low-point in relations at the Nice European Council in 2000. Foreign Minister Fischer played a prominent party in reinvigorating relations with France in the clear tradition of the German Foreign Office.[40] The signing of a new Elysée Treaty on Franco-German co-operation in January 2003 provided for the recalibration of the partnership, producing concrete results in the agreement of common positions (between the German and French Foreign Ministers) on the financial and institutional architecture of an enlarged European Union.

Part III

The Dynamics of European Policy in the SPD

5
The Next Generation

After looking at the *climatic changes* behind German and SPD European policy in Chapter 2 and the actors and structures involved in policy-making in Chapters 3 and 4, Part III will explain the manifestations of this changing policy environment in the form of three 'internal dynamics' in SPD policy. The *dynamics* to be explored are *generational, electoral-strategic* and *ideological*, which together characterise the main developments in SPD European policy since 1990. The SPD's capacity for change was enhanced by its position as an opposition party at the federal level for most of the 1990s. The learning process in the party's European policy was characterised by *pragmatism* in three senses: in the assessment and pursuit of German interests (*generational change*); with regard to the greater responsiveness towards the electorate and other actors within the policy contexts dealt with in the previous section (*electoral-strategic change*); and, in terms of ideological flexibility, which enabled the party to fashion a new response to *climatic change* (*ideological change*). While there were limits to the party's ability to change in all these areas, these forms of pragmatism define the dynamism in SPD European policy after 1990, and highlight the continuity and change in party policy during this period. A further catalyst for change was the transition from a party of opposition to a party of government (Chapter 3). A German Chancellor is always drawn towards foreign policy whatever their natural inclinations, due to the fact that Germany is comfortably the most populous country in Western Europe with the largest economy sharing borders with twelve states. After coming to power, the 'formula which was found read: "continuity in substance, new accents in style". In place of the *historical pathos* [author's italics] with which Kohl had underpinned his foreign policy, was Schröder's pragmatism.'[1] The *pragmatism* in European policy was encapsulated by the

Table 5.1 The development of SPD European policy since 1990 – policy dynamics

Internal dynamics	Impact on SPD European policy
Generational change	The emergence of a new generation of SPD leaders, socialised with European integration around them, allowed a more assertive EU policy, more willing to pursue *hard* German interests (Chapter 5).
Electoral-strategic change	The need for the SPD to maximise votes and construct a credible programme for government made it more *responsive* to public opinion and other domestic actors, while governing Germany brought home the importance of EU-level actors (Chapter 6).
Ideological change	From a state of ideological pluralism in the early 1990s and division over EU policy at the federal level in the mid-1990s, a coherent and comprehensive vision of Europe the early 1990s and division gradually evolved (Chapter 7).

dynamics described in the remainder of Part III and set out in Table 5.1, above.

The first *dynamic* in the development of SPD European policy is *generational change*. A new generation of party leaders came to power in the 1990s, who were less influenced by memory of the War and were more willing to be assertive in their pursuit of what they saw as German interests. The *generation* of party leaders that emerged in the 1990s adopted a more 'pragmatic' approach, which enabled them to interpret *climatic change* into a new style of German policy, ready to articulate material German interests (e.g. on the EU budget) and confident enough to sanction the use of German troops in *out-of-area* activities in Kosovo and Afghanistan. These politicians were determined to move away from *exaggerated multilateralism* towards *normality* in European policy. They made SPD support for European integration *conditional* upon the attainment of certain policy goals, and this approach was carried forth into government (Chapters 9 and 11). Chapter 5 examines the impact of generational change in SPD European policy, first, by looking at the extent to which the party leadership freed itself from the bonds of history; and, second, by focusing in on the more assertive style of SPD and German policy with respect to the EU budgetary policy and external security, to ask if German policy has indeed become more *normal*.

Generational change

Before 1990, a high degree of consensus existed on European policy between political parties and within Germany as a whole. European policy was dominated by conceptual agreement over 'the binding of Germany to France' and 'the economic advantages of the larger market'.[2] It was also founded on an *exaggerated multilateralism* originally designed to restore to Germany, through European co-operation, both political sovereignty and economic prosperity. In the mid-to-early 1990s, German policy under Kohl was largely impervious to *climatic change*, and still based on an historical conception of Germany's role, leading to an *exaggerated* or 'over-accommodating' German policy in the EC/EU.[3] According to one interviewee from the SPD's European policy community, 'when Kohl came back from Edinburgh or any other Summit, he always argued historically – Europe is the result of 1945, Europe is the answer to 1945 ... the return of the German nation to the civilised world'.[4] During the Maastricht debate in the German *Bundestag*, for instance, Kohl emphasised that the question before them was to 'commit ourselves irrevocably to economic and political union' or make possible 'a reversion to earlier times'.[5] In the 1990 election campaign, the SPD likewise claimed that: 'People know that only stability in Europe guarantees the growing together of both German states, but also peace and security ... A willingness to co-operate is therefore demanded of German politicians as opposed to nationalistic power games.'[6] The emerging SPD leadership generation in the 1990s was to use this type of reasoning less and less, and these politicians became the *political entrepreneurs* that would interpret *climatic change*.

Historical memory was, in fact, already becoming less of a factor as the Second World War moved further back in the national consciousness: Korte wrote that since 'the 1970s, at the latest ... the political order had to legitimize itself ... no longer exclusively through comparison with Weimar or the NS regime'.[7] In terms of a German leadership role, however, Kohl's position as late as 1996 was that 'Germany did not want more influence than any other Member State and was committed to making political integration in Europe "irreversible".'[8] The new mood in the SPD leadership and the country at large was epitomised by Schröder's comments in 1997: 'Kohl says the Germans have to be tied into Europe or they will stir up old fears of the "furum teutonicus". I say that's not the case. I believe that Germans have become European not because they have to be, but because they want to be. That is the difference.'[9] After the *climatic change* brought about by unification and the end of the Cold War, the new generation in the SPD was increasingly able to distance itself from the traditional style of reasoning. Schröder therefore felt able to press for Germany to have more votes than France in the Council in the negotiations on institutional reform leading up to the Nice European summit (2000), in direct contradiction – as President Chirac pointed out – to Kohl's remarks quoted above.

The impact of *generational change* on SPD policy was an increased assertiveness in the pursuit of altered German interests, and an increased interest in the detail of policies that would be presented on a more differentiated, case-by-case, basis. This development extended far beyond the SPD, and across the whole of German politics and society. High-ranking figures in the coalition parties were also keen to articulate German aims more clearly. The Christian Democrats, Wolfgang Schäuble and Karl Lamers, introduced the concept of a 'Kerneuropa' (core Europe) in 1994, which could better reconcile German interests in a simultaneous *deepening* and *widening* of the EU (Chapter 10). As European policy guidelines were set by their Chancellor, it was difficult for the coalition parties at the federal level to diverge from Kohl's traditional foreign policy perspective, and any substantive expressions of *wariness with Europe* were left to the Christian Democratic in Bavaria (the CSU). The SPD, on the other hand, was freer to interpret the demands of domestic actors in opposition, whether or not they offended Germany's EU partners. Yet this shift in attitudes towards Europe and European integration was not only due to the party's relative freedom in opposition, but also to a genuine change in values and political beliefs within the SPD leadership, so that the impact on policy was evident after the party's transition to government in 1998.

The more *pragmatic* approach to Europe among the German political elites was not something that has taken place in blanket form from one generation to the next. Instead, it marked the beginnings of a new European policy which, if not free from historical memory, was free from direct, first-hand experience of the period from 1933 to 1945. As a result of this dynamic and the change in perceptions brought about by German unification and the end of the Cold War, the 1990s showed a marked acceleration of this process. Between 1994 and 1997, the percentage of Germans citing 'freedom and peace' as more important in European policy than 'the economy' dropped from 41 per cent to 27 per cent.[10] As an SPD member of the European Parliament explained: 'I am of the post-war generation ... I was socialised with European integration around me.'[11] In sum, the new generation took Germany's place in the European Community for granted, and were more concerned than their predecessors with the details of integration – the immediate political and economic impact of Community policies on Germany.

Leading figures in the SPD in the mid-1990s were major actors in the *Jusos* in the 1960s and 1970s, for example, Schröder, Scharping and Wieczorek-Zeul. Nicknamed the *68ers* for their participation in the radical student movements of that time, they developed a strong sense of individualism. This new generation began their rise to power in the 1970s, when they began to take over the reigns of the SPD Young Socialist (*Juso*) organisation. Although they were – at this stage – imbued with idealism and political radicalism, this was nevertheless – as Walter argues – underlied by a strong pragmatic or 'opportunist' streak.[12] While the SPD had undergone programmatic change in the late 1950s and early 1960s, to bring itself back towards the centre of a prosperous post-war German society, the new generation that flooded into the party in the 1970s were the social products of that new society. According to Walter, 'society had, as a whole, pluralised, was more culturally diverse, more tolerant, more colourful, more open – in short, more liberal'.[13] These youngsters differed greatly from the older generation of party members, who were socialised in the SPD when it was still clearly a *workers' party*. The new generation were more radical but, at the same time, more flexible in their outlook, because their ideals were based less on identification and solidarity with fellow workers than on their own individual 'Weltanshauung' (world view). They were inspired by the rhetoric of Willy Brandt, who talked of the new social and political goals of a wealthy German state. Most of the new generation furthermore represented the spirit of the times, reflecting the *New Left* goals of environmental protection and international *peace*. While most of these politicians opposed the creation of a more *normal* German foreign policy in the early 1990s (e.g. German participation in UN-peace-keeping operations), their individualistic tendencies (sometimes bordering on the egotistical) and different socialisation to former leaders, left them more open to the *climatic change*. In terms of European policy, however, they were too election-oriented to look much beyond domestic issues until they came to power at the national level (Chapter 6).

Paterson argues that the Berlin Republic 'will be more *selbstbewußt* in both senses of the German original. That is, it will be more self-conscious of itself as a separate player and more self-confident.'[14] Germany under an SPD-led Government has been set on achieving this kind of *normality* in European policy, so that 'Germany standing up for its national interests ... [is] just as natural as France or Britain standing up for theirs'.[15] This relates to both the psychological and economic impact of German unity, and the need for consolidation of the EU after the completion of Monetary Union and before enlargement. As mentioned above, the generational change led to the SPD leadership becoming more *pragmatic* in its conception of German interests. The economic problems in Germany in the 1990s, including high levels of unemployment (particularly in the East), caused the party to prioritise these *hard* domestic issues in the context of German payments to the EU budget. Even policy-makers in the Kohl Government had realised by 1997 that a 'more British bottom line view' must be taken,[16] and that German European policy could no longer be based on *cheque-book diplomacy*. The Kosovo conflict and the international security climate post-September 11 critically challenged Germany's view of its role in the world, and Chancellor Schröder emphasised that Germany would no longer ignore its *international responsibility*. The impact of *generational change* can thus be illustrated by changing SPD policy over two issues: the EC/EU budget and defence and security policy.

A more 'normal' Germany?

Germany, as a leading member of the EC and the economic powerhouse of the Community, would have expected to shoulder a large chunk of the running costs. During the 1980s and early 1990s, the Kohl governments had, by their willingness to compromise for the cause of European integration, greatly increased Germany's share of the net burden. In 1984, for instance, they had agreed to pay a large part of the British rebate negotiated by Margaret Thatcher, in order to ease the path of the Single European Act and the creation of the Single Market. Later that decade, Germany agreed to 'double German contributions to the so-called structural funds' after a similar budgetary dispute.[17] Furthermore, in 1992, at the Edinburgh Summit, the Federal Government agreed to take on the lion's-share of the new Cohesion Fund, set up to support the poorer countries in their attempts to meet the Maastricht convergence criteria. As a result of these *acts of generosity*, German net payments more than doubled between 1990 and 1994, from DM 11.6 bn (€5.9 bn) to DM 25.2 bn (€12.9 bn).[18] The fact that Germany was bearing over 60 per cent of the net burden would have been difficult to accept on its own, but with the costs of German unification and the drop of German GDP per capita from well above to below the EU average, for some it became unbearable.

The SPD leadership in the 1980s and the very early 1990s was not concerned with reductions in German contributions to the EU budget. For the German Council Presidency in 1988, it suggested that 'the means for the Structural Funds must be doubled hand in hand with a reduction of agricultural spending'.[19] As an opposition party, the SPD was nevertheless freer to articulate popular discontentment with this situation after 1990. The new generation of SPD leaders did not feel bound by traditional patterns of foreign policy to soften their demands. In 1994, SPD financial expert, Ingrid Matthäus-Maier, accused Chancellor Kohl of 'missing out, in his enthusiasm over Europe, on reducing the burden of a mid-ranking Germany [in the EU table of GDP per capita] after unification'.[20] In the early- to mid-1990s, however, the party's European policy community was not prepared to push this too hard and break with consensus: Detlev Samland MEP rebuked Oskar Lafontaine in a private letter in May 1994 over his comments on 'the theme of the paymaster position', writing that it 'has severely damaged the social democratic MEPs, because it has poured oil on the fire which the "Republikaner"[21] are attempting to ignite – the idea that the Federal Republic is the "Milchkuh" [milk cow] of Europe.'[22] The Federal Government nevertheless came under great pressure, even from its composite parties at the regional level (especially Minister-President Stoiber), to rectify this situation which had become a great embarrassment by the late 1990s.

It was not just the domestic-oriented SPD leadership which had been affected by the impact of unification. Though many in the party's European policy community still stressed the need for structural funds and the benefits Germany had received from the Single Market, they also wanted to see a reduction to Germany's net contribution in line with the economic situation (and an end to German *cheque-book diplomacy*) by the mid-1990s. One SPD MEP stated in an interview in 2000 that: 'we had a major change in the composition of the social democratic MEPs about five years ago ... to a younger generation. We are no longer in the European Union for reasons that have anything to do with history, and we will no longer be blackmailed with this ... it is not a project that we alone should have to pay for.'[23] Another in the foreign policy community in Berlin emphasised that Germany's excessive payments to the EU were 'a thorn in the flesh of German policy'.[24] A top SPD official made a similar point: 'Other countries have shown much trust in Germany, but Germany has proved itself deserving of this trust. We cannot base our responsibilities today on guilt for what happened forty or fifty years ago ... we must show that is simply not on any more.'[25]

As the SPD became a more credible opposition party in the late 1990s, their European policy moved towards that of the government in several areas (e.g. over Monetary Union), yet calls for a lessening of the German budgetary burden remained strong, and the party was not afraid to demand a reduction in the contribution at the expense of Germany's EU partners. By 1997, the Federal Government was also championing this cause. Finance Minister Waigel stated that he wanted 'to see net payments to the EU budget reduced to about 0.4% of GDP from the current 0.6%' for the new budget in 2000.[26] But this was barely credible given the fact that Waigel had helped negotiate the previous budget. Once in government, Chancellor Schröder stated unambiguously: 'the old system of solving European problems with German money doesn't exist any more'.[27] The Government pursued a reduction of its net contribution in three main ways: through the introduction of 'co-financing' in CAP (Common Agricultural Fund);[28] ending the Cohesion Fund since Monetary Union had by then been completed; and, abolishing the British rebate. These proposals meant upsetting three of Germany's major partners: France, Spain and the UK, respectively. In the event, the Red–Green Government was prepared to accept a moderate decrease in German payments in favour of more fundamental European goals. At the European Summit in Vienna (December 1998), the Chancellor stressed that he would seek 'budgetary justice' for Germany in EU financial negotiations, and as late as January 1999 argued strongly for the country's net contribution to 'decrease clearly' from its level of approximately DM 22 bn (over €11 bn), adding that 'more than half the contributions that are burnt in Europe come from Germany'.[29] It could nevertheless be written just two months later, that 'money is no longer so important for Schröder's group' – for Verheugen (Minister for Europe) what 'Europe brings cannot be calculated in Marks, Francs or Guilders'.[30] The Chancellor had therefore modified his initial approach, adjusting his position to the constraints of the EU context. Even within the context of more pressing issues,[31] however, some reductions to the German net contribution were achieved (Chapter 11). The reduction of German contributions has also remained a focus of the SPD's EU agenda, as the party's *Responsibility for Europe* paper showed in its proposals for the re-nationalisation of CAP and Structural Funds.[32]

Another European policy (and foreign policy) area in which the impact of generational change was felt was defence and security policy. At the beginning of the 1990s, the SPD at the federal level was firmly against the use of German military resources in *out-of-area* operations. Many in the party were even opposed to the use of German minesweepers in the Persian Gulf *after* the first Gulf War in 1991, and the party took the Federal Government to the Constitutional Court over the use of German ships to uphold the UN-embargo of the Adriatic during the Yugoslav conflict.[33] Within the SPD, there were fierce public disputes over the use of *Bundeswehr* troops in UN peacekeeping operations. The up-and-coming generation of SPD leaders – such as Lafontaine, Schröder, Scharping and Wieczorek-Zeul – were firmly against German participation, reflecting their *New Left* sympathies. At the Bremen party conference in 1991, Lafontaine said that 'Wars do not fit with human rights', while Schröder argued that 'If the war-mongers think that we should participate in conflicts ... that, I find grotesque'.[34] Socialised in the pacifist and environmental movements, they were opposed to the use of German troops for UN-peacekeeping missions. Hans Ulrich Klose, chair of the SPD parliamentary group from 1991 to 1994, supported German involvement in the Gulf War, but later remarked that – in the *Fraktion* – 'I was the only one in the party who supported participation.'[35]

Engholm, the party chairman, was one of the first in the SPD to go down the route of advocating a more active role for Germany in international operations, explaining how unification had directly affected his position: 'At our 1988 Münster Party Conference, we saw the blue helmet-story [German participation in UN-peacekeeping] ... as not right, because we were – as before – a divided nation with limited sovereignty. This has changed in the meantime.'[36] The linkage of unification to German military action (in a multilateral setting) was an idea that most of the new generation of leaders were to increasingly accept as time moved on, since they were flexible in the way they judged Germany's external climate and interests, and had the capacity to change. The fragile compromise reached at Bremen was expressed in the SPD's 1994 programme for government: 'The *Bundeswehr* should remain as part of the NATO defence force, and take part in UN peace-keeping operations ... [but] their should be no participation in wars ... whether such wars take place under the auspices of the UN, NATO or the WEU.'[37]

The inner-party disputes over UN peace-keeping in the early 1990s lie in stark contrast to the Red–Green Government's decision to use German troops in NATO operations against Serbia from March to June 1999, when there were few voices of dissent to be heard within the SPD on the federal plane. The flexibility element of *generational change* meant that the SPD leadership could adapt to the new post-unity reality and so was less concerned (in terms of historical resonance) by the idea of Germany planes flying sorties over Serbia that were not even sanctioned by the UN. Though Fischer (also a *68er*), the Green Foreign Minister, was inclined to 'modernise' rather than 'de-emphasise' Kohl's historical approach,[38] his *pragmatism* was illustrated by the fact that he had the self-confidence to reinterpret the 'nie wieder Krieg' ('never again, war') motif of post-war Germany into the phrase 'nie wieder Völkermord' ('never again, genocide'), thereby justifying intervention on humanitarian grounds. SPD politicians relied less on historical reasoning in their argumentations, referring to Germany's *responsibility* in the modern world. During the Kosovo conflict, Defence Minister Scharping stated that while a European force would be no substitute for NATO, 'one wants nevertheless to take greater responsibility for the European house'.[39] The Red–Green Government after Kosovo was therefore keen to participate in the emerging European Security and Defence Policy (ESDP) and the nascent rapid-reaction force.

While the Kosovo conflict proved a turning point for German policy, the events of 11 September 2001 altered the whole climate of international security. In its 2002 election manifesto the SPD stated that: 'the return to civil war and genocide in South East Europe, right outside our front door, and the terrible events of 11 September 2001 in the USA, have made us confront our own security tasks in the international community. We have taken responsibility in the framework of our powers and helped politically and diplomatically, humanitarianly and also through the deployment of the *Bundeswehr*'.[40] The German Government's decision to take part in operation 'enduring freedom' in Afghanistan reaffirmed this commitment. The Red–Green coalition agreement in 2002 explained that 'the *Bundeswehr* is taking part in the military activities of the international anti-terror coalition', showing 'solidarity with the United States in the war against international terrorism'.[41] German troops have tended to be used in peacekeeping rather than combat operations, but their level of engagement – 10,000 peacekeeping troops in 2003, second only to the USA – has nevertheless been impressive.

The SPD position on US-led intervention in Iraq was nevertheless quite different. The party and the German population as a whole were overwhelmingly against US military action against Iraq. According to an Emnid poll in 2002, 80 per cent of Germans 'do not want a strike against Sadam Hussein'.[42] The decision of the party to adopt such a firm position against the conflict was, however, dictated more by poor SPD ratings for the upcoming federal elections than by a genuine policy decision. Chancellor Schröder criticised US policy in a number of fierce public statements, speaking of American action as an 'adventure' in which Germany would play no part, and arguing for German's right to oppose US policy in this matter. Schröder further spelt out the position – that Germany would not contribute financially as it had done in the first Gulf War in the early 1990s even with the backing of the United Nations. This was a major step for Germany diplomacy, which had always taken care not to depart dramatically from the line of its American allies or from the position taken by the UN, and distinctly soured German–US relations. Though the SPD was fully behind the Chancellor's stance and the vehemence of his declarations displayed self-confidence, the way it was done smacked of populism – playing to the domestic audience – and in this sense ignored the important diplomatic lessons learnt in the first years of the Red–Green Government.

Although it could not be said that the whole party approved of German participation in the Kosovo conflict (Lafontaine for one opposed the action along with the *Jusos*), voices of disapproval were particularly mute in contrast to the debate over UN peacekeepers only a few years earlier. While participation in the *War on Terror* in Afghanistan was more controversial – the Chancellor had to make participation a matter of confidence to gain the full support of the coalition parties in the *Bundestag* – the fact that Germany took part at all showed that the SPD in government was prepared to make tough decisions on international security (breaking with established patterns of policy i.e. non-participation in *out-of-area* operations) for what they saw to be German interests. The party's position on Iraq similarly broke with traditional policy by actively opposing the US position on military intervention. As with the issue of the EU budget, German policy still showed a high degree of continuity – here, in terms of the sober German perspective adopted on military engagement. This can be seen by the Federal Government's pro-active approach to conflict resolution: Germany was at the fore in diplomatic efforts to secure an end to the Kosovo conflict and, after the end of NATO action, to create a Balkans Stability Pact to stabilise the region. With a view to the Iraq conflict and the *War on Terror*, the SPD adopted a *multilateralist* position that promoted economic integration and conflict prevention. The party, furthermore, wishes to pursue its policy goals through an EU foreign and security policy (CFSP), incorporating so-called 'soft security' issues like trade and aid. The party's manifesto for the 2004 European elections stated that: 'The responsibility of the European Union for security and peace, also beyond Europe's borders, will further increase – we will make sure that Europe stands by its responsibilities.'[43] German troops have, thus, taken an active part in the first two EU missions, to Macedonia and the Congo.

Generational change in terms of SPD European policy implies 'pragmatism' with regard to Germany's altered interests from the perspective of the SPD, and can be seen as a gradual reinterpretation of policy in response to the demands of actors operating within the policy networks. According to 'Die Zeit': 'For Helmut Kohl as for Helmut Schmidt, three iron rules were valid. Europe is a question of war or peace; we bow three times before the *Tricolore* before we bow the head before *Black, Red and Gold*; and to our American friends we stay true ... Schröder was the first Chancellor, who no longer felt emotionally bound to this post-war consensus.'[44] Although the *generational change* did not affect attitudes to Europe for all people in all policy areas, even Lafontaine, an opponent of the NATO operations in Kosovo, characterised a more assertive and self-confident policy. During his brief stint as Finance Minister, for instance, he was prone to lecturing EU colleagues in ECOFIN meetings on the virtue of a growth-oriented and regulatory EU model. At the start of their term in office, SPD members of the Federal Government pursued policies very close to those formulated in opposition. This can be seen in the bold statements on the reduction of German budgetary payments made in the first few months in office.

While the Red–Green Government remains more assertive than its predecessors, the approach of the SPD leaders in government has *softened* as a result of the recognition of what was possible at the EU level and of common European interests, and the Government has adopted a more diplomatic position on most issues – utilising a combination of *direct* and *agenda-setting power*. A recent example of this has been the renewal of the Franco-German motor, producing common agreements on financial and institutional reform for the EU in 2003 (Chapter 11). Generational change, therefore, allowed political leaders to *normalise* EU policy in the sense of becoming more like other large member states, not being afraid to take on a stronger leadership role for Germany, a view shared by one in three Germans who expect the government to 'more strongly shape Europe's future'.[45] Chancellor Schröder has stated that: 'Germany is nowadays ... presenting its national interest more forcefully than in the past. I don't see anything negative about that.'[46]

6
Winning Elections and Strategic Change

The SPD began the 1990s as a party characterised by *loosely coupled anarchy* with its leaders playing mostly to their own followers. After poor performances in the federal elections of 1987 and 1990, the SPD under Björn Engholm began the process (to be continued in fits and starts) of turning itself into a more effective electoral machine, capable of finding its way out of the *30 per cent ghetto*. *Electoral-strategic* change manifested itself in three ways. First, a more 'responsive' policy approach was adopted towards a limited number of actors in the German system (e.g. the electorate). This was characterised with regard to European policy by short-term, sometimes 'populist' or parochial policies, often based on single issues and lacking a holistic perspective (not integrated into policy as a whole). These tactics were frequently employed by the domestic-oriented *Länder* minister-presidents up until the late 1990s and reflected the increasingly *zero-sum* view of the European Community/ European Union held by the electorate. This perspective was further sharpened by the penetration of the European Union into domestic politics, the penetration of the media into politics, and the growth of material concerns in Germany after unity.

Second, a more reasoned political strategy was developed, founded on the views of a broader range of organised interests in Germany, to produce policies of a more realistic kind expected of a *government in waiting*. After the poor electoral performance in 1994 (given the state of the German economy), when the party's appeal was hampered by a lack of cohesion, this strategy became more dominant. Under the chairmanship of Lafontaine (after November 1995), the party became more focused on winning elections and being *responsive* to a broader range of (domestic) actors as it moved towards government. As the SPD moved towards becoming a *government in waiting* and finally gained power, it was prepared to reflect these domestic concerns, but also attempted to represent fundamental German interests in a healthy and integrated European Union. The interdependency of EU politics was finally recognised by the SPD leadership once in government, so that the party also became *responsive* to European-level actors. In short, SPD European policy was increasingly defined by 'strategic actions ... informed by "knowledge" of a structured context'.[1] Chapter 6 will study the electoral-strategic dynamic in SPD European policy by outlining the electoral circumstances of the party in 1990 and its attempts to 'make majorities' between 1990 and 1998; and, then, investigating the party's efforts to respond to a wider range of interests in government, as it recognised the need to lead as well as follow opinion in the domestic context.

Electoral-strategic change

At the point of unification, the SPD found itself in an awkward political situation. The party had not recovered from the bickering and in-fighting that had marked the last years of the Schmidt Chancellorship, and was soundly defeated in the first post-unity federal elections. This was partly due to the unenthusiastic attitude of its Chancellor Candidate, Oskar Lafontaine, towards German unification. A more deep-lying reason was that the SPD had not managed to find a consistent answer to a changing electoral environment. The organisational, strategic and programmatic pluralism outlined in Chapter 3,[2] was compounded by the rise of the Green Party (or 'parties') in the 1980s. Kitschelt explains that, as a result of the party's internal divisions, the SPD 'oscillated over the entire range of alternatives' after it lost power in 1982.[3] This was enabled by what he describes as 'a leadership constrained in its strategic autonomy', which when faced with multiple options found it 'difficult to find a new strategic equilibrium with a consistent approach'.[4] In other words, their electoral strategy was inconsistent, switching emphasis from trying to gain votes from the Green post-materialist Left to seeking votes from the Christian Democrat parties. Furthermore, the SPD was still suffering from the long-term shrinkage of its traditional support base among the working class, which comprised over 50 per cent of party membership in 1950, but only to 40 per cent in 1985. The proportion of 'white-collar' middle class members grew from 20 per cent to 50 per cent in the same period.[5] The SPD also had to cope with the *voter dealignment*, which came about as a result of a more diverse society in terms of individual lifestyles and values (Chapter 1). The heterogeneous party was, therefore, seriously wrong-footed in 1990: split over the merits of unification whilst emphasising the policies of the New Left, just as the those values were beginning to become less important.

Making majorities

Given its electoral failure on the federal level, the SPD was determined to create the majorities necessary to improve its performance, 'to win and maximise votes, to build a voter coalition which extends across class and confessional borders ... to in this way gain and maintain power'.[6] The retreat of environmental issues in the 1990s with the increase in unemployment and the onset of economic recession, emphasised the point that the right direction for the SPD was to move towards the *centre* of the traditional Left–Right spectrum, to gain the votes they had lost to the Christian–Liberal coalition in the 1980s. By the early 1990s, Engholm was being accused of pursuing a 'Schmusekurs' (cosying up to the Federal Government), while Rudolf Scharping in 1993 explicitly expressed the need to move to the *centre*, since it had 'comfortably three times the voter potential ... of the Green camp'.[7] With the growing strength of the Greens at the regional level and their participation in *Länder* governments, the potential for a Red–Green alliance on the federal plane allowed the party to focus on this strategy. To quote one SPD politician, 'the aim of the party has been to get out of the ghetto of defeat. And to that extent, the strategy has been similar to the strategy of Blair in Britain and Clinton in America.'[8] The idea has been to create a modern party, effective in communication and appealing to the areas where votes are thickest,[9] becoming a *Volkspartei* in its truest sense. In this vein, the SPD established the 'Kampa' – a rapid-reaction policy unit to co-ordinate political strategy. Communications strategy was nevertheless only one part of the solution. Matthias Machnig, head of the *Kampa* team, put its success in the 1998 federal elections down to the good co-ordination of party policy in the presidium and the 'systematic work-plan' put in place by the *Schwerpunktkommissionen* after 1996.[10] In terms of the key voter groups targeted, it was clear to Machnig that the party must 'find answers to the necessary processes of change' in society.[11]

European policy, however, was only a side-show at this time, as the EU was not among the list of issues close to the electorate's heart. Public opinion in Germany, similar to other countries, has not rated Europe highly compared to most domestic issues come election time. In the early- to mid-1990s, the key issues of concern for the electorate were domestic economic problems (i.e. low growth and high unemployment). The low-ranking of European issues was further illustrated by the poor turnout in the 1999 European elections, when less than half of Germans turned up to vote. We will see later in the chapter, furthermore, how the SPD found it hard to convince the electorate that Europe was a top issue in the 2002 federal elections.

For the SPD, it was important to plug itself more effectively into the network of domestic interest groups as a whole, focusing in particular on the views of the electorate. In this sense, Machnig argued that even from a position of power, the SPD must sustain this network approach: 'a new programme has no consequence if the party is not in the position to mobilise the majorities for it ... that means it must analyse social trends at the time, taking up new options and chances in central policy fields'.[12] The party had certainly moved in this direction by the late 1990s, enabling it to take power in 1998. This was achieved, according to Schwarz, because 'the politicians adapted themselves to what would become mainstream German positions'.[13] The idea of Machnig's 'network party' has been to create a more intensive process of dialogue within the party to make it more *responsive* to societal change. This plan ran parallel to calls for more participation by citizens in politics and an *opening up* of the party (Chapter 3), was included in SPD election programmes from the early 1990s. The more distant aim was also to effect a change in the German system – some have called for referenda to be allowed by the Constitution as part of a law for more citizen participation.[14] The SPD has, in particular, tried to draw younger people to the party through a number of proposals (detailed on the party's new 'Next' generation website) flanked by organisational initiatives to ensure the representation of young people at all levels of the party (Chapter 3).[15]

The filter through which party policies are presented to the public is, of course, the media. The media has increasingly penetrated into politics, scrutinising politics, policies and politicians to an ever-greater degree (Chapter 1). While the media may often concentrate on trivial, short-term political events, it is essential for political parties to harness its power as their major link to the electorate. This is especially the case when the party is in government, where 'every mistake will be mercilessly registered'.[16] Political parties and governments, as a result, must second-guess media interpretations of their policies and the public response to the news as it is presented to them. The speed with which news is distributed, furthermore, has created a quicker and more direct link to the electorate, whether or not the way policies are presented is reflective of their deeper content. The media, in addition, concentrates on personalities and, in particular, the party leader, chancellor candidate or chancellor, who acts as the focus for the party's electoral ambitions.

The importance of the party leader, or chancellor candidate/ chancellor in playing this role was shown by the election of Gerhard Schröder as Chancellor Candidate for the SPD in 1998. Party chairman, Oskar Lafontaine, while more popular in the party, recognised himself that Schröder, with his media-friendly image and appeal to the political *centre*, stood a better chance of winning the federal elections. Schröder's effectiveness in the media was clearly illustrated by his ratings in the 'TV-duels' between the chancellor candidates and the general 'out-performance' of his party in the 2002 elections. Blondel argues that: a 'good or effective party leader is not only concerned with the activities of his own party. He must relate to the country at large, both guiding the party and providing a link between it and the nation.'[17] In fact, the concept of the *Neue Mitte* was based upon the idea of capturing the political middle ground and harnessing these centrist values.[18] In strategic terms, Olaf Scholz, SPD General Secretary after the party's re-election in 2002, saw the *Neue Mitte* as essentially 'defining social and political transition processes in good time as well as laying down the basis for a successful and modern social democratic strategy'.[19]

The speed and penetration of the media, in addition, have heightened the need for efficiency in decision-making or 'manoeuvrability' with regard to party policy. For social democratic parties, in particular, with their *bottom-up* party structures, this has produced the pressure for the organisational changes mentioned in Chapter 3. According to party strategist, Thomas Meyer: 'to achieve the full effect of this media-oriented communication, the strategic arrowheads of social democratic parties must gain much more freedom of action, leaving the party and its democratic process much more behind than ever before'.[20] In their efforts to square the need for leadership autonomy with a desire for inner-party legitimacy, the SPD leadership recognised that the 'the links to the membership must be strengthened'.[21] In addition to the formal organisational changes, the party elite was in a stronger position to lead debate after the SPD came to power, due to the speed of decision-making and the complexity (and resources) of modern government, when they could more easily embrace the logic of the *Volkspartei*, and aim to represent all Germans. Meyer has argued that: 'centre-left parties across Europe are increasingly adopting Clintonesque campaigning techniques and policy techniques which downgrade the traditional role and structure of political parties ... There remains a crucial political role for parties such as the SPD – both as a large democratic body able through its own actions to energise civil society, and as a network able to communicate effectively with the social groups.'[22]

Figure 6.1, below, shows that there was scepticism towards the EU – or, as Germans would more correctly say, *fatigue with Europe* ('Europamüdigkeit) – through most of the 1990s, peaking in 1997. In 1990, the vast majority of the German population thought that the country had 'benefited' from the EU and strongly supported German membership (Figure 6.1). By 1996, however, more Germans thought they had 'not benefited' from the EU, though this was largely to do with Germany's position as paymaster of the European Union and resistance to Monetary Union (Figure 6.1).[23] As the 'Frankfurter Allgemeine' reported: in Germany's dealings with the EU 'the short-term relationship ... is often troubled. It is influenced by public discussion of European affairs, which concentrates almost exclusively on money',[24] as with the debate over the *paymaster* position. Yet underneath these highly visible issues, despite increasing apathy, membership of the EU was still strongly supported. The advent of the Single Currency in 1999, and its relative success – in the currency markets after 1999 and with the introduction of Euro banknotes in 2002 – removed one of the main reasons

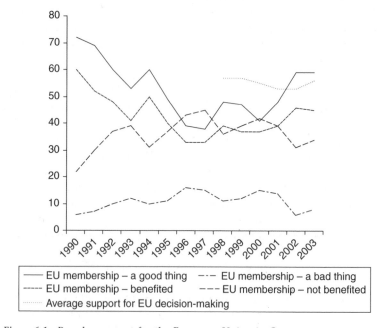

Figure 6.1   Popular support for the European Union in Germany
Source: *'Eurobarometers' 50–59*, European Commission, Brussels.

for discontent. Despite uneasiness over central policies such as Monetary Union and eastern enlargement (Chapters 8 to 11), joint decision-making in the EU still enjoyed relatively strong support (Figure 6.1). As has been implied above, electoral change has influenced the SPD leadership much more than its European policy groups. Even the European policy experts realised, however, after the ratification of the Maastricht Treaty (which pushed through Monetary Union against the will of the German people), that the party must, as one internal paper put it, 'pay attention to the ever greater scepticism and growing disinterest in European Community politics in the formulation of its main European policy objectives'.[25] The difference was that those primarily engaged in European policy were concerned with countering 'the disappearance of trust in the Community to solve important problems',[26] which was something the party leadership only learnt was necessary after its first few months in office. During the mid-1990s, the party's leaders were not yet playing to the electoral middle ground, and SPD core supporters were not keen Europhiles: 'a not inconsiderable part of the voter clientele belong to those who are tired of or disinterested with Europe (Europe is as before a subject for the better trained classes with higher incomes, the so-called "high achievers").'[27] SPD MEPs confirmed in interviews that they had found particularly high levels of *Euroscepticism* among SPD supporters when campaigning for the European elections in 1999.[28]

The greater responsiveness towards the electorate and the domestic agenda in the formulation of SPD EU policy was increased by the prominence of minister-presidents in the party who had a regional or national agenda. These media-conscious leaders, furthermore, realised that the best way of gaining media attention was through breaking political taboos,[29] and this was a key reason behind the negative views expressed by the *Troika* on Monetary Union in the mid-1990s (Chapter 8) as Scharping, Lafontaine and Schröder all vied for the media spotlight. The populist manifestation of electoral change reached its high point in March 1996 with the *Länder* elections in Baden-Württemberg, when the SPD candidate, Dieter Spöri, ran on a explicitly anti-EMU ticket (Chapter 8).[30] This manifestation of *electoral-strategic change* had its limits, because European policy as a whole was not seen as a controversial issue by the public (e.g. due to the support for joint decision-making in the EU – Figure 6.1). EU policy, moreover, was *cartelised* by the two major parties in the *Bundestag* in a pro-European consensus, so that an anti-integration policy could not appear credible.

During the mid-to-late 1990s, as the SPD moved towards becoming a *government in waiting*, discipline increased and the party became a more effective electoral machine as it began to respond to a broader range of actors in German society. Chancellor Schröder later wrote that: 'we shall seek to co-operate with all sections of society, irrespective of formal position or responsibility',[31] and the underlying belief of public opinion and the strong belief of other major actors (such as big business) in European integration. The desire to engage with as wide as possible a range of society actors was illustrated most clearly in government. The party leadership's pluralistic approach to policy-making was illustrated by the establishment of a number of bipartisan Commissions after the SPD came to power to deal with Germany's most pressing political and economic problems. The Federal Government set up the Weizsäcker Commission on the reform of the *Bundeswehr*, the Süssmuth Commission on immigration, the Hartz Commission on labour market reform, and the Rürup Commission on welfare and social policy. The latter three commissions, in particular, produced proposals that were broadly integrated into Government policy and – subsequently – the policy programme of the SPD.

'Selling' policy in government

The SPD pursued an electoral strategy in power that engaged with domestic actors. The problem was that the party had become too responsive to these actors to brave unpopular policies, such as the welfare and labour market reforms advocated by the proponents of the *Neue Mitte* in 1999.[32] By 2003, the economic difficulties in Germany – low growth and rising unemployment – had reached such an extent that unpopular economic and social reforms were unavoidable. The Red–Green coalition's wafer-thin victory in the 2002 elections was fortunate in that it relied heavily on Schröder's (and Fischer's) personal popularity and on the turn of events that focused attention on his leadership qualities – the floods in Eastern Germany and looming US intervention in Iraq.[33] The party's *Kampa* unit was blamed for presenting the electorate with a party that 'lacked substance' yet it was difficult to sing the SPD's praises when it had clearly not performed well in its priority areas – economic growth and employment. The party realised that it would have to *lead opinion* and take some unpopular decisions and try to *sell* Government policy. In a paper published by a young group of SPD members of the *Bundestag* just after the elections, the following case was argued: 'We must be clear that the election victory in 2002 was less about broad enthusiasm about the last four years' work of the Red–Green

Government, and more about the recipes and cultural definition of our opponents ... The SPD fought for the opportunity for further renewal of our country, for modern and pragmatic goals and organisational reconstruction of the party. We want to utilise this opportunity decisively over the coming four years.'[34] In an effort to turn around poor economic performance, the party leadership set forth a centrist, *Neue Mitte* agenda encapsulated in the *Agenda 2010* concept revealed shortly after the elections, entitled 'Mut zur Wahrheit – Wille zum Wandel' (courage for truth, will for change).[35]

Although the SPD began to engage more effectively with the European context after coming to power in 1998 – coming to terms with the interdependent realities of the EU – the Red–Green coalition still needed to represent the central demands of domestic actors in its European policy. At the Nice European Council (2000), for instance, it promoted *Länder* demands for a clearer division of competences in the EU by gaining agreement to a further IGC on institutional reform (Chapter 11). Whatever the reality of inter-governmental negotiations, it was important to the Federal Government to at least be seen to be pursuing German interests – because 'Press reporting concentrates on the description of national interests affected by Europe'.[36] After Council meetings the Government, therefore, tried to emphasise what Germany had gained from any resulting agreements. The consequence of this was a growing gap between the *style* of policy (or at least the rhetoric espoused in public) and its actual *content*.

Once the party had first-hand experience of EU decision-making, it realised that – while continuing to stress key German interests – the common interests that existed between EU states required a more pro-European policy, and, for that, they needed to convince the public of its merits. An SPD member of the *Bundestag* from the party's European policy groups emphasised the point that 'it was a mistake for the previous government to make European policy decisions without recourse to the people and behind the closed doors of the European Council ... One must carry the people with you when taking European policy decisions, otherwise scepticism or fatigue will develop ... If the people are not taken along, European integration will grind to a halt.'[37] With less pressures on European than domestic policy (as the EU was rated far below domestic economic and social issues by most domestic actors), the SPD began to lead opinion on Europe as well as respond to it. This attitude was particularly evident in SPD policy on the eastern enlargement of the EU (Chapter 11). In September 2000, Günter Verheugen spoke of the need to involve the population more in decisions about Europe's future, which – it was reported – 'reflected a fast-expanding stream of thought within Germany's ruling Social Democratic Party'.[38] Chancellor Schröder stated in the *Bundestag* that 'the reaction of citizens to these suggestions [transition periods for the free movement of people after enlargement] strengthens my belief that we may well find support for the enlargement process if we take the worries and concerns of the people very seriously and in a noticeable way'.[39] This was to be achieved by presenting 'a plausible definition of European policy to the people',[40] and responding to public fears over certain aspects of EU policy. With this in mind, party strategy adopted a more sophisticated two-level game. This was the purpose of the SPD's *Responsibility for Europe* paper, presenting European policy as a central programmatic pillar within the context of *globalisation* and a reformed European Union.

The SPD's 2002 election manifesto illustrated that key party objectives were to be sought at the EU level, by placing emphasis on the importance of 'Germany's role in Europe and the World' (Chapter 7).[41] While the SPD in government had recognised the importance of German European policy, the course of the 2002 election campaign nevertheless demonstrated that it was still not seen as a major issue by the electorate. Although foreign and European policy were the lead issues in the manifesto, they were drowned out by the continuing bad news from the economy and the emerging issue of the floods in Eastern Germany and the looming conflict in Iraq. With the placing of European integration at the centre of a social democratic response to *globalisation*, the SPD took on the task of trying to lead opinion as well as respond to it.[42] Yet the 2002 *programme for government* illustrated the limits of this strategy, with the difficulty in promoting European policy given what were viewed by the public as more pressing matters.

In an attempt to counter continuing public disinterest, the SPD set itself the goal of engaging more with the electorate over the European Union. In the run-up to the elections for the European Parliament in June 2004, the party set up a new homepage for its 'Eurokampa', which promoted – for example – brainstorming sessions with campaign activists over European policy issues.[43] Yet, given the prioritisation of domestic issues – in particular, the state of the economy and the levels of unemployment – the challenges for the SPD to engage with the electorate over European issues have been great. Even in the campaign for the 2004 elections to the European Parliament, 'opposition parties campaign on national issues', and European issues play hardly any part.[44] Here, the ZDF 'Politbarometer' (political barometer) broadcast highlighted the lack of discussion of the European constitution.[45]

The development of SPD policy has, therefore, been marked both by continuity and change, moving towards a European policy more inclusive of and *responsive* to actors within the institutional, national and European contexts. Chapter 6 has demonstrated that *electoral-strategic* considerations can have a significant impact upon ideology as expressed in policy programmes and vice-versa, and it is to these policy programmes we must turn to explore ideological change in the European policy of the SPD.

7
A Change of Heart

The third dynamic in SPD European policy is *ideological change.* Ideological change had two key effects on party policy. First, the development of views on economic policy and the role of the state, culminating in the rise of *Neue Mitte* group in the party, had a major influence on the EU model and type of Euro-zone that the SPD wished to establish. Second, the party's perception of the European Union altered substantively – from a complete disinterest in EU policy in the early 1990s, to a prioritisation of the Union (uniquely) in the first section of its manifesto for the 2002 federal elections as a means to achieve social democratic goals.[1] A more long-term social democratic model came with the party's *Responsibility for Europe* paper that integrated domestic and European policy into a *federal* concept that sought the entrenchment of specific social goals within a Charter of Fundamental Rights and a European constitution.[2]

The ideology of the SPD has, of course, been closely related to its electoral strategy. While Downs' assumption that 'parties make use of their ideology in their attempt to mobilize mass electorates'[3] holds true, the relationship is more symbiotic than this might suggest. Socioeconomic change permeates society's values, which – in turn – define the views of the electorate that provide the framework for the strategic concerns of political parties *vis-à-vis* the system of electoral competition. The SPD 'Grundwertekommission' (Basic Values Commission) has stressed the importance of both ideology and political strategy for the party's programme: 'not only the electoral interests of social democracy for forming majorities, but likewise ... the coupling of economic success and social justice require a credible policy of social and political alliances'.[4] This chapter will analyse developments in SPD ideology since 1990 from both a European policy and a more general perspective, detailing the 'rise of the *Neue Mitte'* and the 'rise of European policy' in the party. It will show that the SPD eventually produced a policy platform, which prioritised European policy within the context of a comprehensive vision for the EU.

Ideological change

Ideological change has been epitomised by the ideological flexibility of the SPD leadership that emerged in the 1990s, characterised by Hombach's argument that, in a changing world, 'it is fatal to cling to ideologies'.[5] Even Lafontaine, a bitter opponent of Hombach's ideas and often portrayed as a Left-winger, was characterised by 'strategic flexibility', as illustrated by his work on the 1989 Berlin *Basic Programme*, 'to make the party more attractive to the "affluent majority" containing the "target groups" identified by electoral analysis'.[6] Franz Walter has similarly argued that: 'This generation was never as ideological as they sometimes pretended to be ... But tactical unscrupulousness is no bad virtue for a politician.'[7]

The SPD has been seen as a programmatic party – its key ideological turning points being defined by new *Basic Programmes*. This was true at Bad Godesberg in 1959 and the Berlin Programme, as with the SPD's programmatic review launched in 2000. Programmatic statements have marked attempts to find a synthesis of basic values, to achieve internal consensus (e.g. the drafting of the Berlin text). The main difference with the most recent programmatic review is that it has taken place while the party had been in government, and therefore has had to negotiate not only internal compromises within the party and with regard to electoral strategy, but also with a view to the implementation of policy solutions in the reality of government.

Programmatic pluralism in the SPD in the 1980s and early 1990s was characterised by three different streams of ideology. The first stream supported the traditional social democratic values of *solidarity* and *social justice* with strong affiliations to the trade unions and has often been depicted as representing the core values of the party. It has therefore permeated – to varying degrees – the party's other ideological groupings. A second *New Left* stream held to post-materialist values such as *environmentalism* and individualist values such as *human rights*. The New Left reached its height in the SPD in the 1980s, when many of its ideas were incorporated into the party's Basic Programme: 'We social democrats are struggling for a peaceful world with a sustainable environment, for a human and socially just society.'[8] This was an expression of strong party support 'in the post-materialist section of the working class and the post-materialist section of the new middle class.'[9] The new generation of SPD leaders, *68ers* who were socialised in the student movements of the 1960s, were considered to belong to this New Left group in the early 1990s. A third strand of party ideology was defined by the more centrist positions (along the traditional left–right axis) of the party establishment, which – for example – showed strong support for economic orthodoxy.[10] Then came the shock of unification, which decreased the prominence of post-materialist concerns. Hans-Jochen Vogel, party chairman at the time, described the Berlin Programme as a 'somewhat stillborn post-materialist party platform just at the moment when the most significant problems facing Germany had suddenly reverted to the classic materialist concerns of production, wealth and distribution'.[11] While 'environmental protection' was the top issue for the electorate in 1990,[12] by 1996 it had slipped to ninth place well behind issues such as 'safeguarding unemployment' and 'pensions'.[13]

The competing strands of ideology helped to convey the perception of the SPD as an internally divided party. While New Left ideals did not disappear, they were increasingly absorbed into the Centre-Left position on the traditional Left–Right axis.[14] After Scharping became leader and then chancellor candidate in 1993, the party emphasised its traditional post-Godesberg ideology, with particular regard to policies that would alleviate the growing problem of unemployment in Germany and achieve social consensus. After Lafontaine became party chairman late in 1995, he continued to emphasise social democratic values which could be easily adapted to question the economic and social uncertainties caused by mass unemployment and public sector cuts (de-emphasising many of his own New Left ideas). When Gerhard Schröder became chancellor candidate in 1998, a dual leadership was formed between the traditional and post-materialist Left (Lafontaine) and the Centre-Right (Schröder) of the party. For the SPD, Lafontaine 'embodied the soul of the party, its social conscience ... against that Schröder portrayed himself as a driving moderniser, who talks about the harsh truths'.[15] The final piece of the jigsaw was Schröder's market-oriented, 'economy first' approach that could win on the key issue of *economic competence* and persuade former Christian Democrat voters to turn to the SPD. The title of the 1998 federal election programme, 'Innovation and Social Justice', showed clearly enough how a compromise had been reached between the two major wings of the party for the time being at least.

The rise of the *Neue Mitte*

To study SPD European policy, it is essential – given the penetration of EU politics into all political spheres – to chart the key changes in the party's ideology. The most significant development in recent years has been the rise of the *Neue Mitte*. Gerhard Schröder's victory at the head of the SPD was also a victory for the centrist policy of the *Neue Mitte*, which put forward ideas similar to the Tony Blair's *Third Way* adapted to the German setting. The essence of the *Neue Mitte* approach was, as in the UK, to develop a *pragmatic* party programme 'to make sense of a new world ... while holding true to fundamental values' such as 'social justice'.[16] In other words, they wanted 'to have recourse to the values of pragmatism and anti-*dirigisme* ... to create an effective synthesis of liberal principles and the basic values of the SPD'.[17] This ideological approach meant, first of all, ensuring stability then growth in the economy, while encouraging entrepreneurship and pursuing an enabling role for the state. In 2000, Schröder stressed in a meeting with colleagues that the 'state ought not to do what society can do better', adding that the state 'should not force people into a straightjacket that chokes freedom and individual creativity'.[18] The *Neue Mitte* also advocated a social infrastructure that increased equality of opportunity through public investment in education and training, and a welfare state that is 'gut gemacht' (well made) rather than 'gut gemeint' (well meant).[19] In terms of industrial relations, the *Neue Mitte* sought to create a stability and growth-oriented social dialogue between business, the unions and government (pursued, once in power, through the *Bündnis für Arbeit*). The ideological grouping became increasingly prevalent in the SPD leadership after the resignation of Lafontaine as Finance Minister and party chairman in March 1999 and his replacement in these offices by politicians from the centre-Right (Eichel and Schröder). Beyond the *Enkel*-generation, younger members of the parliamentary party have also tended towards these views – the SPD *Youngster* group[20] has called for the promotion of 'individual initiatives' rather than the 'subsidy mentality', arguing that 'Justice is whatever creates jobs'.[21]

Another factor behind the rise of the *Neue Mitte* after 1998, is that they aimed to respond to the broader set of pressures within which governments must work. Lafontaine's more interventionist plans alienated big business and the markets. This reflects the importance of the *opposition–government* axis: while in opposition the SPD leadership criticised various privatisations and cuts in public spending, but in government economic pressures and the demands of the European Single Market have ensured that many of these policies were continued. With their willingness to engage with a broader range of societal actors, the *Neue Mitte* were better suited to government. In fact, as with the Schmidt governments of the 1970s and early 1980s, it could be argued that such an 'open' ideology was necessary to achieve economic success in the country. Even the Jospin Government in France, despite its social market rhetoric to the contrary, felt obliged to increase the pace of privatisation. In Germany, Finance Minister Eichel (with the support of the Chancellor) implemented budgetary cuts aimed at reducing the annual deficit to zero by 2006, which produced the lowest budget for 13 years in 2002. Tax reforms were also introduced which – while closing tax loopholes for companies – significantly reduced corporation tax. A central pillar of the *stakeholder* economy was, furthermore, removed with the abolition of Capital Gains Tax on the sale of company cross-holdings.[22]

As with the *generational* and *electoral-strategic* changes described in previous chapters, *ideological change* was ultimately determined by the SPD's domestic and institutional setting. In terms of the party as a whole, these policies have not been popular with the *Basis* and the party's labour wing. Concessions, therefore, have had to be made: in the case of the 1999 savings package and the reduction of corporation tax, an increase in inheritance tax on property and a stepping up of efforts at the EU level to close tax loopholes for investors were offered in return. While internal ideological divisions persist, the problem of ensuring consistency in policy was circumvented to a large extent after the party leadership (i.e. the presidium) became dominated by 'modern' or *Neue Mitte* social democrats, many of whom had an independent power base in the apparatus of the federal government. This is not to say that the lower levels of the party do not have the ability to disrupt the course of the government, but that the party will bring the leadership or Government policy to book if it moves too far and too fast. An attempt was made to bring the main body of the party closer to the position of the *Neue Mitte* leadership through the discussion of a new party programme: 'a programme in the centre of society … binding economic dynamism with social responsibility.'[23] This was shown by the composition of the Programme Commission itself, which – under the leadership of Schröder and Scharping – also initially included Reinhard Klimmt (a former associate of Lafontaine in the Saarland) as well as Klaus Zwickel, chairman of the IG Metall. The interim report for the new party programme subsequently took up the slogan 'Security in Change', characterising the two wings of the party's ideology much the same as the 1998 federal election slogan, 'Innovation and Social Justice', had done.

The SPD in government had to face serious economic challenges that threatened the social state, and tough policies could no longer be avoided after the 2002 federal elections. The secular processes of an ageing population and the increasing costs of healthcare added to low growth and rising unemployment set within the context of budgetary stability (dictated by the EMU Stability and Growth Pact), placed immense pressure on the Red–Green Government to reform Germany's taxation system, welfare state and labour market. These reforms were brought together in the Chancellor Schröder's *Agenda 2010* package, which offered distinctly *Neue Mitte* solutions to these problems. These reforms were, however, counter-intuitive for a social democratic party like the SPD, given that they sought to lower taxation, cut social spending, and introduce *penalties* for those not accepting work. In his speech to the November 2003 party conference Gerhard Schröder explained: 'We will have to cut the obligations of the state, promote individual responsibility and the efforts of each individual ... We have brought the rights and duties of those seeking work into a new equilibrium ... Whoever refuses reasonable work must face penalties.'[24] The focus was now to be placed on *equality of opportunity*, which was at the heart of the SPD's 'politics of the centre'.[25] This meant prioritising *social investment* in education and training relative to *benefit spending*. The new Minister for Economics and Employment, Wolfgang Clement (SPD), argued to the country and the party that the purpose of the reforms was: 'to adjust political and economic structures to the global economy but also to demographic developments, in order to free the resources for urgently needed, significantly higher investment in the future – above all in education and further training, in science and research.'[26] Despite vocal opposition to the reforms,[27] they were passed at an extraordinary party conference in June 2003 with an impressive ninety per cent of the vote.

The ideology of the *Neue Mitte* sought to resolve the tensions between an emphasis on individual freedom (New Left) and the SPD's traditional belief in collective goods (traditional Left) within the party. A synthesis of these contradictions was to be found in the *Kantian* idea of 'enlightened self-interest', which would be achieved through a *Third Way*-style mixture of rights and responsibilities. The *Neue Mitte* elements of the party leadership tried to feed these ideas into the ongoing programmatic debate in the party. Of particular significance was General Secretary Scholz's paper on 'justice and the solidarity of the centre in the 21st century'.[28] Here, Scholz provided a new interpretation of social justice: 'The question of what a politics of justice should look like was discussed in Western post-war Germany as – above all – a question of the just distribution of growth through prosperity and income ... This perspective, with the current challenges, is no longer just ... What is decisive here is the insight that the future belongs to an active and activating welfare state.'[29] He further argued for the removal of the term 'democratic socialism' from the party's vocabulary. This was too much for some senior members of the party establishment, who refuted the suggestion that redistributive justice and opportunity were contradictory, stating that redistribution was still necessary and that 'democratic socialism' remained a relevant term.[30] The main body of the party was unhappy with the ideological content of Scholz's position, and – by the time of the party conference in November 2003 – were also dissatisfied with the emerging details of the *Agenda 2010* reforms. Scholz and Clement, seen as the architects of these changes were duly punished at the party conference, with the General Secretary only narrowly re-elected with 52.6 per cent of the vote, and Clement achieving only 56.7 per cent in his re-election to the presidium. Until a political compromise can be reached, the new ideological positioning of the party leadership will therefore remain dependent upon the success of its policies in both economic and electoral terms. Having looked at the rise of the *Neue Mitte* and its impact on the SPD as a background to ideological change, it is now necessary to turn – more directly – to the party's changing perceptions of the EU, and *the rise of European policy*.

The rise of European policy

The conception of European affairs in the SPD changed dramatically in the decade after 1990. Before unification, European and foreign affairs were dominated by an *internationalist* perspective supported by New Left and traditional social democrats alike. *Internationalism* promoted the redressing of the North–South divide (along the lines of the 1980 Brandt report), disarmament of 'nuclear, biological or chemical weapons of mass destruction', an international response to 'pollution of the soil, water and air', and was against 'huge multinational companies ... evading democratic controls'.[31] When German participation in military operations became an issue in the early 1990s (Chapter 5), it was firmly rejected by party leaders with New Left roots such as Lafontaine, Schröder and Wieczorek-Zeul. At the Mannheim Conference of 1995, Lafontaine reiterated that 'we want to remain a peace power ... we stand back when it comes to military operations, and so it shall stay'.[32] The party leadership and the federal SPD in general, however, devoted little attention to European policy. This can be confirmed by briefly looking at party programmes in the early- to mid-1990s. The 1989 *Basic Programme* focused on international issues, and only allocated two pages to European policy, consisting of vague statements about the good of European integration.[33] The lack of interest in European Community issues was evident in 1990 in an election manifesto that merely reiterated SPD support for a 'united states of Europe'.[34] The 1994 document similarly neglected European issues, although the areas for further integration were, at least, mentioned: 'foreign policy', 'development policy', 'economic policy'.[35]

By the mid- to-late 1990s, the belief began to emerge in the SPD leadership that many social democratic goals could be best achieved through the European Union, and that the development of a social union to accompany Economic and Monetary union could be realised. For the SPD's European policy groups, political integration and political union had long been viewed as objectives for the European Community, but these ideas had been manufactured under the umbrella of cross-party consensus in the *Bundestag*. The new formulation of EU policy gave it a social democratic flavour that could appeal to the SPD leadership or other policy groups within the party. Support for the incorporation of key social democratic policies like employment into the party's European policy platform began to take off in the late 1990s as a result of European integration (Chapter 8), and with the realisation that increasing *globalisation* left less room for manoeuvre for national governments. The idea of responding to economic globalisation was not a long leap from the often-expressed socialist and social democratic concern about the internationalisation of capital.

The first leader to integrate Europe into a serious ideological perspective was Lafontaine. One interviewee confirmed in 2000 that 'Oskar Lafontaine, who had been very sceptical of the single currency, changed his policy about six or seven years ago having studied the matter.'[36] In this, his ideological flexibility was clear. Drawing on the *internationalist* perspective, he saw the EU as a potential instrument with which to reign back the markets and powerful multinational corporations, and create an 'ecological, social market economy'.[37] One SPD Left-winger spoke of Lafontaine's policies as a marriage of New Left and traditional social democratic ideas: 'he said – and here I agree – that the European states compete over taxes and social security ... we must have minimum tax rates and minimum social and ecological standards'.[38] Many of Lafontaine's internationalist demands were nevertheless very unlikely to be achieved. International co-operation was needed (both inside and outside the EU), to support the main planks of his policy such as the 'regulation' of 'the international financial markets', 'a stabilisation of exchange rates', 'a stability- and growth-oriented interest rate policy' and an 'employment-oriented budgetary policy'.[39] Agreement on these points was inconceivable given the importance of equity markets for the

UK economy, the improbability of the US agreeing to controlled exchange rates, the stability-oriented remit of the European Central Bank, and the budgetary restrictions of the EMU convergence and stability criteria. Furthermore, given Germany's export-oriented economy, it was against the wishes of domestic business interests.

Under Wieczorek-Zeul's stewardship, SPD European policy nevertheless began to be linked more markedly to its domestic policy and to the goal of a European social union in the late 1990s. A platform for exercising these new ideas was the 1996 IGC, when the Kohl Government was isolated from its main European partners in trying to block the creation of an EU employment policy (Chapter 8). This issue was something tangible for the SPD hierarchy, which could be utilised to attack the Federal Government's economic policy. The 1998 manifesto thus reflected the willingness to attach conditions to European integration: 'we want Germany to be a motor of integration', but 'Monetary Union must bring with it [EU] economic and fiscal policy' (Chapter 9).[40] A large section of the SPD at the federal level still remained reluctant to embrace European policy, placing it well behind the pursuit of social democratic goals in the domestic policy field. Although Wieczorek-Zeul, as a presidium member, gave European policy a certain amount of prestige in the SPD, there were few other influential figures involved in the policy formation process in the mid- to-late 1990s with the notable exception of Norbert Wieczorek. While European policy became important for a few SPD leaders (e.g. Lafontaine) in the late 1990s, its general weight among the party elite only really grew after the SPD had attained power. As the leading economic power in Europe, situated at the centre of the continent, with an export-oriented economy, Germany could not ignore the reality of interdependence. The business-friendly approach of the emergent *Neue Mitte* was, for instance, focused on domestic reform and creating majorities within the domestic electorate, so that their conversion to the EU as a *shaping mechanism* was to come relatively late, when the party was in office. To quote Klaus Hänsch, former (SPD) President of the European Parliament: 'It may be that authority in European policy is not needed to win elections, but it is certain that one cannot govern the country without it.'[41]

EU Policy in the SPD was, at this time, characterised by the differences between Lafontaine, the European policy convert, and Schröder, whose domestic-orientation was reflective of the broad disinterest in the lower levels of the party and in the electorate as a whole. At the Hanover party conference in December 1997, Lafontaine's 'pro-European and

anti-business tone threw into starker contrast his differences with
Gerhard Schröder'.[42] The diversity of the approaches can be observed in
a book entitled *'The Challenge of Globalization for Germany's Social
Democrats'* published in the run-up to the 1998 elections, in which
Lafontaine called for international rules to provide a political framework
for globalisation while Schröder wrote of 'economic and social
modernisation' essentially in a national context.[43] The transition to government made European policy a reality for the SPD and the new
Chancellor, whose responsibility it was to set the guidelines for policy.
During the first few months, Lafontaine acted on his belief in EU policy,
placing Europe near the top of his ministerial priorities: this was demonstrated by his immediate success in moving powers for the co-ordination
of European policy to the Finance Ministry. He also sought to establish
an alliance with the French Finance Minister, Dominique Strauss-Kahn,
to help secure interventionist policies such as an accord on binding
growth and employment targets and an EU-wide minimum wage to be
included in a European Jobs Pact. He further proposed amending the
ECB's remit to incorporate a commitment to growth as well as price stability. For the reasons mentioned above, however, these efforts were
doomed to end in frustration and failure.[44] For Schröder, national action
for growth and employment was the priority. In the end, the Jobs Pact
agreed at the Cologne Summit in June 1999 merely advocated a macro-
economic institutional dialogue between the social partners (employers
and trade unions), finance ministers and the ECB, aimed at producing
'a non-inflationary wage dynamic' upon which growth could be built.[45]
This was very much a *Neue Mitte* goal and mirrored the Government's
domestic *Bündnis für Arbeit*.

The German Presidency of the European Council in the first half of
1999 demonstrated to even the most domestic-oriented leaders of the
party that it was impossible to govern without Europe. And gradually, it
was recognised that Europe could act as an important instrument for
supporting national policies through active co-ordination. For the *Neue
Mitte*, pursuing measures at the EU level could act as a spur to the 'modernisation' of the economy and the welfare state. The Blair–Schröder paper
(May 1999), called for the creation of 'conditions in which ... businesses
can prosper and adapt, and new businesses can be set up and grow'
along with a 'modernisation' of the welfare state and 'political benchmarking in Europe'.[46] Controversially for social democrats, it also argued
that 'public expenditure as a proportion of national income had more
or less reached the limits of acceptability'.[47] Although hardly a stir was
created by this document in the UK, it produced a barrage of public

attacks on the Chancellor from inside the SPD, particularly as the document had been created outside the formal machinery of the party. This soon persuaded the party leadership to place more stress on the traditional social democratic aspects of these proposals. The measures emphasised were life-long learning and retraining, and an 'active labour market policy' (e.g. tax cuts for the low-paid and training for the unemployed).[48]

The final phase in this *ideological change* began with the promotion of EU policy to the forefront of SPD policy embodied in its 2001 *Responsibility for Europe* paper, an impressive step for the erstwhile domestic-oriented Gerhard Schröder (the review group was headed by the Chancellor himself). Through a mixture of further European integration, democratic reform of the EU institutions and subsidiarity, the aim was to formulate a response to *globalisation* that could capture the support of the German people and work as a tool for both German and social democratic interests. As one European policy expert stated: 'Globalisation has often been seen as a terror, but the new Government emphasises the chances.'[49] Political control would be regained through further European integration, including the formation of 'a European executive', but on the basis of *subsidiarity* under which policy areas best undertaken at national and regional levels would be returned to the competences of Member States.[50] The characterisation of EU policy as a response to *globalisation* was seen as providing a *plausible concept* for the electorate[51] that combined *Neue Mitte* and traditional social democratic goals to offer *security in change*. The creation of a competitive European model was considered essential for social democratic policy, to create employment based upon a healthy national economy. The Chancellor emphasised the Lisbon accord, which aimed to modernise the EU and to use this modernisation for growth and employment (Chapter 9).[52] A framework for the governance of a *social market economy* was also set out in the form of a binding Charter of Fundamental Rights, which would include social regulations (Chapter 11). The European policy review launched in 2000 thereby not only prioritised European policy goals, but also integrated them into a multi-level policy programme to be pursued both on the domestic and EU planes.[53]

The SPD's 2002 *programme for government* placed European policy at the heart of its policy programme. The novel approach of the party, in prioritising the EU to achieve its domestic goals, nevertheless failed to catch on in the media or the electorate (Chapter 6). This one innovative message in the manifesto received hardly any attention for the reasons mentioned in the previous chapter. The fact that the Government was facing the possibility of a 'blue letter' from the Commission with regard to its exceeding the 3 per cent deficit criteria also made it inadvisable for the SPD to profile itself on EU policy at that time. The paradox was that, despite its strongly pro-integration platform, the party had profound objections to the penetration of EU policy into domestic policy on issues like the funding of public provision and German industrial policy in general. While the Chancellor's and Finance Minister's public criticism of the Commission over Competition Policy and Economic Policy (Chapter 9) greatened the desire for deeper integration in these policy areas in the party, the positions of other Member States (notably the UK) made integration in these areas unlikely. The Red–Green Government therefore held out the option of the *structured* co-operation of an advance group of states (Chapter 11). European policy was nevertheless submerged – as a salient political theme – by domestic economic problems, so that the SPD vision of a social democratic EU remained a strategic (ideological) rather than a political (electorally significant) goal.

Part IV

EU Economic and Monetary Union

8
EMU in Opposition: Consensus, Conflict and Conditionality

After the Second World War, the Bretton Woods International Monetary System was established by the Western market economies. Under US dominance, this system was designed to ensure the monetary stability necessary for economic regeneration to take place. By the 1960s, however, it had come under great pressure through exchange rate fluctuations, which led to the devaluation of the French Franc and the revaluation of the West German Mark. The problems in France and Germany, in turn, 'threatened the stability of other [European] currencies',[1] challenging the increasing levels of trade and the solidity of EU policies inside the European Community. Within this context, the Hague Summit of December 1969 first made economic and monetary union a goal of European integration through proposals to create narrow margins of exchange rate fluctuation within the EC (the Werner report, 1970). In March 1972, the so-called 'snake in the tunnel' was launched, which consisted of a managed floating of currencies ('the snake') within narrow margins of fluctuation against the US Dollar ('the tunnel'). Thrown off course by oil crises, the weakness of the dollar and differences in economic policy, the *snake* lost most of its members in less than two years, and was reduced to a 'Deutschmark' area (Germany, Benelux and Denmark). In 1979, a new initiative was launched by French President, Valery Giscard D'Éstaing, and German Chancellor, Helmut Schmidt, to create greater monetary stability through a European Monetary System (EMS). The Single European Act launched the Community's Single Market Programme, which, when combined with the success of the EMS, further enhanced the integrative logic of a Single Currency. The political will to actualise this logic emerged in the late 1980s as a response to *climatic changes* that included German unification.

This section will look at SPD policy on European Economic and Monetary Union after 1990. EMU is an especially apt case study, since it has not only been a high-profile subject of European integration spanning the entire period since 1990, but has itself also shaped the EU policy *climate*: it is what Anderson calls a 'constitutive' policy by virtue of its ability to 'establish or amend the Community rules of the game'.[2] SPD policy will be analysed using the model set out in the introduction (Figure I.1), reflecting on the *climatic change* that has remoulded the policy environment (Chapter 2) and demonstrating the influence of the *internal dynamics* (Chapters 5–7). The policy of the party, or – to be more precise – the various strands of European policy within the party at the federal level, will shed further light on the policy contexts described in Chapters 3 and 4, as the SPD has moved along the opposition–government axis.

Chapter 8 presents a chronological examination of SPD policy on Economic and Monetary Union between 1990 and 1996. This will be achieved, first, by looking briefly at the background behind the Treaty on European Union (TEU or 'Maastricht Treaty') and the SPD's views on Monetary Union at its conception. Second, the agreement of the Maastricht Treaty itself through an Intergovernmental Conference will be examined, studying the input of key German actors in the negotiations and the SPD's assessment of the accord. Third, the chapter will analyse the evolution of SPD policy on EMU through the mid-1990s, charting the rise of scepticism in the public and, then, among certain elements of the party leadership. The chapter will explain and interpret the development of SPD policy – from the cross-party consensus at the conception of EMU and the signing of the Maastricht Treaty to the questioning of the Single Currency by major figures in the party leadership in the mid-1990s – which came to challenge institutionalised patterns of European policy in the SPD and Germany as a whole.

Creating monetary union

As argued above, the need for stable exchange rates between members of the European Community, combined with a desire to draw the natural conclusions from a Single Market (to incorporate the free flow of goods and capital), created a certain degree of economic logic behind EMU, especially for an export-oriented country like Germany. Germany supported the concept when, at the Hanover Summit in June 1988, the European Council called for the setting up of what became known as *the Delors Committee* to more closely define Monetary Union and the mechanisms by which it could be achieved. Many German policy-makers nevertheless saw Economic and Monetary Union as part of a broader, and more integral, political union, which was not the view taken by Germany's closest EC partner, France. While this 'economic logic' made politicians consider a single currency as a real option, the political catalyst for Monetary Union came in the form of German reunification. Unification enabled the proponents of EMU in the Federal Government (notably Foreign Minister Genscher) to convince Chancellor Kohl that Monetary Union was an end in itself, allowing Kohl to 'seize it as an opportunity to make an historic contribution to unifying Europe and to reinvent himself as an historic Chancellor'.[3] Kohl thereafter took the view that the unification of Germany and the unification of Europe were *two sides of the same coin*.

The prospect of German unity was something the French political elites, like other Member States (particularly the UK), found hard to face. What would Germany's attitude to West European integration be now that full political sovereignty was imminent? How could France contain this new Goliath, which – even as West Germany – had been economically dominant? How could Germany be tied to West European integration now that the East was, once again, open? For Mitterrand, EMU was a solution that would gain greater political influence for France with respect to the previous dominance of the Deutschmark in Western Europe. A European Central Bank would base its monetary policy on the economy of the whole European Community. Mitterrand himself admitted: 'While we stand today under the hegemony of the German Mark, we will tomorrow count with our full weight in monetary decisions.'[4] For most Germans, however, the process of unification towered above any consideration of Economic and Monetary Union. Although the German Government was won over to the idea of EMU, given the predominance of unification and upcoming federal elections, Chancellor Kohl would have preferred to concentrate on domestic affairs for a time.

Many in the German political and economic elites subscribed to an 'ordo-liberal' approach, which placed economics ahead of politics in determining economic and monetary policy.[5] These actors favoured a 'coronation theory' (*Krönungstheorie*) of Monetary Union.[6] In short, the Single Currency should come as a crowning of the political integration process. Kohl supported this view but, under pressure from Genscher and Mitterrand, was prepared to agree to the launch of an IGC on EMU, if it meant the speedy resolution of German unity and if a parallel IGC on political union was convened. The advantages of EMU for Germany were not, however, entirely clear-cut. Though the country's export-oriented economy might benefit from the stability of exchange rates in the Single Market brought about by Monetary Union, the loss of the de facto dominant position of the *Bundesbank* and the stable Deutschmark, led central actors in the national context to question the overall profitability of the project.

EMU and the Maastricht Treaty

The *Delors Report* submitted in 1989 marked the first agreement of a concrete definition for Economic and Monetary Union. It was defined as the 'total and irreversible convertibility of currencies' whose essential elements were a free and complete 'single market', an economic policy resting on fiscal and budgetary discipline and Monetary Union itself.[7] A three stage process for Monetary Union was also set out in the report which was broadly accepted by Member States at the Madrid European Council (1989). Stage I was to initiate the free movement of capital. Stage II was to launch the European System of Central Banks (ESCB), to *monitor and co-ordinate* Member States' economic policies. Stage III was to herald the currency union itself. The *Bundesbank*, played a major part in the development of EMU. Its President, Karl-Otto Pöhl, was a member of the *Delors Committee* and strongly promoted the goals of budgetary and fiscal discipline outlined in the report. Though the *Bundesbank* was fairly lukewarm towards Monetary Union, subscribing to an *ordo-liberal* conception of a *coronation* process, Pöhl was nevertheless convinced by his central bank colleagues that, if Monetary Union was to take place, it was better to influence the process from the inside.[8] The *Bundesbank* was instrumental in negotiating the details of Monetary Union (in co-ordination with the Finance Ministry), championing the pre-condition of economic convergence and designing the resultant convergence criteria. The institutional nature of EMU was of fundamental importance to both the *Bundesbank* and the German Government. They were resolved to ensure the independence and stability-orientation of the future European Central Bank at all costs, and in the face of French reservations. If they were going to give up the strong and stable Deutschmark, they were determined to guarantee the same credentials for the ECB. These dual goals were duly set into the resulting Treaty.[9]

For the IGC on Economic and Monetary Union, the attitudes of the German Government were split between those of the Chancellor and the Foreign Minister, who were willing to accept a *softer* approach to the convergence criteria (supported by France) with flexible rules for the inclusion of poorer Member States, and the *ordo-liberal* view of the *Bundesbank*, represented by Finance Minister Waigel, which argued that *harder* convergence criteria were necessary for EMU to be a success. The *soft* approach was characteristic of a conciliatory attitude towards the French position which was 'less rigorous ... on the convergence criteria for EMU and the independence of the ECB'.[10] It was underpinned by the belief of Kohl and Genscher in established patterns of German European policy and the continued significance of historical memory. The level of public respect accorded to the *Bundesbank* in Germany nevertheless exerted enough pressure for Waigel to convince Kohl of the economic and political importance of the convergence criteria. The political reasoning of Kohl and Genscher did, however, overcome the *harder* economic concerns of the Finance Ministry and the *Bundesbank* in two central areas: in the formula laid down for the convergence criteria and the timetable for Monetary Union. Originally, the *Bundesbank* had proposed that they represent fully binding pre-conditions for entry into EMU. In the end, the Federal Government was willing to accept criteria which, when viewed in detail, were subject to a large degree of political interpretation by the Council.[11] Kohl was also prepared to see an automatic transition into Stage II of Monetary Union (by January 1994), and even Stage III (by January 1999), thereby threatening German parliamentary control over the evaluation of the convergence criteria in particular and the process of Monetary Union in general.

The policy of the Federal Government on the formulation of the Treaty of European Union was less successful in the IGC on political union. Despite a formal change of name from a European Community to a European Union, the objective of achieving significant advances in integration outside monetary policy met with failure. While there were some differences between the Member States over Monetary Union, the central goal of currency union was at least clear. There were, on the other hand, large conceptual differences over what was meant by a 'European Political Union' (EPU). While the Kohl-Mitterrand *joint letter* in April 1991 had put an IGC on political union on the agenda, it only offered the vague goals of strengthening democracy in the EC and the efficiency of its institutions; achieving greater economic and political co-ordination; and, establishing a common foreign and security policy. Germany was eventually forced to compromise in this area, for an agreement to be reached at Maastricht. In terms of political union, only a very modest array of co-decision rights for the European Parliament were gained, leaving a decision on a significant extension of majority voting in the Council to a later date. The economic dimension of Economic and Monetary Union was therefore very much limited to the convergence criteria for the single currency. On another level, the Maastricht Treaty had also failed to establish a social dimension to its policies. Commission President, Jacques Delors, also had social policy in mind when he wrote of economic co-ordination as one of the pillars of EMU, and this he further elaborated upon in the so-called 'Delors White Paper' on 'Growth, Competitiveness and Employment' in 1993.[12] Although the Federal Government would have been highly unlikely to have achieved agreement in this area given the position of the UK Government (as their opt-out from the final 'social protocol' showed), the failure to achieve deeper integration in economic and social policy formed the basis of SPD criticism of Maastricht for years to come.

German attitudes to EMU

The political elites in Germany were embedded in a European policy consensus, which extolled the virtues of European integration, and this consensus was particularly evident in the *Bundestag* (Chapter 4). Within the Federal Government, changes had begun to surface as result of further integration. The fact that EMU was negotiated, to a large extent, by the Finance Minister rather than the Foreign Minister was an important turn of events. It meant that the details of pre- and post-Maastricht policy were dominated by an economic rather than a political interpretation, often the result of close interaction between the Finance Ministry and the *Bundesbank*. While the *Bundesbank* was pleased to have achieved key goals such as the independence and stability-orientation of the future ECB, its hard-nosed attitude made the Federal Government's presentation of Monetary Union to the media and public more troublesome, by laying out the costs as well as the benefits of a single currency. The *Bundesbank*, for example, underlined the potential risks to currency stability and the problems of a Monetary Union that lacked any real political union, particularly in the form of a common economic policy. These firmly articulated views did not make the *Bundesbank* President a popular figure with the Chancellor,[13] who – with the support of the Foreign Minister – allowed the *softening* of the convergence criteria in the Maastricht Treaty described above.

Neither of the *social partners* in Germany exerted much influence over the negotiations that led to the Maastricht Treaty. Dyson and Featherstone explained that the 'distributional effects [of EMU] remained too unclear for sectoral interests to be able to specify their interests in an unambiguous manner'.[14] Business interests were, however, generally supportive of Monetary Union as a spur to free trade – 70 per cent of executive managers were in favour of Monetary Union in September 1995,[15] over double the rate of the general population (Figure 8.1). The unions, while also supporting EMU and EPU, were keen to see social rights incorporated into the Treaty, as well as the development of a Community social policy. IG Metall, for example, stated in 1999 that it had 'supported European Monetary Union and the Euro from the very beginning – at the same time, it is a sharp critic of a one-sided monetarist economic policy … the one-sided economic policy set on price stability and deregulation increases unemployment and social inequalities'.[16] The unions were, thus, limited in their praise for the eventual Treaty.

At the time when negotiations were taking place for the creation of a European Union, the public as a whole was both apathetic to and ignorant of these changes. This was largely due the opaque nature of intergovernmental negotiations in the Council, which could engage the attention neither of the media nor the public at large. This was hardly surprising given the historic events of German unification that were unfolding, which – according to one SPD MEP – 'totally overshadowed the European integration that was taking place'.[17] Yet by the end of the

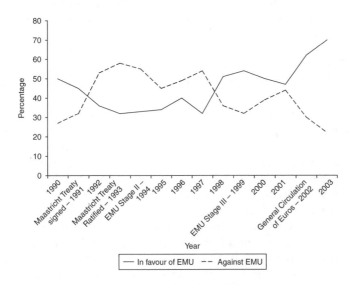

Figure 8.1 Support for EMU in Germany, 1990–2003

Source: *Eurobarometers 34–59*, published by the European Commission in Brussels, 1990–2003.

ratification process in 1993, widespread ambivalence to Monetary Union had turned into clear opposition. To contemplate Monetary Union with traditionally weaker currencies was a difficult psychological jump for most Germans to make, especially as the huge costs of unification were becoming more obvious. EMU was agreed by the political elites and presented to the public as a *fait accompli*. There was little attempt to inform them about the decisions that were being taken, and there was even less opportunity for doubts to be articulated due to elite consensus on this issue. Emerging public concern was reflected in a series of articles published by 'Bild' magazine during the Maastricht Council (December 1991), citing 'the end of the D-Mark'.[18] Opposition to the Single Currency rose markedly in Germany between 1990 and 1993, from 27 per cent to 58 per cent (Figure 8.1). Looking more deeply at public opinion, however, one can see that opposition was aimed specifically at currency union rather than the Treaty itself. In 1993, while only 32 per cent supported Monetary Union (with 58 per cent against), 39 per cent were in favour of the Maastricht Treaty (with only 24 per cent against).[19] The lack of support for Monetary Union was partly a result of a deep-lying German fear of inflation (that the new currency would be less stable), and – perhaps more importantly – because the Mark was the most potent symbol of German post-war prosperity and stability: 'Germans had, for a long time after the war, few points of orientation or symbols of identification, and the D-Mark was the strongest of them by far.'[20]

The SPD and EMU

The European policy consensus in the early 1990s meant that while the emphases of the CDU and SPD may have differed on, for instance, the social dimension of European integration, their policies were almost identical (Table 8.1). On the agreement of Monetary Union, the views of the SPD *Bundestagsfraktion* were clear: the 'advantages of the European Single Market will only reach their potential if the monetary borders between Member States also fall away ... the SPD is for a Single Currency ... We advocate the agreement of dates for further steps'.[21] The SPD, free from the difficult intergovernmental negotiations, could even criticise the Federal Government for missing out on 'constructive steps towards the creation of a European Economic and Monetary Union', complaining that the Franco-German initiative in April 1990 only 'proposed that decisions for European economic and monetary union should be ratified by the end of 1992, but went no further.'[22] The SPD also supported an independent European Central Bank, 'obligated to the primary goal of monetary and fiscal stability'.[23] In addition, internal party documents show that the party was fully aware that the EMU convergence criteria were 'built on ... the political evaluation of the European Monetary Institute, the Commission and finally also the Council',[24] and thereby open to political interpretation. This contrasts with later demands by the party that *hard criteria* must be observed according to the Treaty. The SPD was half-hearted in its criticism of the Federal Government's failure to push through an agreement on social policy equal in status to EMU. It only expressed disappointment that, despite the agreement of all except the UK to a *Social Charter* in December 1989, 'we will reach the completion of the Single Market on 1.1.93 without the completion of the social dimension',[25] offering little detail to supplement its general support for 'widened EC competencies in social policy and an active employment policy'.[26]

In 1992, SPD European policy was, in fact, more concerned with the lack of political union and democratic checks on European policy in the Maastricht Treaty than the neglect of a social or ecological union (Table 8.1). The parliamentary party stated that its 'central demand was

Table 8.1 Federal government/SPD support for aspects of European integration

	Economic and Monetary Union (EMU)	European Political Union (EPU)	European social and ecological policy
The Federal Government	*Strong*: given the pre-condition of a stability-based, independent central bank, viewed as a natural outcome of the Single Market.	*Strong*: even threatened to veto EMU due to lack of political union – in the end they accepted a small extension of the European Parliament's powers as a short-term compromise.	*Weak*: while notionally supporting social and ecological minimum standards, was more concerned with the economic and political aspects of integration.
The SPD	*Medium*: at the federal level at least. Despite some concerns about the lack of a social dimension, government policy was supported.	*Strong*: critcised the Federal Government for not doing enough to ensure political union and economic policy co-ordination, championed greater inclusion of the *Bundestag* in future decisions.	*Medium*: stressed the importance of social and ecological policy, but they were not yet *linked* to economic issues at home or made a pre-condition of Treaty ratification.

therefore that EMU and a democratically legitimate European political union ... would be decided upon and realised at the same time'.[27] In other words, if the control of monetary policy was to be taken away from the national plane, steps should be taken to close the legitimacy gap and to make the co-ordination of economic policy a reality (Table 8.1). The relative neglect of the economic side of Economic and Monetary Union was an issue the party would return to with increasing vigour. The SPD, for instance, proposed the control of ECOFIN by the European Parliament, and criticised the Chancellor for giving away the Deutschmark without ensuring political controls at the EU level.[28] The importance that they attached to democratic controls to accompany Monetary Union can be seen in the efforts made by the party to gain greater parliamentary involvement in the European integration process (Chapter 4). With the help of Brunner ruling, the SPD helped to establish a *Bundestag* European Affairs Committee to scrutinise government policy, and secured amendments to the German *Basic Law* in the Maastricht ratification process obliging the Federal Government to report to parliament *at the earliest possible opportunity*, to give the *Bundestag* an opportunity to form an opinion before the agreement of EU legislation.[29]

There were still those in the SPD who opposed the Maastricht Treaty on the basis of what they saw as a bias towards free market interests. Lafontaine, for instance, toyed with the idea of voting against the Treaty if improvements were not made to harmonise Member States' 'wage, fiscal and social policies'.[30] The party, what is more, was in a position to block the Treaty in both chambers given the need for a two-thirds majority in parliament. Calls to make the party's support for the Maastricht Treaty conditional on the agreement of political, social and ecological dimensions to integration came mostly from isolated voices in the *Länder* and from the labour wing of the party. The general view in the SPD was that a rejection of the Maastricht Treaty would not be productive, because the party was 'already striving to get Kohl to rectify his bad mistakes', and gain post-hoc 'improvements to the EC decisions at Maastricht'.[31] Taking into account the 'Yes–No' decision in parliament on the ratification of the Treaty, even the most avid proponents of political and social union backed down. One Left-wing member of the *Bundestag* commented in retrospect: 'I don't think [voting for the Maastricht Treaty] could be avoided ... To not support it would have meant coming across as an opponent of Europe.'[32] The SPD did, however, demand a further concession from the Government. They insisted on a voice in further revisions of the Treaty, but especially in future decisions on German participation in Monetary Union: 'a central point therefore is the evaluation of the political and economic risks at each stage of integration ... the decisions of the Federal Republic in the Council should have parliamentary consent and ... no automatic rule for the introduction of the third stage of EMU (1999) may be given'.[33] After the constitutional changes referred to above, it was clear that parliament would have to agree to the start of Stage III.

In the final analysis, the SPD voted for the Treaty and managed to come to a broad agreement with the Federal Government over the further goals of European integration that would complement the European policy consensus in the *Bundestag*. Engholm declared in the ratification debate: 'The Yes to Maastricht is a clear vote for the Community ... Now it remains to continue the European unification process with perspective and reason.'[34] Yet this 'constructive' approach to EMU emanated not from the coherent European policy of a *government in waiting*, but from a party that lacked interest in European issues and instrumentalised the cross-party consensus to cover up a lack of ideas on Europe. European policy was largely left to the European policy groups, which throughout the 1990s believed that 'without a common currency the single market remains incomplete' and that exchange rate fluctuations lead to 'distortions in competition'.[35] The consensus reached in favour of Maastricht was epitomised by the fact that an SPD motion on the Treaty[36] was integrated into a joint CDU/CSU, SPD and FDP motion in support of a 'a unified Europe',[37] though small differences of emphases remained on social policy.

Questioning EMU

By 1992, the German economy was suffering under the weight of unification and the general slowdown in world trade. The national debt was increasing rapidly as were unemployment rates, and economic growth had been slowing since the mid-1980s (Chapter 2). Furthermore, the high level of public spending necessitated by unification had required the *Bundesbank* to raise interests rates significantly, to prevent an increase in inflation. As *Bundesbank* interest rates rose and remained high, great pressure was placed on other currencies in the ERM, as speculators moved more and more money out of other European currencies (notably Sterling, the Italian Lira and the French Franc) and into the Deutschmark. The UK and Italy were forced into embarrassing and costly withdrawals from the ERM in September 1992, while only concerted French and German central bank intervention prevented the devaluation of the French Franc. This raised a serious question mark over whether Italy, in particular, would be ready for Stage III of Monetary Union. After further exchange rate turbulence in the summer of 1993, Finance Ministers resolved to broaden the EMS bands from 2.5 per cent to 15 per cent. The experience of the exchange rate crises hardened opinion against EMU in some Member States such as the UK and Denmark, while in others politicians became even more convinced of the need for EMU to prevent such crises from happening again in the future. Public opinion was another thing entirely, since Monetary Union was widely seen as the root of the problem. As Dinan explains: 'Currency turmoil may have strengthened the rationale for EMU, but it widened the already growing gap between political and public opinion in most Member States.'[38] The unpopularity of the Euro can be observed in German opinion polls through this period (Figure 8.1). While over 50 per cent of Germans were in favour of EMU in 1990, this figure had dropped below 45 per cent in 1991 (the year the Maastricht Treaty was signed), to just over 35 per cent in 1992 (the year of the ratification crises), and fell below a third in 1993 (Figure 8.1). Support for EMU was to remain at these low levels until the Euro drew near in the late 1990s, and confidence was gained by the launch of the currency in 1999 and the general circulation of Euros in 2002 (Figure 8.1).

The ERM crises further increased the problems of Monetary Union with regard to the ratification of the Maastricht Treaty within individual Member States. Although, as mentioned above, the German Government could rely on a broad pro-EMU consensus in the *Bundestag* and *Bundesrat*, other governments were not in such a fortunate position. Luckily for the process of Monetary Union, the UK government did not require direct popular ascent to pass the Treaty, but – even so – it won only a narrow victory in the House of Commons. In Denmark, however, the Treaty was rejected by referendum in June 1992, casting further doubts on currency union. In France, the joint *motor of European integration*, the 'Yes-vote' only achieved the most marginal of victories. The unpopularity of Monetary Union was exacerbated by the effects of the Maastricht convergence criteria at this time. In a situation of low growth, high interest rates and high unemployment, it was difficult for countries to get a grip on public spending, and austerity measures were acutely felt. Furthermore, now that one of the convergence criteria had already been amended (the increase of the ERM band to 15 per cent), there was distrust over whether the other criteria would or could be maintained. In Germany itself, the ratification process ended with a ruling by the Constitutional Court, which was commonly seen as another public rebuke for Monetary Union, undermining popular support and emboldening political opposition. Assailed by these economic and political problems, the future of the EMU project looked distinctly shaky, just as the political consensus behind the Single Currency began to be challenged by an increasingly vocal group of SPD politicians. The new generation of party leaders was not afraid of articulating its doubts over the economic problems Monetary Union might bring, like Lafontaine who had described it as *a barrel without a bottom*.

A new SPD strategy?

The election of Rudolf Scharping as party chairman in May 1993 was a turning point in SPD European policy. As explained in Chapters 5 and 6, he was part of a new generation of SPD leaders who felt less constrained by traditional policy positions and more *responsive* to public opinion than previous leaders. Though responding to public opinion meant that European policy remained – as before – a low policy priority, it also precipitated a more intense questioning of the Federal Government policy on certain issues, and the desire to establish the contours of a more distinct SPD position. The new leadership strategy on Europe – such as it existed – had two general thrusts: first, a strong criticism of the lack of a common European social policy as a means to attack the government's economic record at home; second, a greater emphasis on popular concerns over the nature of EMU. The first part was not so much a European policy goal, but – in its formulation – a strategic arrow aimed at the Government's domestic economic policy. The second part manifested itself as a policy designed to guard against (or appear to guard against) the *softening* of the Maastricht criteria by the Federal Government, to ensure that the future European currency would be as stable and non-inflationary as the Deutschmark. For this, the opinions of the *Bundesbank* and Constitutional Court were used as *institutional markers* (Chapter 4) – as sticks with which to beat the Government and policy guidelines for the SPD. This entailed an emphasis on closing the *legitimacy gap* in the EC/EU, safeguarding economic stability post-Monetary Union as demanded by the Constitutional Court, and an emphasis on the strict adherence to the *Bundesbank*-sponsored convergence criteria.

While primarily designed to attack the government record on unemployment, the use of institutional markers was also an attempt to gain public confidence in SPD European policy and to foster a sense that the party could be trusted in government. At the same time, the influence of the Constitutional Court and *Bundesbank* were used to promote party unity over Monetary Union when genuine disagreement existed as to how far it should be used to promote stability or growth. By taking the *Bundesbank* line, the SPD tried to portray itself as the party of the stable Euro. The party's 1994 federal election programme stated: 'We will prevent Monetary Union weakening the Deutschmark. There will not be a weakening of the Maastricht criteria with us.'[39] 'The time-table laid down' at Maastricht, it was further underlined, 'was no goal in itself'.[40] Yet this new style of policy also heralded the evolution of a more sceptical approach to the Monetary Union, questioning the European policy consensus among the political elites. Scharping caused uproar after commenting in an interview with 'Der Spiegel' in June 1993 that he had 'decided upon bringing European integration forward as a step by step process, not sticking slavishly to some or other goal or timetable [in reference to Monetary Union]'.[41] This displayed a more *pragmatic* but also a more *populist* attitude to currency union. He was willing to question Monetary Union on economic grounds, but this also reflected the fact that support for a single currency had reached its low-point of 32 per cent in this year (Figure 8.1). On the other hand, the SPD argued for further steps towards an EU social and employment policy in line with union demands for an inclusion of 'binding statements on a common economic, financial and employment policy'.[42] The programme for the 1994 elections was, however, strongly focused on domestic unemployment, so that the area of EU policy was barely mentioned.

In terms of the contexts for European policy outlined in Chapters 3 and 4, we can see that the SPD was strongly influenced by the *Bundesbank* and the unions at this stage, but with a growing responsiveness to popular feeling. Though the Federal Government had a major publicity victory with the agreement to locate the ECB in Frankfurt (October 1993), it was obvious that the growing opposition to Monetary Union had to be countered. The coalition parties began to respond to some of these fears by stressing the *hardness* of the convergence criteria, but it was difficult for them to alter their pre-unity style of European policy. The Federal Government was often concerned with appeasing other Member States, to smooth the path of European integration in a policy marked by *exaggerated multilateralism*. By the mid-1990s, however, domestic actors were beginning to become more important for the Christian Democrats, which manifested itself in an attempt to offer a more *pragmatic* position. The Schäuble-Lamers paper of 1994,[43] for instance, wrote of a 'variable geometry' of European integration, accepting the fact that some Member States (including Italy) would not be able or willing to join Monetary Union in time for its launch (Chapter 10). While Chancellor Kohl was in power, however, Germany remained more responsive to the concerns of its EU partners, so that this type of proposal could not easily become government policy.[44] Even if CDU/CSU minister-presidents in the *Länder* were prepared to articulate domestic concerns, Kohl asserted that the 'construction of a European house is a vital issue. My political fate is associated with it'.[45]

Within the SPD, a gap was beginning to emerge between the consensus-oriented views of those working in the European policy committees and groups in the *Bundestag* and at party HQ, and the high-profile leaders of the party in power in the *Länder*. Norbert Wieczorek, chair of the *Bundestag* European Affairs Committee, drafted a European policy paper in the summer of 1995 supporting the promotion of 'monetary integration', and suggesting that the SPD concentrate its efforts in the 1996 IGC on the so-called 'Maastricht left-overs'. The acceptance of the paper by the *Vorstand* in June 1995 'strengthened the far-reaching consensus between the Federal Government and the SPD opposition'.[46] While the SPD European policy groups promoted consensus and constructive criticism *vis-à-vis* government plans, they had failed to capture the minds of key figures in the party with a distinctive conception of European integration. The SPD *Troika* stepped into this vacuum of ideas, seeking to lend 'the key European issues a domestic perspective ... as with European Economic and Monetary Union'.[47] Despite Rudolf Scharping's position as chairman of the SPD parliamentary group (as well as party chairman) after the federal election defeat in autumn 1994 and his closer proximity (in both a literal and a figurative sense) to the consensual European policy atmosphere of the *Bundestag*, he retained the desire to use Monetary Union as an electoral tool for reasons of *pragmatism* (in terms of *generational* and *electoral-strategic change*) and the wish not to be outdone by his *Länder*-based rivals in the party leadership, Lafontaine and Schröder.

The SPD against EMU?

It is obvious from opinion polls and from the evidence given above (Figure 8.1) that the average German was not convinced about the economic benefits of Monetary Union, even though the political will in Bonn, Paris and Brussels was clear enough. This was particularly the case given the economic burden of unification described in Chapter 2. Germans became more aware of their large contribution to the EU budget and more ambivalent about the benefits of EU membership in general (Chapters 5 and 6). In the same sense, giving up the

Deutschmark, the main symbol of post-war prosperity and stability, was seen as a further sacrifice for European integration which would entail costly transfer payments at a time when the country could ill afford it. Unpopular austerity measures introduced by the Government to help slow down the burgeoning national debt were, furthermore, often blamed on the strictures of the convergence criteria (sometimes by the Federal Government itself). Worse still for supporters of the Single Currency in Germany, the Madrid European Council in December 1995 conceded that Stage III of Monetary Union would not be launched in January 1997, since the Member States had not reached the necessary levels of convergence. Although support for EMU among elite actors was still strong, they were not totally impervious to the doubts and fears of the public over the new currency.

The views expressed by Schröder from the mid-1990s onwards articulated an anti-Monetary Union or anti-European integration stance in a way not seen in the upper echelons of the SPD since the 1950s. While Scharping had, in 1993 and again in 1995, questioned the value of sticking to the EMU timetable, his position as chairman of the party meant that he had a responsibility to official SPD policy which quite clearly supported currency union. Therefore, his 'dismissive remarks about EMU' were officially portrayed as 'a lapse', and it was emphasised that he was 'a convinced European and had wanted simply to underline that it would be wrong to give up the D-Mark for a European currency that was less stable'.[48] Scharping's views on Monetary Union were therefore couched in terms of support for *hard criteria*. This position was shared by Schröder, who also took the *Bundesbank* line that called for 'countries to be obliged to stability' even after the conclusion of Monetary Union (this was also a priority for the Federal Government).[49] Schröder broadened these views into a more detailed criticism. Like Lafontaine, he believed in a broad-based single currency, and 'advocated Italian, Spanish and British membership as a precondition for EMU'.[50] He rejected Finance Minister Waigel's assertion that Italy might not participate in Monetary Union by 1999 because of its untidy public finances, insisting that all 'important Member States' must take part.[51] Although there was certainly a populist dimension to Schröder's views, he was also speaking for a specific section of German industry when he advocated as wide as possible a Single Currency. On the board of Volkswagen in Lower Saxony, he saw the threat of other countries outside Monetary Union devaluing their currencies against the Euro as a threat to the competitiveness of the German car industry. Schröder went on, however, to make some clearly populist assertions. Speculating on the unknown cost of Monetary Union, he made explicit Scharping's earlier criticisms, remarking that it 'would be no great mistake, for Monetary Union to come a few years later.'[52] This was a clear breach of the German European policy consensus. Lafontaine's opposition to Monetary Union, on the other hand, rested more on his belief that the Maastricht Treaty needed to be renegotiated before currency union took place, and that an EU economic government should be established along the lines of Delors' Common European Economic Authority.

The timing of Monetary Union became an increasingly important issue for the SPD leadership *Troika*. Schröder considered his views to be 'completely rational' from an economic point of view, stating that he was 'in principle for a Monetary Union', but that the 'economic and political risks ... were greater than the difficulties that would be brought about by a postponement'.[53] Lafontaine, while laying more emphasis on the achievement of a European social and employment policy, also questioned the time-scale: 'Before Monetary Union blows European unification apart, it would be better to correct the timetable of the Maastricht Treaty.'[54] Much of the sharpness of the *Troika*'s rhetoric on Monetary Union nevertheless came from the great personal rivalry between the three figures – the desire not to be outdone and to show themselves as defining the contours of party policy. One SPD MEP confirmed this point: 'I remember a radio interview with Rudolf Scharping, where because of anti-European statements made by Schröder in the papers the day before, he spoke out against the Euro himself.'[55]

Roth argues that it 'was less the content and much more the style of Scharping and Schröder, which let loose an avalanche of responses from inside as well as outside the party, that raised doubts about the seriousness of SPD European policy'.[56] The party's European policy groups were quite capable of saying similar things, but in a more Euro-friendly and constructive way: Norbert Wieczorek stated in the *Bundestag*, for example, that 'I find that the ECOFIN Council was realistic when it said that it is not conceivable that a majority of the countries will fulfil the criteria of the Maastricht Treaty in the next year; therefore it would be sensible to orientate towards the date, 1 January 1999.'[57] There were, however, genuine differences in the detail of policy, as the European policy groups also believed that it was 'important that the Federal Government pushes for the maintenance of the timetable'.[58] Schröder's comments, in particular, provoked savage attacks from the older generation of politicians and the European policy establishment outside the federal party machinery. Former Chancellor, Helmut Schmidt, for one, sided with Kohl in his anger at the rising tide of Euroscepticism in

Germany: 'It lies in the central strategic interests of Germany to avoid a return to a situation in which our many neighbours join together against a real or imagined German threat, in order to keep us Germans in check. If the Federal Chancellor, in this context, has so far all too pathetically spoken of war and peace in Europe, he nevertheless is completely right! Against that, his party colleagues, Tietmeyer and Stoiber, and my party colleagues, Schröder and Spöri, are strategic pygmies.'[59] The manner in which Schmidt criticised Schröder epitomised the often haughty view of European politics taken by older politicians from the German political establishment, who balked at the breaking of European policy taboos. They too readily dismissed genuine concerns with the details of European integration. Schröder, therefore, could pertinently reply that: 'Helmut Schmidt overlooks the fact that we must deliver legitimacy for the abolition of the German Mark.'[60]

The European policy experts away from Bonn were equally critical. Klaus Hänsch spoke against a 'populist–nationalist agitation', and European Commissioner, Monika Wulff-Mathies (SPD), warned against 'D-Mark nationalism'.[61] Even mainstream SPD politicians criticised what they saw as the counter-productive, populist agitation from the Troika. Heidi Simonis, Minister-President of Schleswig-Holstein, for instance, warned the party against a '*Stammtisch* [pub] debate'.[62] The parliamentary group, embedded in the *Bundestag* consensus, was – furthermore – drafting a paper on Monetary Union with the coalition parties through the European Affairs Committee at this time. Wieczorek, the chair of the Committee, stressed that it was 'right that we have made Monetary Union a cross-party consensus ... Monetary union lies in our political, but also in our economic interests'.[63] Although the SPD European policy groups disagreed with populist style of the *Troika*'s comments on EMU, they stopped shy of publicly condemning their outspoken views, while other members of the *Bundestag* simply stressed that 'the SPD will not deviate from its traditional European policy'.[64]

The coalition parties were incensed by the comments of the *Troika*. Foreign minister Kinkel accused Scharping and Schröder of 'cheap populism', and Peter Hintze, General Secretary of the CDU 'warned that the SPD would make a "serious historical mistake" if it abandoned the European idea'.[65] Big business, furthermore, attacked the SPD leaders for casting doubt upon the introduction of the Euro: Siemens chief, Heinrich von Pierer, reminded the party that 'the meaning of Monetary Union for business was far-reaching'.[66] The SPD leadership was not, however, alone in the German political scene in articulating its reservations. Their views were mirrored by Christian Democrat politicians at the *Länder* level, such as Edmund Stoiber (CSU), Minister-President of Bavaria, who talked of a 'splitting of Europe' if EMU did not include at least two-thirds of the EU Member States and was not flanked by further political and social integration,[67] and Kurt Biedenkopf (CDU), Minister-President of Saxony, who labelled the project 'premature, and without a state superstructure too risky'.[68] Although none of these politicians were against Monetary Union in principle, their criticisms could only help to undermine public confidence. The CDU/CSU did not question the premises of Monetary Union or call for its delay at the federal level, so that there was never any real danger of it becoming party policy. Some in the SPD leadership, on the other hand, intended to use the Monetary Union issue as an electoral weapon. According to Schröder: 'Finally we social democrats again have a national theme.'[69]

The supposition of Scharping, Schröder and – to a lesser extent – Lafontaine that electoral support could be won through a sceptical position on Monetary Union was mistaken for two reasons. First, it over-looked the nuances of public opposition to a currency union. Public scepticism over Monetary Union as with European integration as a whole was more subtle than it first appeared. The composition of countries included in the new currency was seen to be crucial by the public: according to polls in 1995, 'Just under 80% expressed support for currency union if it excluded the poorer Mediterranean members',[70] differing significantly from the 34 per cent who expressed support for Monetary Union as a whole in polls conducted in the same year (Figure 8.1). Furthermore, 'a large majority (68 per cent) thought that Germany should join if the single currency were introduced'.[71] Second, the profiling of the SPD on an anti-Euro line had no chance of success because the majority of the party at the federal level was strongly in favour of a timely introduction of Monetary Union: 'Although the politicians' statements on EMU were generally interpreted as a funda-mental shift in the SPD's position on monetary integration, their move was neither co-ordinated nor coherent, and had not been formally endorsed by the party's executive.'[72] This was aptly illustrated by the *Bundestagsfraktion*'s attempts to adopt a position of constructive criti-cism in a 'questionnaire' to the Federal Government on German policy towards Monetary Union.[73] Schröder and Scharping's portrayal of them-selves as defenders of the Deutschmark and currency stability, therefore, appeared opportunist rather than credible. The apparent U-turn by the party's three most prominent leaders resulted in 'a loss of credibility for the SPD leadership', and the party's competency ratings in European affairs plummeted to 8 per cent in November 1995 compared to 46 per cent for the CDU/CSU.[74] While the *Troika's* positions were not politically astute and did not reflect the views of the party at the federal level, they characterised a dynamism in SPD European policy that increasingly saw EU integration in a *pragmatic* light – in terms of what they thought to be German interests, in their focus on the views of (selected) domestic actors and in their ideological and strategic flexibility (Chapters 5–7).

The controversy manifested itself at the SPD party conference in Mannheim in November 1995. The main highlight of the party conference was the Lafontaine's *coup d'état*, when he – in a surprise move – stood against and defeated Scharping in a contest for the chair of the party. It was also marked by a 'violent inner party dispute over the European policy course for Economic and Monetary Union'.[75] By this stage the European policy groups in the party were fed up with the leadership for allowing the stream of European policy statements which ran against or undermined the party's official views. Willi Görlach, head of the SPD group in the European Parliament, criticised the lack of discipline: 'Enough is enough; Scharping must practice damage limitation.'[76] The Single Currency was nevertheless a central issue as Lafontaine and Scharping helped to draft a motion on Monetary Union in the first days of the Conference. The sharp formulation of SPD policy adopted by Scharping and Schröder was not welcomed by the main body of the party at the federal level or the conference delegates. Original passages of the motion were redrafted, so that in 'the opinion of observers, the SPD's previously sceptical comments were withdrawn'.[77] The motion accepted, entitled 'Wir brauchen Europa' (we need Europe), while retaining many of Scharping and Schröder's demands for a 'stability community' and Lafontaine's emphasis on the agreement of 'common minimum social standards', clarified that the party 'supports the Economic and Monetary Union'. It also declared that for 'economic and political reasons as many countries as possible should take part in Monetary Union', rather than speculating on a postponement as Scharping and Schröder had done.[78] The changes to the original draft furthermore ensured that 'a social union will no longer be named as an unconditional pre-condition to EMU',[79] as Lafontaine had previously argued.

This was not the end of the debate over Monetary Union or the end of remarks by leading SPD politicians about a possible postponement of the new currency, but by summer 1996 the anti-EMU rhetoric became more isolated. The difficulty of using Monetary Union as an election issue had been illustrated by the SPD campaign mounted by Dieter Spöri for the Baden-Württemberg regional elections in March 1996, which sought to use Monetary Union as a key issue in its election strategy.

Posters were put up declaring 'No Way CDU! A stable currency rather than even more unemployment: 1999 – No Euro!'[80] This caused a furore in Bonn, and Lafontaine had to insist that these posters be removed. The telling factor here was that, as Reinhardt argues in an article on these elections, 'the Social Democrats did not profit from their strategy but lost a considerable share of the vote'.[81] The period from autumn 1995 to summer 1996 had marked a troubled time for SPD European policy. Policy confusion and opportunism led to a loss of public credibility. This is not to say that the party's European policy groups and the German political elites in general were totally in the right. In their unwillingness to respond to genuine fears over Monetary Union, other than to argue that Germany would profit most, they failed to offer any direct antidote to these concerns.

The move towards a more complete European policy worthy of a *government in waiting* was to be assisted by the launch of a European policy review at Mannheim: the role of the *Schwerpunktkommission* was to 'to develop an SPD position on European problems and events and mediate it through the SPD'.[82] It was also significant that criticism of certain aspects of European integration was – for the *Troika* at least – no longer off-limits. European policy would be judged on its own merits, according to Germany's new political environment. The *Troika* had, furthermore, hit upon a source of discontent over European Monetary Union in Germany that could not be ignored. The European policy review, explored in Chapter 9, sought to find a synthesis between these positions.

9

Governing the Euro-zone

Chapter 9 examines the development of SPD policy on Economic and Monetary Union as the party moved along the opposition–government axis, when it became a *government in waiting* in the late 1990s and entered office in 1998 to be faced by the governance of the Euro-zone after the establishment of Monetary Union on 1 January 1999. The chapter will, first, chart the development of a more cohesive European policy in the mid-to-late 1990s as the party moved along the 'road to government' with reference to the policy confusion described in the previous chapter. Here, SPD European policy sought to establish *issue-linkage* between Economic and Monetary Union and European social and employment policy during the 1996–97 IGC leading up to the Amsterdam Treaty (1997). The party also sought to press the Federal Government on the maintenance of *hard* convergence criteria for the transition to Stage III of Monetary Union. Both of these policies were bound to the domestic aims of the party in attacking the Kohl Government on its performance in economic and social policy in Germany as the SPD developed its *policy for government* in the run-up to the 1998 federal elections.

Second, the chapter will study the course of SPD policy in relation to the 'governance of the Euro-Zone' after it came to power in 1998. In the first few months in power, the party had to come to terms with *living with the Single Currency*. The dramatic failure of Lafontaine to realise his goals for the European Union illustrated the need to come to terms with the new network of pressures and constraints in government. In a second phase in government, party leaders focused on the achievement of economic and social policy goals on the national level, satisfying themselves with the *open method* of co-ordination on the EU plane. The penetration of EU politics – with particular regard to the completion of the Single Market – nevertheless demonstrated to the party the urgent need for closer co-ordination of economic and social policy to protect and promote the German social market model. Finally, the SPD European policy review published in 2001 set out the party's goals for a social democratic EU.

The road to government

After the Mannheim Conference, with Lafontaine as party chairman and Schröder as a likely chancellor candidate, many had expected the SPD to adopt a more sceptical stance on European policy than was the case under Scharping,[1] who – as chairman of the parliamentary group – could be reigned in by the *Bundestagsfraktion*. Lafontaine, under pressure from the European policy groups within the party, nevertheless sought to make Europe an uncontroversial topic within the SPD. The aim was to formulate a policy that could incorporate different strands of thought within the party, so that European policy would at least cease to be a weakness in electoral terms. Lafontaine and Wieczorek-Zeul also aimed to use European policy for the party's electoral advantage. Rather than simply focusing on the *pros and cons* of Monetary Union, the SPD would take the opportunity of *linking* Monetary Union to other issues with more electoral potential and more resonance to the party's domestic political agenda. In immediate terms, the European policy groups – with the support of the party leadership and party chairman – were to increasingly link EMU to EU reform at the Maastricht revision conference in 1996.

Monetary Union and European social policy

Lafontaine's opposition to the Maastricht Treaty was based on his view of EMU as a one-sided currency union. Agreeing to a social dimension to Monetary Union was not something that the Kohl governments were totally averse to, but any accord had proved impossible given the stance taken by the Conservative Government in the UK and the prominence of liberal economics-oriented governments in the EU. Many of the original architects of Monetary Union regretted this state of affairs. Lafontaine repeatedly cited the proposals of the 1993 *Delors White Paper* on the harmonisation of economic, fiscal and social policy. The foundation of EU social policy was, for Lafontaine, substantial integration in EU economic policy: 'Only such a policy that is bound to the name of Jacques Delors and his proposal for a European economic government has the prospect of success.'[2] This position marked a strategic change in

Lafontaine's vision of the EU. He had called for the SPD to vote against the Maastricht Treaty in 1992, but – after some consideration of European issues and after the experience of the defeats of an anti-Monetary Union policy at Mannheim and in Baden-Württemberg – he had developed a more constructive approach to achieve a more social democratic EU: 'We make European policy for the workers and not for the owners of capital.'[3] This new tack was something that the party's European groups could easily live with, since it could be integrated into their policy objectives for the 1996 reform conference. While the party leadership offered guidelines for European policy after Mannheim – insisting that the social aspects of European integration become more of a focus – EU affairs once more became the preserve of the experts in the party under Wieczorek-Zeul.

European social policy centred on the creation of an EU employment policy. The party's European policy groups had, by the time of the Madrid Summit in December 1995, produced a position paper calling for the incorporation of a Chapter on employment policy into the EU treaties.[4] A central task of the European policy review in the *Schwerpunktkommission* in 1996 was accordingly to examine the 'possibilities and perspectives for a European employment policy and the strategic meaning of the European plane to ensure fully effective social protection'.[5] The party also expressed the goal of inserting the European Social Charter into the EU treaties. Confirming the objective of establishing workers' protection on the European level, they stressed that 'the fight against unemployment must be a central task of the European Union' with a 'European Growth and Employment Pact'.[6] Furthermore, a 'corridor model' was proposed for national tax regimes in the EU. This aimed to relieve the pressures placed upon Member States' social policies by tax competition, a process known as 'social dumping'. Taking a more constructive role in the pursuit of these policy goals at the IGC launched in March 1996, the SPD began to show a firm commitment to Monetary Union itself, so that by the end of 1996, Günter Verheugen (SPD foreign policy spokesman) could state that the party was 'moving out of isolation on the European Union', and 'would be on the same side as the Bonn coalition in supporting the Euro'.[7]

The two most important domestic actors for the SPD on EMU at this time were the *Bundesbank* and the trade unions. The *Bundesbank*, aside from its support for a hard interpretation of the Maastricht criteria and a post-Monetary Union stability pact, also warned that 'Monetary Union could fail if it was not backed by increased political integration.'[8] *Bundesbank* President, Hans Tietmeyer, complained that, despite the fact that EMU was based on a Single Market in goods, services and capital, 'Economic and social policy was mostly in national hands and would thus be determined by national interests.'[9] Though Tietmeyer's hawkish stance may not have been good for public opinion on Monetary Union, it gave credence to the SPD's new concepts for the Maastricht revision conference. The unions, with particularly close ties to the SPD in opposition, were in full accord with the party's focus on social and economic integration, calling themselves for an 'employment programme', the 'incorporation of the social protocol into the Maastricht treaty', and 'target goals for growth and employment policy'.[10] Beyond these national actors, the SPD was also improving its European contacts with other social democratic parties in the EU. As chairman of the Party of European Socialists, Scharping had, for example, made a joint declaration with former French Prime Minister, Michel Rocard, in 1994,[11] and made speeches at both the Austrian Social Democratic and British Labour party conferences in 1995.

The party made specific proposals for the 1996 IGC through its parliamentary group on the revisions it wanted to the Maastricht Treaty. One long-term objective was the establishment of a Charter of Fundamental Rights, within which would be included 'binding basic social rights ... secured in the same measure for all Member States'.[12] More immediately, it called for the 'creation of a European employment pact and a European social union ... the most important themes of the revision conference'.[13] Many of the social policies forwarded by the SPD – for instance, 'positive measures in favour of the equal position of women', the enshrinement of 'consultation rights' for the social partners and the extension of 'co-decision for workers ... Europe-wide'[14] – were, in fact, measures that the Federal Government could agree with. And although there were differences over the nature of minimum social standards and the harmonisation of taxes to prevent tax competition, there was general agreement on the concepts themselves. Little co-operation took place, however, over employment policy. One interviewee, heavily involved in SPD European policy at the time, stated that 'employment policy ... [was] the one really clear controversy [between the parties] that I can remember ... the one area where you could see a really well-defined social democratic point of view'.[15] It created the most conflict because it focused attention on unemployment in Germany, which was in the process of passing the politically significant four million mark.

At the start of the IGC the SPD called for a 'European Alliance for Work' that included the following elements: the obligation of the

European Council to 'regularly define the important guidelines on economic and social policy for the whole European Union'; the duty of the 'relevant Council of Ministers ... to lay down annual employment guidelines for Member States and the European union'; and, the demand that Member States 'publish programmes lasting several years for an active employment policy'.[16] These goals were not only clear and well researched, they were also worked out in co-operation with the SPD's sister parties (which were increasingly coming to power in the EU in the late 1990s), and therefore had a decent chance of success. With pressure mounting for an employment pact from other Member States, the SPD was confident of forcing a U-turn from the Federal Government. Before the Dublin Summit in December 1996, it officially made its support for the ratification of the new Treaty conditional upon the agreement of an 'active employment policy'. In a statement delivered in the background of a *Bundestag* European debate and signed by Lafontaine and Scharping, among others, the party declared plainly: 'Without binding rules on an active employment policy, no ratification.'[17] They repeated the call for social policy to form a central part of the new Treaty. In terms of the harmonisation of taxes, the SPD laid down the specific goal that a minimum corporation tax rate should be introduced along with the closing of tax oases for businesses and individuals. Explicit *issue-linkage* was evident in the assertion that, as Delors had argued, a social dimension was necessary to give equilibrium to EMU: 'The goal of economic and monetary union is to advance growth, employment and stability in all participant states.'[18]

Just a year after the Mannheim conference, given the internal divisions that were paraded there, this was an impressive and forthright display of a coherent SPD EU policy. The election of the British Labour Party in summer 1997, and their willingness to accept the Maastricht social protocol removed a large obstacle in the path of a European social policy. The Amsterdam Council in June 1997 could, therefore, remove the UK *opt-out* and incorporate the *social protocol* into the EC Treaty, whilst expressing an 'attachment to fundamental social rights'.[19] The Labour Party's more market-oriented approach nevertheless contributed to the watering down of the measures included in the new *Title* on employment in the EC Treaty. Lionel Jospin's victory in France was of equal importance to the SPD, which had cultivated strong bilateral ties to its French sister party over a number of years, offering the prospect of EU-level support for a more integrated social policy.

The Federal Government of Germany had been reluctant to allow the agreement of an EU employment policy, despite pressure from their partner states in the EU and the SPD in Germany to accept Dutch draft proposals. In this context, the SPD organised a European Congress in Bonn, to push for the implementation of an employment policy with the support and attendance of representatives of their social democratic allies across the EU. Dutch Employment Minister, Ad Melkert, for instance, stressed that that the fight against unemployment was 'the key to future competitiveness'.[20] Increasingly isolated, the Federal Government was forced into an embarrassing climb-down and accepted the inclusion of an Employment Chapter, if remaining sceptical about its content: 'We all want to create jobs ... but it can't be done with articles in treaties.'[21] The Amsterdam Treaty agreed that 'the Commission shall encourage co-operation between Member States and facilitate the co-ordination of their action in all social policy fields', especially in areas that included 'unemployment'.[22] Concrete proposals instructed the EU 'to formulate a European strategy' and for Member States to draw up 'national programmes', to be assessed by the Council each year.

The European policy pursued by the SPD from summer 1996 through to June 1997 was an undoubted success after the chaos of the previous year. A coherent policy was defined – essentially by the European policy groups within the party, but with the support of the party chairman – which was both coherent in its aims and could satisfy the electoral ambitions of the SPD and its leadership. Strident support for social policy and its *linkage* to EMU was further evidence of a *generational change* at the heart of SPD policy as the party was for the first time prepared to attach conditions to EU integration. Its policies were built on a new *electoral pragmatism* that went beyond the populism of late 1995 and early 1996 to encapsulate a broader set of domestic actors. Rather than merely playing to its own supporters, the SPD was producing the credible policies of a *government in waiting*. The Federal Government's acceptance of a Jobs Chapter at Amsterdam was a much needed victory for the SPD, which could gloat that 'After the Federal Government had denied the need for entrenching ... rules on an active employment policy for such a long time, it is to be greeted that they now recognise the need for the entrenchment of such a chapter.'[23]

EMU stage III

The Federal Government of Germany was under extreme pressure by the mid-1990s to demonstrate that it was seeking to safeguard the stability of the future European currency. This pressure came not only from public opinion, *Länder* minister-presidents (Stoiber had insisted that, in a conflict between the goals of the Maastricht timetable and the criteria, 'the criteria have precedence'[24]) and from the SPD leadership, but also from the *Bundesbank* itself. Tietmeyer, was not afraid to speak about his doubts, arguing in an interview with the ZDF TV channel that the Maastricht Treaty was 'not sufficient to guarantee the stability of the planned European currency on an enduring basis', and demanded 'a contract between the participants of Monetary Union'.[25] During the IGC in 1996, the German Government managed to push through a *Bundesbank* concept for a 'stability pact', which – given the pressure for the agreement of a social dimension to EMU – became a 'stability and growth pact'. The pact was primarily designed to prevent 'excessive' public spending by Member States after the introduction of the Euro, and comprised two main elements: 'a preventative, early warning system for identifying and correcting budgetary slippages before they bring the deficit above the 3% GDP ceiling', and a 'dissuasive set of rules with a deterrent effect to put pressure on Member States to avoid excessive deficits or to correct them quickly'.[26]

Finance Minister Waigel sought an even tighter *Bundesbank* proposal for a system of automatic financial penalties for Member States who breached the stability pact's deficit criteria, but the Government agreed to a *soft* penalty system (fines were made subject to Council approval) in deference to French sensitivity over the issue.[27] For the Federal Government, it was important to sell EMU as a strong, stable currency, so the new stability pact was very necessary. Tensions over Monetary Union were nevertheless exacerbated by the state of the domestic economy, because – although things were beginning to improve by 1997 – Germany itself had failed to meet any of the convergence criteria in 1995 and 1996. Despite the problems it was causing for the coalition parties, the commitment of the Government and Chancellor Kohl to Monetary Union remained strong, and Amsterdam saw the launch of the ERM II, to govern the exchange rates between participating and non-participating states after currency union.[28]

From the early 1990s, the SPD had used *Bundesbank* policy on currency stability to guide its own policies. Even the European groups in the party were keen to stress that 'keeping to the convergence criteria' was 'unconditional',[29] so the stability pact was keenly supported. The parliamentary party regularly clarified its view that 'the convergence criteria laid down in the Treaty are not softened.'[30] Ever since the agreement of the Maastricht Treaty, the SPD had argued strongly that there ought to be no automatic transition to Stage III of Monetary Union, and that the convergence criteria should have clear precedence over the timetable laid out (Chapter 8). By 1997, however, it had adopted a more *pragmatic* policy that was beginning to take into account the political realities at the EU level, starting to concede that Monetary Union was a political as well as an economic decision. In the *Bundestag*, therefore, the party could call for 'those participating [in EMU] to under-take everything so that the target date for Monetary Union, 1 January 1999, will be achieved through the use of the stability criteria as laid down in the Treaty',[31] knowing full well that the Treaty allowed for a loose, political interpretation of these targets.[32] In truth, SPD politicians, much like the coalition government, cared less for the strict application of the convergence criteria than was often admitted. In December 1996, Verheugen made the rare concession that, while the party 'will argue that membership of Economic and Monetary Union should be decided through an interpretation of the criteria that conform with the treaty ... it would be absurd to let EMU collapse if a country had a deficit of 3.1%'.[33] Attacks on government EU policy were, therefore, oriented towards the social and employment dimensions of integration. The con-vergence criteria were only used against the coalition parties as a means of criticising their handling of the national economy: 'On the realisa-tion of the so-called deficit criteria, the Federal Government stands before the shattered heap of its mistaken economic, financial and budgetary policy.'[34]

This is not to say that SPD policy was totally cohesive during this period. Rather than taking on the more constructive approach adopted by the European policy groups and the party chairman, Gerhard Schröder continued to state his opposition to the timetable for Monetary Union laid down in Maastricht, maintaining that the Single Currency should be a 'crowning of the integration process'.[35] If sharper in his rhetoric than the *Bundesbank*, his doubts continued to be based on a similar economic evaluation of currency union. *Coronation theory* suggested that the EU might have to 'wait with Monetary Union until the far-reaching structural adjustment of the participating economies is completed'.[36] Like Minister-President Stoiber and Henning Voscherau (SPD Mayor of Hamburg), he wished to have an inclusive Monetary Union strictly fulfilling the convergence criteria, arguing that the 'time for the start of Monetary Union is not as important as keeping to the criteria'.[37] He stated that, since the criteria were unlikely to be met by 1999, rather than giving the project up it 'would be no great mistake if Monetary Union comes a few years later'.[38] Tietmeyer similarly made a point of disagreeing 'with those who argue that a delay to the Euro would cause the heavens to cave in or the economy to come off the rails'.[39] These barbs were aimed at politicians like Kohl, who made the case that 'to postpone the Euro ... could possibly be a postponement for all time'.[40] This is not to say there was not a populist side to Schröder's remarks, given that opposition to the Euro peaked at 54 per cent in 1997 (Chapter 8), but more that his *pragmatism* (Chapters 5–7) led him to adopt a strident economic assessment of EMU that went against the *Bundestag* consensus.[41] The voices of scepticism were nevertheless isolated in the SPD by this time, as the party prepared policies for government that took more account of the political realities that power would bring (i.e. the fact was that the Euro was going to happen on 1 January 1999) and more heed to domestic actors other than the electorate.

Consensus therefore reigned between the two major parties after Amsterdam in their support for a broad-based Monetary Union, according to the Maastricht timetable, assuming that member states – if not meeting the convergence criteria – had made good progress in that direction. For its part, the SPD continued to relate what it saw as government failings over EMU to economic problems in Germany (e.g. employment and public debt). Its position was strengthened by the Government's failed attempt to revalue German gold reserves in May 1997, in order to meet the Maastricht debt criteria.[42] Official SPD policy now actively praised the 'great advances that have been made in currency stability through the Maastricht Treaty', complaining only that these benefits had not been 'made clear enough to the public'.[43] The Government was even rebuked for using the Maastricht criteria to justify austerity measures and social cuts: Scharping described Waigel's remarks 'that further savings will be made above all in social welfare because of the 3 per cent criteria' as the 'kind of argumentation which only raises citizens' fears'.[44] SPD EU policy had, by this stage, reached a new plateau of competence, worthy of a *government in waiting*.

A policy for government

In May 1997, the SPD finally published the findings of its European policy review initiated at Mannheim. The document entitled 'Reform for Europe: interim report of the *Schwerpunktkommission*', was the culmination of the efforts made over the previous eighteen months to incorporate a coherent EU policy (capable of support within both the party and the country) into the overall policy programme being chiselled out for the 1998 federal elections. The proposals were characterised by strong support for Monetary Union along with demands for the conclusion of an EU employment policy and further economic and social policy integration, reflecting the European policy concepts of both the European policy groups and the party chairman.

The new policy paper not only backed Monetary Union, but also saw the SPD's role as 'to distribute information, dissipate fears, work against risks and make clear the advantages' of the Single Currency, because EMU was an 'integral instrument against the damaging of employment and competition through currency speculation and fluctuations', which would 'above all profit export-dependent Germany'.[45] The EU policy document went on to state that the 'realisation of the third stage of Economic and Monetary Union inclusive of the timetable is of central meaning ... a postponement of Monetary Union would have clear political and economic consequences'.[46] The paper, formulated by the party's European policy groups but in tune with the (revised) ideas of Lafontaine also called for a 'harmonisation of taxes' to end harmful tax competition,[47] including minimum tax rates 'in particular for corporation tax and the taxation of capital earnings' and the co-ordination of social and employment policy, repeating the threat that the 'SPD will only agree to the revised Maastricht Treaty if a chapter on employment policy is included'.[48] These views were reiterated at the party conference, 'Politikwechsel in Deutschland' (political change in Germany), in 1997 at Hanover. After the agreement of employment policy at Amsterdam, the SPD could commit itself to 'vote for the transition to stage three of European Economic and Monetary Union in the *Bundestag* in April 1998'.[49]

The employment policy agreed at Amsterdam was to be followed by the Luxembourg Summit in November, to ensure a rapid implementation of the accord. The SPD's *programme for government* called for a 'European employment pact ... with binding goals', and 'European co-ordination of national economic and fiscal policies'.[50] The *issue-linkage* between European employment policy and EMU was clearly underlined by the party in the months leading up to the Summit. At the launch of the SPD's European policy resolution for the party conference in Hanover at the end of the year, Lafontaine asserted that the goals established for cutting unemployment policy should 'rank equally with, if not have priority over' the Maastricht stability criteria, while Wieczorek-Zeul stated that 'cutting unemployment could not be left to national policies, but required a European action programme'.[51] The Luxembourg European Council agreed to the drawing up of national employment action plans to be reviewed in December 1998, to 'improve employability' through training (focused on the young) and by closing 'the gap between rates of male and female unemployment'.[52] The German Government, however, helped prevent stricter targets being set, by refusing to accept the Commission's proposal of a 65 per cent employment rate target, to be achieved within five years.[53] Though supporting the results of the

Luxembourg Summit as a step in the right direction, the SPD – along with its union allies – criticised the Federal Government for opposing 'the laying down of quantitative goals at the EU level'.[54]

Although the SPD as a whole was very much behind Monetary Union by this stage, the views of Gerhard Schröder – soon to become the party's chancellor candidate – even up to the spring of 1998 were far less positive. In addition to previous comments that Monetary Union without meeting the Maastricht criteria would suffer a 'sickly premature birth',[55] Schröder continued to argue that it 'would cost jobs in the short term'.[56] An SPD European policy expert explained that in 1998, in contrast to 1995, 'SPD opinion completely distanced itself from such positions'.[57] Schröder's views nevertheless reflected continuing public scepticism, with levels of support for Monetary Union still at only 40 per cent in 1998 just months before the launch of the new currency. The *Bundesbank*, furthermore, had cast 'serious doubts' over some of the countries recommended to join the Single Currency, referring in particular to the level of public debt in Belgium and Italy.[58] The *Bundesbank* could, therefore, only give its 'qualified support to the [positive] assessment of the convergence presented by the Commission'.[59] By spring 1998, however, the Constitutional Court had ruled two complaints against German entry into Monetary Union 'clearly unfounded', the European Monetary Institute had recommended a broad-based Monetary Union (omitting only Greece from those Member States wanting to join), and the *Bundesbank* had given its formal (albeit 'qualified') support for Stage III to go ahead. With Member States in favour, it was clear, therefore, that currency union was going to take place as planned on 1 January 1999.

By the end of March, Schröder had become the SPD's chancellor candidate, and – in his 'partnership' with party chairman, Lafontaine – was far more restricted in his ability to diverge from the party's official policy. He could not use EMU as an election issue even if he had wanted to, because the need to conform to official SPD policy was too great. Despite his well-known views on Monetary Union, Schröder's nomination was not of concern to those in the party involved in European policy, who surmised that while 'there are domestic policy orientations there, it does not matter that much since [if he becomes chancellor] he must stick to the duties of the Federal Republic.'[60] Schröder accepted the fact, by April 1998, that 'the Euro would be irreversible by Germany's general election'.[61] Official party policy only articulated SPD concerns through constructive criticism, without questioning the timetable for currency union. As early as December 1997, the SPD seemed to indicate that Monetary Union would be supported whosoever was recommended for participation. According to an internal letter: the 'participants in EMU will be named by the European Council on 2 May 1998. We should consider making a joint statement with the coalition government in the German *Bundestag* as in the case of the Maastricht Treaty.'[62]

Schröder switched the emphasis of his European policy to attacking Germany's high level of contributions to the EU budget during the election campaign, vowing to put it at the top of an SPD government's agenda for the forthcoming German Council Presidency. This was a change of focus from concentrating on the possibility of a postponement of the Euro. Summing up the party's European policy programme in a newspaper interview, Lafontaine prioritised 'Monetary Union, the employment pact, tax harmonisation and social minimum standards.'[63] Lafontaine's influence over European policy for the elections was substantial as he was in charge of European policy (in addition to financial affairs) in the SPD's election team. His *internationalist* perspective on the need to construct a social democratic EU in the face of *globalisation* and Wieczorek-Zeul's emphasis on the *linkage* of EMU to social and employment policy were clearly illustrated in a subsection of the party's electoral programme entitled 'the Euro for Work and Social Stability'.[64] Here, it was argued that 'European Economic and Monetary Union offers a chance to shape things under the new conditions of globalisation', and that this should be complemented by a 'common economic and financial policy', and used 'to dismantle mass unemployment in Europe'.[65] It was revealing, however, that the section in the manifesto on Europe was still only the twelfth point in the document, reflecting that EU policy still did not feature as a top-ranking issue for the German electorate or the SPD. Despite the coherence achieved in SPD EU policy by 1998, formulating policy within the different constraints and networks of government was to prove quite a different matter.

Governing the Euro-zone

On coming to office, the SPD had been out of power for sixteen years. As a consequence, those in the party leadership had no real experience of government at the federal level. While the party had adopted many centrist policies in its pursuit of power, there was little appreciation of the constraints of policy formulation in government compared to opposition. The first months were a learning process for the new Government, as key members of the SPD tried to adapt themselves (with varying degrees of success) to the altered policy context. This was no more true than in the area of European policy. Policy objectives had to be channelled through strongly institutionalised patterns of decision-making to succeed at the EU level. Within the SPD itself (the institutional context), the leadership in government gained more autonomy from the party through the resources and independent apparatus of office (Chapters 3 and 4). The role of the European policy groups was, for the time being at least, to *complement* Federal Government policy and 'anticipate possible domestic discussions',[66] rather than to initiate policy. Among the actors whose importance was greatly enhanced with regard to SPD policy were the party's Green coalition partners (particularly Foreign Minister Fischer) in the national context, and the various EU institutions and Member States (especially France) on the European level. On the other hand, in the *Bundestag* they faced the Christian Democrat parties minus the influence of Kohl, who felt freer – as the SPD had done in opposition – to question government European policy.

Living with the single currency

One of the first actions of the incoming government was the decision to move co-ordinative powers for European policy from the Economics to the Finance Ministry (Chapter 4). This was of particular bearing to Finance Minister Lafontaine in the context of Government policy on EMU. Lafontaine's support for the social and employment dimensions of EU integration was well known, as was his advocacy of a growth as well as a stability-oriented European economic policy. It was unclear, however, to what extent he would try to achieve these objectives when faced with the new constraints of government. The launch of the Euro had huge implications for the application of these ideas, with the creation of an independent and stability-oriented European Central Bank to govern monetary policy. Article 108 of the Treaty Establishing the European Communities stipulated that the ECB shall not 'seek or take instructions from Community institutions or bodies or from any government of a Member State ... The Community institutions or bodies and the governments of the Member States undertake to respect this principle.'[67] The 'primary objective' of the ECB, modelled on the ethos of the *Bundesbank*, was 'to maintain price stability'. Yet this did not sit well with Lafontaine's growth-oriented perspective. Soon after taking office, he appeared to question Central Bank independence by arguing that: 'In view of the stability-oriented fiscal and wage policy, the ECB has more room for a monetary policy that supports growth and employment.'[68] He furthermore advocated the banding of the major world currencies, arguing that 'the trading range of the Euro against the dollar and yen should be managed' to avoid damaging exchange rate fluctuations.[69] Not only did Lafontaine advocate these exchange rate controls, but actively sought support for such measures (backed initially by the French government) in G7 meetings – despite the almost certain disagreement from the USA and Japan.

The connection or *issue linkage* between the Single Currency and employment policy was key for Lafontaine: employment would be increased through a 'macroeconomic stimulus to demand, to come from monetary policy and fiscal policy'.[70] This is why the reduction of interests rates was necessary – to enable an expansionary budgetary policy, which ran against the stability criteria laid down at Madrid. Accordingly, the Commission criticised the German budget in 1999 for its 'minimal position' on the reduction of public debt.[71] Although Chancellor Schröder's top EU priority for the German Presidency of the Council was the reduction of German net payments to the EU budget, Lafontaine stated that 'For me the most important question as before is the fight against unemployment ... that means that monetary policy, fiscal policy and wage policy must work together.'[72] In his position on an EU employment policy, he was supported by the socialist government in France, and formed a strong axis with French Finance Minister, Dominique Strauss-Kahn, to promote strict employment targets and public investment projects as well as a looser interpretation of the EMU Stability Pact.

Lafontaine, having projected his domestic policy goals into a vision for Europe, was, even so, too inflexible in the pursuit of these goals: for instance, his insistence that EMU 'must be placed at the service of job creation'.[73] Schröder, on the other hand, had recognised many of the flaws in his own (domestic-oriented) approach by the end of the German Council Presidency. An interviewee revealed in summer 2000 that 'only yesterday in the *Vorstand*, Gerhard Schröder said that criticising the launch of the Euro was a mistake'.[74] While many of Lafontaine's ideas, such as the harmonisation of taxes in the EU and the closing of 'tax-havens', were uncontroversial within the party, the SPD at the federal level had a long tradition of stability-oriented, monetary orthodoxy. Though Chancellor Schröder agreed with the need for greater integration in the area of EU economic policy, his position on the ECB was much closer to the overwhelming support for a *Bundesbank*-styled stability ethos and autonomy of action among the German political elites. Schröder argued that 'Monetary Union means, next to the communitisation of monetary policy through an – and I emphasise this – independent central bank, the co-ordination of economic and financial policy.'[75] Although Schröder's top goal was also the reduction of unemployment,[76] the more business-friendly *Neue Mitte* was opposed to an 'interventionist' EU employment policy based on demand-side economics. Lafontaine's attitude to the ECB was, therefore, untenable, and his position was further undermined by the fall of the Euro partly as a result of his comments.[77] Schröder, a *pragmatist* and a *fixer* by nature, after a few months' experience of EU policy at the governmental level, had tapered his objectives more readily to those goals that could realistically be achieved. His *pragmatism* was needed to help solve the emerging crises that arose in the first few months of the German Presidency in addition to the EU budgetary negotiations. As one SPD politician remarked: 'In Berlin, Gerhard Schröder became a European', doing a deal for Europe amid the crises that arose in spring 1999.[78]

For the SPD, it was not difficult allying with the Green Party over European policy. The Greens, if anything, were more pro-Europe and EU integration, placing less emphasis on *national interest*. Government policy on Monetary Union and the economic governance of the Euro-zone, however, was very much the domain of SPD politicians in the Finance Ministry (Lafontaine, then Eichel),[79] under the general policy guidelines of the Chancellor (Chapter 4). For their part, the Christian Democrat parties, after the departure of Kohl and their removal from the strictures of government, began to articulate what they saw as German interests more clearly in their European policy. The main body of the CDU at the federal level was not, however, convinced by Stoiber's efforts to effect a change in CDU/CSU policy (illustrated by his populist attempt to out-bid Schröder in his demands for a reduction of German payments to the EU budget). The Union soon reverted to its traditional pro-European approach, if increasingly characterised by the *climatic changes* that had affected SPD policy in the 1990s. The German *Länder*, on the other hand, while supporting the forthcoming currency union, were now more concerned with securing institutional reform in the EU (Chapter 11). The initial growth in public support for the virtual currency union concluded in January 1999 had been reversed as the Euro rapidly declined in value against the US Dollar in the currency markets (Chapter 8). By September 2000, the Euro had lost about a quarter of its original value, increasing the feeling among Germans that 'their leaders may have traded away the D-Mark, historically one of the world's strongest currencies, for a lame duck'.[80] The tide nevertheless turned with the strengthening of the Euro after 2001 and the successful introduction of the Euro into general circulation in 2002. As opposition to the Single

Currency waned, the SPD turned itself more fully to the pursuit of (Europeanised) domestic political goals at the EU level.

EU social policy and the constraints of the Euro-zone

The relative weight of the social partners in the SPD policy formation process had, of course, changed on coming to power. For an SPD-led government, it was much more important to have the support – or at least co-operation – of business interests in running the country than had been the case in opposition. Though both *social partners* supported Monetary Union in itself, they had quite different views on the governance of the Euro-zone. The BDI, the German industry federation, in addition to stressing that the ECB 'must be supported through a stability-oriented budgetary and financial policy', warned that politicians should not try to 'soften the adjustment process' for companies with the onset of the Euro, and strongly rejected the need for 'quantitative binding targets' for an EU employment policy.[81] In contrast, IG Metall argued for 'employment goals to have at least the same value as stability goals', urging 'the Federal Government to lead a change of course towards an active employment policy and social regulation' at the EU level.[82]

The SPD's main election pledge was to reduce unemployment in Germany. And while views on the type of EU employment policy differed, the party was united in its aim to further European integration in this area, 'to give Monetary Union an employment policy and social policy profile' through an 'active labour market policy'.[83] The employment policy agreed at Luxembourg in 1997, which sought to co-ordinate employment policies through the assessment of national action plans, was supplemented by a further accord at Cardiff in June 1998 that aimed to boost employment through structural reforms (e.g. deregulation) and more flexible working practices (e.g. flexible working hours). A blueprint for a 'third pillar' of employment policy was set out by Lafontaine and Strauss-Kahn later that year, with annual growth targets, an EU-wide minimum wage and an annual growth and employment conference (also supported by Denmark, Sweden and France). After Lafontaine's resignation in March 1999, however, when Schröder's *Neue Mitte* had become dominant in the Federal Government and the SPD presidium, these elements of the agreement were jettisoned by the German Presidency (despite the French Government's efforts to win the Chancellor over at a Franco-German Summit in June 1999).[84] The centrepiece of the European Employment Pact agreed at the Cologne Council later that month was, in fact, a macro-economic dialogue between the European social partners, finance ministers and the ECB on the co-ordination of economic policy, wage developments and monetary, budgetary and fiscal policy,[85] very much in the spirit of Schröder's domestic *Bündnis für Arbeit*. This dialogue, in contrast to the Lafontaine-Strauss-Kahn proposals, was to promote a 'non-inflationary wage dynamic', reasoning that growth must be built on the solid platform of price stability.[86] Actual EU investment was limited to an extra €500 million for the European Technology Facility and €1 billion of loans to fund Small to Medium size Enterprises (SMEs) working in high-technology industries.

Added to the new European policy networks that existed in government, SPD policy on the Euro-zone faced a number of constraints that came with the Single Market and the Single Currency and economic integration in general. These constraints convinced the SPD and the Red–Green Government of the importance of the *rules of the game* at the EU level. Member States participating in EMU were not only being bound to the monetary policy of the ECB, but also to the accompanying stability criteria, which keep a strict reign on public spending. ECOFIN ministers regularly hold meetings on the prospective budgetary policies of Member States, and national governments can be publicly rebuked by the Commission for over-spending. The Commissioner for Economic and Monetary Affairs, Pedro Solbes, has emphasised that: 'in Economic and Monetary Union you have to do what is coherent at the European level'.[87] The tighter reign on public spending after EMU was an added reason for Finance Minister Eichel's national *savings package*. The Blair–Schröder Paper published in May 1999 stated that 'In a world of ever more rapid globalization and scientific change we need to create the conditions in which existing businesses can prosper and adapt'.[88] It was argued that 'public expenditure as a proportion of national income has more or less reached the limits of acceptability'.[89] The backlash to this paper, which went too far for many in the party is described in Chapter 7. It should be noted, furthermore, that both Schröder and Blair were – at this time – speaking in a favourable economic climate, which saw an increase in growth and a decrease in employment in both countries. For Germany, in particular, the economic optimism was short-lived, and – as we shall see later in the chapter – strict limits to public spending were not so attractive in a low-growth scenario, making the Government and the party more critical over EU-level dictates on the Stability Pact.

The SPD was already sensitive to the economic direction of the Euro-zone on two accounts. First, the economic reforms imposed by the *completion of the Single Market* entailed the restructuring of 'state-funded' or 'state-run' enterprises. One example is the deregulation precipitated by the targeting of 'anti-competitive' state provision. EU liberalisation directives have forced Member States to open domestic markets in, for example, the telecoms and energy sectors, while Mario Monti, Competition Commissioner after 1999, stepped up attacks on state aid as in the case of the German *Landesbanks*. Monti summed up the Commission's position, when he declared that 'whoever tries to protect themselves from the pressure of the market ... runs the long-term risk of weakening themselves in their structural and competitive position.'[90] The coming of the Euro, along with the Single Market, has therefore effected an economic reform in the EU that has greatly impacted on Member States' European and domestic policy. This raised a heated debate in the SPD at both the federal and *Land* level over what many saw as the Commission's undermining of 'Daseinvorsorge' (state-funded social provision), the traditional bedrock of social democratic policy. As previously mentioned in the book, this was illustrated most graphically by the Commission questioning state support for regional and local banks (*Landesbanks* and *Sparkassen*) and local transport.

In addition to the pressures of the Single Market and the Single Currency, the German economy has been affected by the level of exposure of large German companies to Anglo-Saxon shareholder value,[91] which has increased the pressure on social democrats to redefine their concepts of economic governance. A particularly thorny issue for the party has been the question of *hostile take-overs* of German companies. Although the Red–Green Government, as stated above, abolished Capital Gains Tax on the sale of cross-holdings, they still sought protection for German companies from predatory attacks through the use of 'poison pills' to discourage the target companies' acquisition. The SPD leadership could nevertheless only offer a few populist gestures to its supporters in this area: Schröder, for instance, criticised Vodafone's €120 billion take-over of the German company, Mannesmann, with the claim that hostile bids 'destroyed the "culture" of the target company'.[92] German MEPs from both sides of the political spectrum nevertheless combined to torpedo an EU directive on take-overs that would have removed limits on individual shareholdings and restrictions on the transfer of shares. Both the imposition of Competition Policy and the attempts to set common rules for European industry increasingly antagonised the SPD and its leader, Chancellor Schröder, who 'repeatedly accused the Commission of attacking his country's industry'.[93] The penetration of the EU polity and a worsening economic climate, thus, increased the desire in the party to actively shape a social democratic Euro-zone.

A social democratic Euro-zone?

At the same time, the SPD was attempting to draft a European policy concept that could deal with the effects of European integration and *globalisation* (such as the spread of *shareholder value*), as demanded by actors within the institutional context (reflecting the party leadership's wish to guarantee *social justice* to accompany *Neue Mitte* reforms), and produce a distinctive social democratic model for the Euro-zone. One top official from the SPD European policy group underlined some of the key issues at stake: 'The question of social provision in Europe is a very important point ... Will Europe go the way of the USA in terms of social provision, the so-called hire-and-fire approach, or will the typical European social model be maintained – though, of course, altered?'[94] He further underlined the point that this was 'a very hot issue inside the SPD, because the majority, I think, stand for a regulated Europe in the tradition of the European social model ... [against] those who, similar to neo-liberals, say that people should be able to create as much personal wealth as possible'.[95]

The solution devised by the European review group under the leadership of the Chancellor, was a holistic concept (for domestic as well as European policy) within an overall policy programme that offered 'Security in Change'.[96] This represented both a synthesis of different views within the party (*modernisation* and *social justice*) and between European and domestic policy. The aim was 'to use the common currency for growth and employment' through a 'fully functional Single Market' and 'a stable Euro', which includes the 'opening of the electricity, gas and postal markets', but also the 'harmonisation of taxation policy'.[97] The party's *social* objectives were to 'modernise the European economic and social model' by 'making the social security system sustainable', 'creating the conditions for full employment' through investment in 'training and lifelong learning', 'technological innovation' and 'social dialogue', but without reducing social standards.[98] The SPD leaders in the Federal Government, thus, not only aimed to soften the short-term effects of increasing market competition, but also to establish a regulatory framework and an active labour market policy that could maintain the most important aspects of the social market model.

The emergence of an SPD vision on EMU and the governance of the Euro-zone can be seen as a *pragmatic* attempt to initiate change both in Germany and the EU, in order to form the framework for a social democratic Europe. The co-operation of the SPD-led government in Germany with like-minded governments in other Member States further manifested itself in the conclusions of the Lisbon Summit (March 2000), which expressed many of the goals contained in the SPD paper the following year. It set non-binding targets for the raising of the 'employment rate from an average of 61% today to as close as possible to 70% by 2010' as well as 'using an open method of co-ordination based on the benchmarking of national [employment] initiatives'.[99] As one interviewee pointed out, however, 'These European norms must be interpreted through national instruments' as far as possible.[100] Emphasis was therefore initially placed on national plans for policy implementation – rather than the EU-level approach advocated by Lafontaine – in a multilayered economic policy based on the principle of subsidiarity.

The limits of national approaches to economic and social policy, and the limits of the *open method* of co-ordination at the EU level nevertheless gradually became more apparent to the SPD in government. This was highlighted by the perceived *attack* on German industry by certain aspects of Commission policy with regard to the completion of the Single Market, as referred to above. The pressures placed on the slowing German economy by the EMU Stability Pact reinforced the idea in the party leadership that change was needed. In the run-up to the 2002 federal election, the Red–Green Government narrowly avoided receiving a warning 'blue letter' from the Commission on its growing deficit that was due – again – to exceed the 3 per cent deficit criteria. The situation became more serious in 2003, when the Commission demanded that Germany reduce its expenditure for 2004 by about €6 billion or face proceedings and financial penalties. The Commission's stance was, in fact, supported by the *Bundesbank* and German industry, which warned against a *soft interpretation* of the Stability Pact and for the punishment of offending Member States.[101] The Red–Green Government, however, took the view that the pact should be subject to a 'flexible' interpretation.[102] Writing in the *Financial Times*, Finance Minister Eichel argued strongly that nowhere in the Stability and Growth Pact does it 'call for sovereign states to be placed under an obligation to adopt a pro-cyclical fiscal policy approach ... Hence I consider it unacceptable for Member States that conform to the measures agreed in the ECOFIN to be subjected to additional procedures and sanctions. This sort of discipline is devoid of all logic and contradicts the spirit of the pact.'[103] Although the Federal Government – with the aid of France, which was also being threatened with proceedings – managed to postpone the threat of financial sanctions in the Council, it was clear to the SPD leadership that EMU and the rules for the Euro-zone had to be reformulated to defend the German model.

Low growth and rising unemployment in Germany after 2000 had made budgetary austerity less attractive. Public spending in this environment was required to aid economic growth, but – with diminishing tax receipts – this meant more debt. The SPD leadership, as in its national economic policy, had to find a synthesis between support for the Single Market and adaptation to a changing economic environment (as illustrated by its *Agenda 2010* reform package, including proposals for tax cuts, balanced budgets, welfare reform and labour market reform) with its wish to preserve key elements of the German social market model. As with the *Neue Mitte* agenda set out in Chapter 7, the party wished to see public spending maintained and even increased in specific areas of public investment. Chancellor Schröder explained, for example, with reference to the Stability and Growth Pact that: 'Phases of economic weakness ... must not only be compensated for through procyclical policy ... We are obliged, particularly in times of low growth or economic stagnation, to maintain a high level of public investment.'[104] Though the emphasis on European policy had not proved effective in the 2002 federal election campaign, the strictures of the EMU Stability and Growth Pact demonstrated to the SPD in government – as Lafontaine had earlier recognised – the interdependence of domestic and European policy and the importance of further economic integration to achieve a social democratic EU. The difference between the *Neue Mitte* approach and Lafontaine's position was that the former sought to spur growth through tax cuts and public investment balanced by cuts in social spending, and the latter, though increases in public spending in preference to tax cuts.

SPD plans for a social democratic EU therefore sought both to maintain the scope for *directed* public spending (the 'growth' dimension of the Stability and Growth Pact), and to improve economic co-ordination as far as possible (the 'economic' dimension of EMU). The Red–Green Government, in the light of Germany's poor economic performance, launched a joint growth initiative with the French Government in September 2003 – 'To make Europe a place of growth and competitivity through necessary investment in infrastructure and in the area of human capital, research and development.'[105] The initiative combined proposals for the 'necessary structural [market-oriented] reforms' in France and Germany (characterised by *Agenda 2010*) with ten projects for growth focused on 'telecommunications and data networks, research and development, transport and sustainable development' without losing sight of 'budgetary consolidation'.[106] Second, the SPD promoted deeper integration in EU economic policy where possible. Significant progress in the area of tax harmonisation was, for instance, warmly greeted by the Federal Government in January 2003, when it was agreed that Member States would either share information or charge a basic tax rate on the interest accrued on the savings of residents from other Member States.

The SPD's position on this issue was made clear in its *programme for government* in 2002, which argued, in a subsection on 'strengthening the European societal and social model', for the 'maintenance and further extension of the European welfare model ... using the advantages of the Euro for growth and employment'.[107] These ideas filtered into the SPD position on the European constitution with respect to the constitutional convention (2002–03) and the forthcoming intergovernmental conference on institutional reform (Chapter 11). Again a common Franco-German position was agreed by the Government and subscribed to by the party. The Government sought formal recognition of the Euro-group within ECOFIN, clarification that the penalty procedure for breaching the Stability Pact rules lay in the hands of the Council, and majority voting on taxation policy.[108] The emphasis placed on the need for closer economic policy co-ordination among the Euro-group furthermore illustrated that the Red–Green Government would accept 'structured co-operation' of an advance group of countries where necessary.[109]

In these ways, SPD leaders attempted to finally redress the imbalance between stability and growth, as they saw it, by supporting the replacement of 'non-inflationary' growth with 'balanced growth' in the EU draft constitution. This was to provide the necessary support for the German social market model within the context of an enlarged European Union and the process of *globalisation*. Whilst supporting the European Single Market and the further liberalisation of the energy markets as well as the basic tenets of the Stability and Growth pact, the party rejected a *Dow Jones interpretation of history*. Gerhard Schröder stressed this point at the SPD's European delegates conference in November 2003: 'Europe is more than a market. It is not just a place of economic interaction. No, it is a place of cultural and social interaction ... It has a European social model that differentiates it from how people live in America ... This we should defend.'[110]

Part V

Eastern Enlargement of the European Union

10
Eastern Enlargement of the European Union

The historic events that took place in 1989 triggered the end of the division of the European continent into two ideologically opposed political, economic and military systems. The reunification of Germany was accompanied by the emancipation of central and eastern Europe from an era of Soviet domination. This not only had huge implications for Germany and German interests, but also for the European Community as a whole, which quickly sought to stabilise the fledgling democracies and harness their potential through Trade and Friendship Agreements (removing import quotas on several products) and, in following years, 'Trade and Co-operation Agreements with Bulgaria, the former Czechoslovakia, Hungary, Latvia, Lithuania, Poland, Romania and Slovenia'.[1] The new geopolitical reality meant that strong German interests lay in ensuring the political and economic stability of central and eastern Europe as well as in taking advantage of trading opportunities. Germany's geographical location in the *Mittellage* of a soon-to-be-enlarged EU, thus, reinforced the view that 'we have lots of neighbours with whom we must get on … [and] cannot afford isolation'.[2] In this context, Chancellor Kohl saw eastern enlargement as a natural extension of German unification, a second 'decisive step towards overcoming the division of our continent'.[3] The proposed eastern enlargement of the EU was, however, without precedent, since the transition from a 6-member EC to a 15-member EU took place over a time span of 22 years, and of those new members only four countries – Ireland, Greece, Portugal and Spain – were significantly poorer when they joined.[4] In contrast to these earlier developments, the applicant states from central and eastern Europe were high in number, extremely poor in comparison to the EU average and were brand new democratic systems.

Part V focuses on SPD policy with regard to the enlargement of the EU to those CEE states. Eastern enlargement has been chosen as a case study for the book, because it offers a central insight into the interpretation of the new constellation of German interests across the time span of the study. It will concentrate on the three key states as far as Germany was concerned – its close neighbours Poland, the Czech Republic and Hungary. Chapter 10 identifies three phases of SPD policy in opposition: first, German and SPD policy on the EU's initial advances towards the CEE states through what became known as the 'Europe Agreements' and the financial assistance offered through the 'Poland-Hungary: Actions for Economic Reconstruction' (PHARE) programme; second, policy in the period covering the setting of the 'accession criteria' at the Copenhagen European Council (June 1993), and the push for enlargement made under the German presidency in the first half of 1994; and, finally, SPD policy on the *linked* issues of EU reform at the 1996–97 IGC and their response to the Commission's 'Agenda 2000' reform proposals, and the place of eastern enlargement in the party's *policy for government*.

Opening out a hand to the East

As German politicians grappled with the not inconsiderable problem of unification, the question of how to deal with the former Communist CEE states was being posed as a result of the events mentioned above. The geopolitical necessity of ensuring political stability and liberal democracy in these newly independent countries demanded a speedy response from both the German Government and the European Community. For Germany, it was particularly important to strike up good relations with its neighbours to the east – Poland, Czechoslovakia and Hungary. Geopolitical interests also necessitated good relations with Russia as part of an eastern strategy. Although relations with the countries under the Soviet sphere of influence had been improved through the policy of *Ostpolitik*, Germany now had to deal with new regimes. Furthermore, older historical tensions remained. Difficulties arose from lingering suspicions of German intentions given the events of the National Socialist era and taking into consideration the existence of sizeable German-speaking minorities in Poland and Czechoslovakia.

The Federal Government sought to overcome these difficulties and stabilise these states through both the strengthening of bilateral ties (political, economic and cultural) and the promotion of links between the CEE states and the European Community and NATO. This strategy was strongly supported by the whole of the *Bundestag*: the SPD, for example, argued with the Greens that, with regard to 'the shaping of relations between Germans, Czechs and Slovaks', it was good for mutual understanding that 'like the process of reconciliation and understanding with France, [it] has a European dimension'.[5] Aside from the need to stabilise and the opportunity to trade with the CEE states, Germany also felt a moral obligation to act as the sponsor or *advocate* of these countries in their efforts to enter into institutional relationships with the European Community. This sense of duty emanated from the part Germany's eastern neighbours had played in the events leading up to German unification, and from continuing guilt over Germany's actions during the Second World War. For Chancellor Kohl, it 'would be a betrayal of European ideals if we were not to respond to the justified hopes of our neighbours to the East'.[6]

Germany began to make political and diplomatic overtures towards its eastern neighbours almost immediately. Despite a brief period of hesitation, the Federal Government had concluded treaties with Poland on the 'confirmation of borders' and 'good-neighbourliness and friendly co-operation' by January 1992. A *good-neighbourliness* treaty with Czechoslovakia in February 1992 was followed by similar agreements with other CEE states in the same year. Germany also made a point of cementing ties with Hungary, whom it thanked for the major part it had played in German unification through the opening of its borders to East German refugees in May 1989. Although the question of the treatment of German-speaking minorities raised its head later in the 1990s, Germany showed a willingness to compromise and admit past wrongs, for example, the 'German-Czech Declaration on Mutual Relations and their Future Development' (January 1997). The political elites sought to develop good lines of communication with their colleagues in the CEE states through regular meetings between government officials and exchanges between respective parliamentary committees and groups. Contacts with Poland, for example, soon became formalised in a 'German-Polish Summit' which was designed to mirror the success of Franco-German relations since the War, an approach that was fully supported by the SPD.[7] Efforts were also made to strengthen bilateral ties through financial aid for reconstruction and the promotion of cultural links: the 'Transform' Programme for 'advice to central and eastern Europe for the Construction of Democracy and a Social Market Economy', established in 1990, had contributed almost DM 2 billion (€1 billion) to this end by 2001.[8] Cultural ties were encouraged through the opening of Goethe Institutes[9] and DAAD (German Academic Exchange Service) offices in the larger of the CEE states.[10]

SPD policy on relations to the East after the events of 1989 was deeply connected to the *Ostpolitik* in which the party had engaged both in government (from the late 1960s to the early 1980s), and through bilateral contacts when in opposition in the 1980s. There was consequently a strong strain of thought in the party (emanating from Brandt), that saw the unification of *all* of Europe as a goal more important than the Single Market and Monetary Union. While some Social Democrats were suspicious of the market-oriented policies of deeper integration (Chapter 8), an increase in political, economic and cultural ties to the CEE states was something they could embrace wholeheartedly. Lafontaine, for example, was opposed to a *one-sided* monetary union in the early 1990s, but quite supportive of an eastern enlargement of the EC as an expression of his *internationalist* credentials. At the same time, the SPD was wrong-footed by the changes in central and eastern Europe just as it had been over German unification. This was partly because *Ostpolitik* had been a policy of *rapprochement* focused on the now deposed *regimes* of central and eastern Europe. The SPD did not react swiftly to these developments, and the 1989 Berlin Programme devoted only two sentences to them, expressing a vague wish to 'offer our help in the renewal of these states', but with no concrete policies to achieve this end.[11] The lack of interest in central and eastern Europe reflected the party's lack of interest in European policy as a whole.

The Federal Government, on the other hand, was actively involved in seeking closer ties with the CEE states, but was nevertheless obliged to respond to French fears that enlargement would damage the political equilibrium of the European Community. The timing of Chancellor Kohl and President Mitterrand's *joint letter* to the Commission (April 1990), showed French determination to use deeper integration as a counterweight to enlargement: 'Instead of discussing German unification and relations with Central and East European countries, the European Council focused on the IGC for EMU ... and the possibility of a parallel IGC on EPU.'[12] Though distracted by the focus on EMU, Germany still promoted the interests of the CEE states when it could, supported in this by a strong cross-party consensus that was far more stable through the 1990s than support for Monetary Union.

In advocating closer relations between the EC and CEE states, Germany was forthright in backing Commission attempts to establish a formal basis for these stronger ties. The Community quickly established 'trade and co-operation' agreements for greater access to EC markets, which soon covered the major CEE states. For its part, the SPD somewhat idealistically advocated a 'complete lifting of import restrictions by the EC and EFTA [Economic Free Trade Area] states for Hungary and Poland',[13] with the goal of 'an opening of the EC to the countries of

central and eastern Europe' for the purpose of 'security and peace'.[14]
From 1991 onwards, more comprehensive 'Association Agreements'
(soon to become known as *Europe Agreements*) were concluded with
Czechoslovakia, Hungary and Poland, and later with Bulgaria, Romania,
Slovakia, Slovenia and the three Baltic states. These concords aimed to
increase *trade and economic co-operation* through the further lowering of
trade barriers, with the long-term aim of improving political and economic interaction between the Community and these states.[15] The trade
agreements that were reached were not, however, the easy success portrayed by the Commission, as trade barriers were maintained in most
key areas.[16] Overshadowed by the Maastricht European Council, SPD
chairman, Björn Engholm, summed up the long-term strategy of the
Bundestag when he stated that the CEE states 'must be in the next stage
of European co-operation after the entry of the EFTA states, which will
open the possibility of entry to the EC for those who wish it'.[17]

Dwarfing its bilateral transfers, Germany invested a substantial
amount of aid through multilateral organisations such as the International
Monetary Fund and – of course – the European Community. By 2001,
Germany could rightly claim to be 'the largest donor of aid' to the former Eastern Block, having placed 'a sum of DM 210 billion (€107 billion)
at the disposal of the states of central and eastern Europe and Russia
since the end of the Cold War'.[18] A significant proportion of this was
provided through the EC's PHARE programme launched in 1989,[19]
viewed as a flanking strategy for the opening up of trade with the CEE
states. 'PHARE', the French word for lighthouse, was 'intended to signal
that the aim was to mark *the way back to Europe* for the CEE states'.[20]
Further money was used to support the new private sector in central and
eastern Europe through the creation of the European Bank for
Reconstruction and Development (EBRD) by the EC (providing 51 per
cent of its capital) and the other 'G24' countries in 1990.

The SPD, once more, fully supported these measures, strongly advocating that the 'EC Member States, together with the EFTA states, should
simultaneously develop and implement a financial programme to support the reform countries of central and eastern Europe'.[21] Along with
the Federal Government, the party more generally called for 'the
European Commission to extend and strengthen its co-operation with
the Central and East European states, in order to help the democratic
and economic reshaping of their societies'.[22] The only real difference
with Government policy was that the SPD placed more emphasis on
the ecological dimension of support for the CEE states – 'the construction of a European capital fund for modernisation and environmental

protection in these countries'.[23] While the SPD was in favour of an eastern enlargement, it was not yet a close enough reality or of sufficient interest to the party for it to construct an accession strategy that went beyond the goals set out by the Commission and the Federal Government.

The criteria for enlargement

The need for political stability in central and eastern Europe was brought home by the escalation of fighting in the former Yugoslavia in the early 1990s. In the context of the Bosnian conflict, Chancellor Kohl called European integration 'the most effective insurance against a re-emergence of nationalism, chauvinism and racism'.[24] The flood of refugees to Germany from Yugoslavia (and other countries like Romania)[25] was a clear reminder to German politicians that, if they did not export stability to these CEE states, instability might be imported instead. This imperative was nevertheless tempered by the danger that too quick an enlargement might dilute the newly launched European Union, and the further deepening of the EU towards which the Franco-German alliance was working. The 'main priority of German foreign policy', therefore, remained 'the drive to deepen integration'.[26] The Federal Government was, on the other hand, keen to stress that the CEE states would experience a quick accession to the European Union. Kohl promised that Poland would be a member by 2000. The SPD's European policy community, aware that this enlargement would take place more slowly (as was the Federal Government behind closed doors), warned against 'quick and easy statements about the rapid entry of the central and east European reform states', arguing that 'the countries of eastern Europe ... should not be disappointed'.[27] This was symptomatic both of their *pragmatic* concern about the potential cost of enlargement so soon after unification and their recognition that these early accession dates were unlikely to be achieved given the need for the approval of Germany's EU partners.

The necessity of political stability added to the rapidly growing levels of trade with the CEE states, however, provided strong motives for Germany to promote eastern enlargement. The country soon became the dominant EU Member State in terms of trade, topping the tables for both EU (about 50 per cent of CEE–EU trade) and OECD states in 1995.[28] The volume of German trade with CEE states was approximately DM 85 billion (€45 billion) in the same year.[29] Figure 10.1, shows the speed of economic integration with Germany's close neighbours, Poland, the

Czech Republic and Hungary. The graph, in addition, highlights the difference in the intensity of trade between Germany and specific CEE states, implying different economic benefits from the accession of the 'Visegrad' states (the Czech Republic and Slovakia, Hungary and Poland) to those of more distant and undeveloped countries like Romania (Figure 10.1).

Although the Federal Government could not differentiate between CEE states in its advocacy of enlargement (for its policy to remain credible with its EU partners), it is clear that stronger geo-political and trade interests lay in the entry of the *Visegrad* states than Bulgaria or Romania. Germany soon developed, furthermore, large trading surpluses with the CEE states. A DM 300 million (€150 million) surplus with Poland in 1995 had, for instance, rocketed to DM 7.7 billion (€3.9 billion) by 1998.[30] The EU trade surplus with the CEE states was something that the SPD recognised as a problem by the mid-1990s (as it increased debt, hampering their economic progress towards the EU's economic criteria),

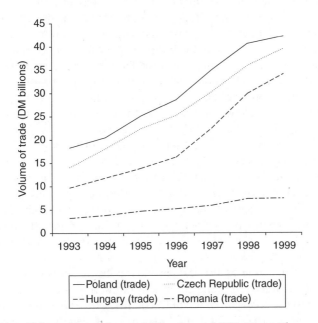

Figure 10.1 Volume of trade between Germany and CEE states with populations of more than ten million

Source: Statistisches Bundesamt.
[1] Figures from Deutscher Bundestag (07/02/01), pp. 83–5.

and the party called for an 'unconditional ... further opening of the European Union market to these countries',[31] emphasising the party's overall commitment to eastern enlargement. Outside the European policy groups in the party, however, enlargement was of little interest to SPD politicians at the federal level. While European policy in general had been seen as a remote domain and the preserve of experts, eastern enlargement – though wholly supported in a symbolic sense – was not tangible enough to engage SPD politicians' attention. Public opinion showed a similar lack of interest (as did the mass media), which reinforced the neglect of this area by the party leadership.

Public opinion, in its view of eastern enlargement, clearly differentiated in its support for the accession of specific CEE states (see Figure 10.3 below). *Eurobarometer 42* (Spring 1995) wrote of a 'diffuse' image of eastern enlargement in Germany, which was among the more sceptical countries with regard to the accession of Romania and Slovenia.[32] The speed of enlargement was a further concern to Germans. In 1994, therefore, only 24 per cent approved of 'the extension of the European Union to countries like Poland, Hungary, the Czech Republic and Slovakia in the *next five years* [author's italics]' with 34 per cent against.[33] The position of the social partners on eastern enlargement, however, contrasted markedly with one another. Big business supported the continuation of enlargement along the trajectory of the Europe Agreements towards the Single Market, given the potential trading advantages of eastern enlargement to these countries (several of whom could boast a highly trained workforce), and on the condition that the CEE states maintained their political stability and adopted the existing body of EU law. The unions, however, were worried about the threat that a further lowering of trade barriers with these states might have on their members' jobs, taking into account the much lower wages in eastern Europe and the existing high levels of unemployment in Germany. Despite the solid cross-party support for enlargement in the *Bundestag*, these views – held by the SPD's core constituency – gradually filtered through into the approach taken by the party leadership, as it began to attach *conditions* to the enlargement process.

At the same time as the framework was being set out for a future eastwards enlargement of the European Community, Member States were agreeing to the accession of the EFTA countries: the states that eventually joined were Austria, Finland and Sweden. The Federal Government and the SPD were fully behind this enlargement, since the new countries were wealthy and would become net contributors to the EU budget, thereby relieving Germany of a small slice of its financial burden. The SPD were also enthusiastic about the EFTA enlargement, because of the likely support of these countries for a 'social Europe'. The Copenhagen Summit in June 1993 stated the aim that these countries should join by the beginning of 1995, and this goal was duly achieved. The accession negotiations were nevertheless punctuated by fierce battles over national interests such as fishing rights, which was a large factor behind the eventual decision of the Norwegian people not to join. This also had the effect of dimming enthusiasm among existing members for a further enlargement to the countries of central and eastern Europe, since – because of the great disparities of wealth – the disputes were likely to be even more intense.

Promoted by the European Commission and the Federal Government, criteria for future accessions, including those of the CEE states, were set in Copenhagen. The Summit (significantly) recognised that eastern enlargement would take place in the not too distant future and agreed to begin a 'structured dialogue' with a broad range of accession states with regard to fulfilment of the criteria. The Council Conclusions clearly stated that: 'Accession will take place as soon as the applicant is able to assume the obligations of membership by satisfying the economic and political conditions required.'[34] The criteria themselves were designed to ensure the 'stability of institutions guaranteeing democracy, the rule of law, human rights and respect for and protection of minorities'; 'the existence of a functioning market economy as well as the capacity to cope with competitive pressures and market forces in the Union'; 'the ability to take on the obligations of membership including adherence to the aims of political, economic and monetary union'.[35] In short, the criteria demanded political and economic stability as well as the adoption by new members of existing Community law. Another important point was the admission by the Council that, in order for eastern enlargement to be a success, the European Union would have to reform itself, to have 'the capacity for accepting new members, while maintaining the momentum of European integration'.[36] This was a clear case of *issue-linkage*: EU enlargement would – from now on – be bound to internal reform. Although the SPD argued for the EU 'to fully utilise the perspective on the accession of the Central and East European states through an active policy of co-operation, opened at the European Council in Copenhagen', this was not highly prioritised and the party's European policy was dominated by EMU at the time.[37] The degree of consensus among the political elites and the lack of interest among the public resulted in the SPD devoting only two lines of its 1994 *programme for government* to this theme: 'We want to offer the central and east Europeans a perspective through pan-European co-operation.'[38]

The party's European policy groups at this time, reflecting the position of the Federal Government, were worried about the dilution of European integration should a quick and broad eastern enlargement take place. This differed from the stance of the foreign policy groups who were more keen on eastern enlargement as part of the larger geopolitical picture.[39] For this reason, the EU policy groups took a *pragmatic* position on eastern enlargement, placing emphasis on the conditions needed for eastern enlargement to take place. As social democrats, the SPD also prioritised employment as an issue, showing their natural sympathies with the unions, and began to express the need (though only timidly at this juncture) for 'transition periods in certain areas', arguing that 'the free movement of workers should belong to this, because of the job situation in all European Union Member States'.[40] This was to become a central plank of SPD policy in government.

Political consensus and lack of interest over enlargement had meant that SPD policy remained underdeveloped. The party's contribution to the German Council Presidency in the second half of 1994 was, therefore, minimal. The Federal Government made several important advances as a result of Germany placing a 'special emphasis on eastward enlargement during its otherwise lacklustre Council presidency'.[41] At Essen (December 1994), the Commission was set the task of constructing a White Paper on the state of candidates' preparations for participation in the Single Market.[42] The Madrid Council a year later agreed that the Commission should provide an assessment of the impact of enlargement after the IGC on the *Maastricht left-overs*, further declaring that accession negotiations would start with a first group of states six months after the end of the Conference. The agreement of the accession criteria, and the transfer of the planning arrangements to the Commission meant that the accession negotiations were to become an *acquis*-driven process, and – in general – external to German and SPD policy. EU reform, on the other hand, was now integrally linked to eastern enlargement. The first area of *issue linkage* was *institutional reform*. The SPD's ideas (or lack of ideas) on this subject were soon to be highlighted by the IGC launched in 1996. The second area was the debate over the financing of the EU after enlargement, raising the question of Germany's position as *paymaster* of the Union, and this was to prove a more attractive issue for the SPD leadership. These two areas were embodied in the Commission's *Agenda 2000* (1997) blueprint for reform examined below.

Reforming the European Union

The acceptance of the principle that CEE states who fulfilled the Copenhagen criteria could join the European Union shifted the focus of enlargement policy to the themes of institutional and financial reform. Weidenfeld wrote that 'the reforms of the Central and East European states and the European Union's structural reform must be speeded up simultaneously. Both reform processes are interdependent.'[43] Put another way, there was a high degree of *issue-linkage* between the two objectives. Along with the capacity of the CEE states to integrate the current body of EU law into their own respective systems, much rested on 'the Union's willingness to create the preconditions for an eastern enlargement by internal reforms ... within the framework of differentiated integration',[44] making the EU what Germans term 'erweiterungsfähig' (capable of enlargement).

Eastern enlargement and EU reform

One response to the challenge of institutional reform was the concept of *differentiated integration* brought to the fore by the Schäuble-Lamers paper, 'Reflections on European Policy', published in September 1994. Although this paper was released in the midst of a federal election campaign, it was nevertheless a serious attempt by senior figures in the coalition parties to formulate a coherent and *pragmatic* framework for European policy. The idea was to develop a concept that could maintain the advances in integration made in the late 1980s and early 1990s – and hold out the prospect of further integrative steps – whilst enlarging the European Union to the states of central and eastern Europe. Schäuble explained that: 'We want advances in European integration, and indeed now. Enlargement is necessary, but we want deepening at the same time. If one wants both simultaneously, then reality forces some Member States who are ready and/or in the position to do so, to move further ahead in integration for a certain period.'[45] The paper called for a *variable geometry* of integration in the EU, which would de facto contain a *hard-core* of states. Flexibility, in this sense, was a reform concept that might overcome the tension between the *deepening* and *widening* of the European Union. The paper went further than this, however, naming the core to consist of the six original EC members minus Italy. As explained previously in Chapter 5, the diplomatic consequences of the proposed exclusion of Italy and the fears of other Member States about the exclusive nature of a 'core Europe' led the Federal Government to distance itself from the document. The paper was nevertheless an important contribution to the EU debate over institutional reform, and its main ideas were to later re-appear in German and SPD policy as a *pragmatic* response to a lack of progress with further integration (Chapter 11).

The SPD at this time had no detailed position on the institutional reform of the EU beyond its long-standing yet vague commitment to strengthening the powers of the European Parliament and extend the use Qualified Majority Voting (QMV) in the Council, as re-affirmed at the Mannheim Conference (1995).[46] The party had not yet become a *government in waiting*, and did not possess a European policy that was far-reaching enough to deal with these issues. SPD European policy in the mid-1990s was, furthermore, dominated by the growing doubts of the SPD *Troika* over Monetary Union (Chapter 8). The complex issue of institutional reform was highly unlikely to appeal to the election-oriented instincts of Lafontaine, Scharping and Schröder. The 1996–97 IGC was likewise to be overshadowed by the efforts of the SPD to force the Federal Government to accept the creation of an EU employment policy to accompany EMU (Chapters 8 and 9): 'If a new European chapter is to be battled out in Turin ... the key questions must be on the agenda. That is the question of the fight against mass unemployment ... we have therefore concentrated on this theme.'[47] The lack of a policy on institutional reform was shown by the fact that, while arguing that 'the *Kerneuropa* concept laid down by the CDU/CSU' went against 'the principle of equality between members of the European Union', Wieczorek-Zeul could offer no real alternative view.[48] Roth confirms that the 'lack of a social democratic model became observable with the presentation of the CDU/CSU-*Bundestagsfraktion*'s core-Europe thesis. The SPD had – like all other parties – barely anything to put against this position'.[49]

In contrast to the low public profile of the institutional reform debate, the re-ordering of the EU financial architecture Union was a much more prominent theme in the context of the growing debate in Germany over the country's *paymaster* role. Given the economic problems at home in the mid-1990s, public support for engagement in Europe was waning, especially as this engagement seemed to be costing Germany a lot more (relatively speaking) than other countries. This is illustrated by Figure 10.2, which shows how Germany, despite the fall in its GDP per capita since unification to below that of France, Austria and Belgium was, by 1997, still contributing a disproportionately high net amount (after redistribution) to the EU budget in comparison to other large Member States. Germany's payments over the 1991–98 budgetary period averaged over 60 per cent of all net payments (Figure 10.2). To solve this problem and

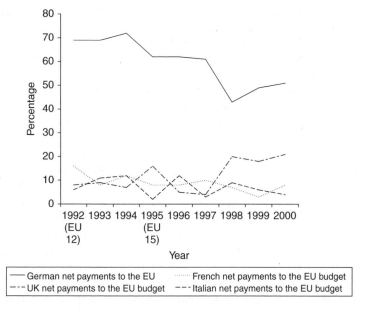

Figure 10.2   Net payments (after redistributions) of Germany, France and the UK, 1992–2000, as a proportion of overall not payments

Note: Calculated from figures published in European Commission, *Allocation of 2000 EU operating expenditure by Member States* (September 2001), www.europa.eu.int, p. 126; and, European Commission, *Allocation of 1998 EU operating expenditure by Member States* (1999), www.europa.eu.int, p. 94.

Source: European Commission.

to make EU financing more 'efficient', the SPD, in its European policy motion at Mannheim, called for the European Union to 'make reforms in the areas of agricultural and structural policy'.[50] The party was quite specific in its plans to close Germany's budgetary 'justice gap': 'a corrective element (co-financing) should be built in which takes into account the relationship between wealth indicators (GDP) and agricultural redistributions. This would also mean an end to the British rebate'.[51]

This marked the start of a new strategy, developed by Wieczorek-Zeul, which – like EU employment policy and EMU (Chapters 8 and 9) – provided *issue-linkage* that could appeal to the growing *electoral pragmatism* and continuing domestic policy orientation of the party's federal leadership. CAP reform was a particularly promising issue for the SPD for two reasons. First, it was an area that required reform before eastern enlargement: if agricultural subsidies *c.* 2000 were applied to the ten CEE states, the cost would have grown by an estimated 14 per cent and the EU budget by 7 per cent.[52] The Federal Government, on the other hand, had previously helped block attempts to reform CAP in deference to the CSU (with its rural support in Bavaria) and the French government.[53] The SPD had no such *veto players* in this field. Furthermore, the *paymaster* issue was difficult ground for the Government to defend, since it had signed up to the previous financial agreement itself.

The IGC that opened in Turin in March 1996, was to look primarily at the issue of institutional reform, one of the main pre-conditions for eastern enlargement. Reform was to cover decisions on the size of the Commission, the policy areas to be governed by QMV, the allocation of votes in the Council, and the size and powers of the European Parliament. The ambitions of the Federal Government for the IGC were fairly modest. Large-scale European reforms would not have been propitious due to the growing economic problems at home and difficulties with key actors in the national network: with the *Länder* (particularly CSU-governed Bavaria) over what was seen as the 'encroachment' of EU competences; with the growing scepticism of the public; and, with SPD opposition to EMU. The UK government's obstructionist stance towards the EU also greatly reduced the likelihood of any significant advances at the Conference. The SPD, concentrating on the promotion of an EU employment policy and mindful of the European policy divisions in the party, also took a minimalist position on the IGC. According to Roth, this was also because the party had 'recognised its own conceptional deficits', so that Wieczorek-Zeul 'wanted to know nothing about "abstract institutional or constitutional models" '.[54]

The results of the Amsterdam Council were an undoubted failure for institutional reform in the context of eastern enlargement. It was also a failure for German Government objectives, even if they had expected little else. The SPD claimed that the Amsterdam Treaty had not made the EU capable of enlargement with regard to the re-weighting of votes in the Council and majority decision-making, but they had contributed little to the debate themselves. QMV in the Council was extended to a much smaller degree than had been the suggested by the Commission: areas in which unanimity was at least partially ended included 'employment' and 'customs co-operation'.[55] The limiting of the size of the Commission (to no more than twenty members) was accepted in principle as was the need for a redistribution of votes in the Council.[56] Despite the commotion caused by the Schäuble-Lamers paper, the Franco-German partnership had played a large part in securing the inclusion of 'enabling' clauses to make closer co-operation between

Member States possible. For the SPD, the Federal Government's eventual acceptance of an EU employment policy was a significant political victory (Chapter 8), but within the field of European policy institutional reform was too *remote* an area for the party and the electorate.

Eastern enlargement, however, remained a central (common) objective for the SPD and the Federal Government. Parallel to the IGC leading to the Amsterdam Treaty, were Commission preparations of the groundwork for accession negotiations with the CEE states (plus Malta and Cyprus). The SPD and the Federal Government shared a pragmatic approach to eastern enlargement in that it should be 'carefully prepared' with regard to 'reform of the European Union' and the fulfilment of 'the conditions already laid down in the European treaties' by the applicant states.[57] The SPD, however, pressed by the unions, went further than the Government in seeking to respond to the concerns of those in the electorate who felt that they would be negatively affected by enlargement: 'the free movement of workers from the accession countries' was not, for example, 'imaginable for the foreseeable future' in the view of the party *Vorstand*.[58] Despite the occasional articulation of these public concerns, the SPD adopted a consensual and constructive approach in the *Bundestag* to the accession arrangements, reflecting German interests in integration with the most advanced CEE states (in particular, their Visegrad neighbours to the East). It was the Commission, however, rather than the Member States, which had the task of designing a *road-map* for enlargement.

Agenda 2000

In July 1997, the European Commission published its *Agenda 2000* proposals 'for a stronger and wider Union'.[59] This was a 1300 page report on the progress of membership applications, the impact of enlargement on the EU, and a plan for the road ahead, which could be used as 'a yardstick for the beginning of negotiations' with the applicant states.[60] The report *linked* the accession of the candidate countries to both reform in the applicant states and reform of the EU's institutional and financial architecture. The evaluation of candidates' readiness for accession stated that, of the ten CEE states, only Slovakia failed to meet the political requirements for 'democracy and the rule of law'; that 'all countries have made good progress in their transition to a market economy'; and, recommended that 'accession negotiations should start with Hungary, Poland, Estonia, the Czech Republic and Slovenia ... in early 1998',[61] while leaving the door open to Bulgaria, Romania, Latvia, Lithuania and Slovakia in the near future. With regard to institutional reform, knowing full well Member States' contradictory positions, the Commission only argued for a decision before 2000 on 'the weighting of votes' and 'the generalised use of qualified majority voting in the Council' and on a reduction in the size of the Commission.[62] It called for another IGC in 2000 to resolve such issues. A more detailed plan for the financing of the EU was, in addition, submitted. This involved a reform of the CAP that would reduce price support subsidies, and achieve a greater concentration of Structural Funds through stricter criteria for *Objective 1* areas (two areas that used up about four-fifths of the Community budget).[63]

The accession strategy was duly accepted by the European Council in Luxembourg (December 1997). There were two particularly important dimensions to the proposals. First, the EU had now demonstrated the willingness to get the negotiation process for enlargement under way. This was a position firmly backed by Germany's political elites. Foreign Minister Kinkel could, therefore, tell the *Bundestag* European Affairs Committee that, in the Council of Ministers, 'the "whether" of enlargement is uncontroversial'.[64] It was no small step for those countries that saw no economic gain from eastern enlargement (e.g. France and Spain) to have agreed to this. The GDP of the first wave of applicants identified by the Commission, after all, was only equivalent to 45.7 per cent of the EU average even by 1999,[65] meaning that they would require a large slice of the EU budget. The Federal Government, with a domestic political consensus behind it on this issue, could take a good deal of credit for persuading reluctant Member States to agree to the start of accession negotiations.

Agenda 2000 also established the principle of *differentiation* between the accession candidates. While the German Government's policy was to declare its commitment to EU enlargement to all the CEE applicant states, it was quite happy to accept the practical decision to create a *first wave* of accession countries, though stressing that 'catching-up by other states remains essentially possible'.[66] SPD European policy experts were equally satisfied with the Commission's interpretation of the Copenhagen criteria. Norbert Wieczorek, chair of the *Bundestag* European Affairs Committee, agreed with the Commission that the 'deciding factor against the starting-line concept is ... the more countries that take part from the beginning of negotiations, the higher the "potential threat" to the more advanced countries.'[67] He candidly revealed that such a strategy 'would make the accession of those countries in which Germany has a particularly great interest more difficult as a result'.[68] This differentiated approach to the eastern enlargement of the EU was

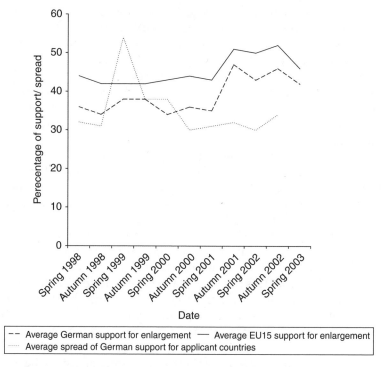

Figure 10.3 Average support for enlargement in Germany and the EU and spread in support for different candidate countries, 1998–2003

Source: Eurobarometers 49–59.

both an expression of German economic interests and public opinion. Figure 10.3 shows that the spread of support in Germany between different applicant states was significant.

Political opinion on EU institutional reform in Germany at this time was – with the notable exception of the Schäuble-Lamers paper in 1994 – if not without form, then without a coherent long-term perspective. European policy experts from all major parties at the federal level were reluctant to outline long-term visions of the EU. This was due both to a conceptual vacuum and to the fact that major European policy goals were traditionally articulated through the Franco-German alliance. That Germany had different aspirations for institutional reform from France was, therefore, a further obstacle to policy formation. Another difficulty for the Government was the position of the Bavarian CSU which, though a coalition party, opposed what was seen as the encroachment of the EU. The Federal Government, as a result, preferred to pursue small, *pragmatic* steps towards its goal of closer EU integration when it could (e.g. through the extension of QMV in the Council), while otherwise pursuing greater efficiency within the context of a future enlargement (e.g. limiting the future size of the Commission). The SPD, on the other hand, neither had the option to pursue European policy through negotiations at the EU level nor had addressed its policy deficits in this area on the issues raised by the IGC. While the *Schwerpunktkommission's* interim report had developed ideas for further integration in, for example, the areas of 'asylum and immigration', tax policy and 'elements of foreign policy', as well as promoting an 'EU Charter of Fundamental Rights' that would strengthen the European Parliament through 'full co-decision rights',[69] these policies did not offer a clear picture of the balance of power between the institutions or between the institutions and the Member States.

The financial framework for an enlarged EU was bound to be a topic that was hotly disputed by Member States, as the distribution of the budget would most clearly bring about winners and losers in a short-term material sense. This was particularly the case for two of the largest recipients of subsidies, Spain and France, who gained most from the Structural Funds and CAP respectively. In addition to securing the financial reforms necessary for enlargement, Germany also sought to reduce its own high level of contributions (Figure 10.2). Regional leaders such as Stoiber in Bavaria and Schröder in Lower Saxony cranked up the pressure on the Government to rectify this situation. The Bavarian CSU was 'conspicuous in the debate about the EU budget',[70] and Schröder also felt that 'in the face of the burdens of German unity, we can not afford any additional engagement in Europe'.[71] This stance was backed by public opinion: in the spring of 1997, 60 per cent of Germans were worried that enlargement would bring extra costs for the country, the second highest figure in the EU.[72] Under intense pressure, the Federal Government began to demand financial relief for Germany – 'to about 0.4% of GDP from the current 0.6%'[73] – in the Council in the run-up to the 1998 federal elections.

The references by some SPD leaders at the time – in particular, Gerhard Schröder – to German money being *burnt in Brussels*, was not, however, indicative of official party policy or the position adopted by the party's European policy groups. While seeking reform of the Union's finances, the *Schwerpunktkommission* report also stressed that the 'debate over EU finances must be rationally led: for the Federal Republic of Germany, as a country that greatly profits from the Single Market, our net contribution is not only to be calculated by payments and returns from the EU budget'.[74] Wieczorek-Zeul, in fact, pleaded with the party's high-profile leaders not to get drawn into the debate over German payments to the EU (as recorded in a presidium protocol).[75] The party's European policy groups were nevertheless beginning to show more *electoral pragmatism*. Realising that cuts in German monies paid to the EU might relax popular opposition to the further deepening and widening of the Union, they integrated these demands into a more holistic financial reform concept for CAP and the Structural Funds. Together with the SPD Presidium, they supported the 'the EU Commission's proposal that an upper limit of EU income' should be set 'at 1.27% of GDP'.[76] Schröder and Lafontaine, on the other hand, were only too happy to refer to Germany's *paymaster* position, to heap more pressure on the government: according to Lafontaine, it 'was Kohl and Waigel who signed the treaties and so are responsible for the inequilibrium'.[77]

Unlike the area of institutional reform, the SPD had concrete proposals for a new financial framework. *Agenda 2000* had stated the very real need to 'further the movement towards world market prices' in agriculture because of the 'the prospect of a new [world] trade round' and 'not least the prospect of enlargement'.[78] The SPD called for an even more ambitious reduction of agricultural subsidies, highlighting how this would benefit Germany's position: 'more justice for the net payers could only be achieved through the reduction of the agricultural part of the budget ... which would make the British rebate unnecessary'.[79] The party also advocated, in line with the Commission, the concentration of EU Structural Funds on genuinely poor regions – for areas receiving Structural Funds to be reduced from over half to 'about 35% of the EU population'[80] – as well as an end to the Cohesion Fund payments for countries participating in Stage III of Monetary Union.[81]

There remained, however, other areas of *issue-linkage* for the SPD (that attached *conditions* to enlargement) that lay outside the *Agenda 2000* proposals. Primary among these was the issue of transition periods for the free movement of workers to Germany from the accession countries once enlargement had taken place, to prevent the threat (real or imagined) of Germany being swamped by low-wage workers from the CEE states. By the late 1990s, this was not only a matter of concern for the SPD's immediate constituency of low-paid workers and trade unions, but had become a concern for the country at large: in 1997, 47 per cent of Germans agreed with the proposition that 'the more countries there are [in the EU], the more unemployment there will be in our country' (second only to Austria), and a figure of 48 per cent was recorded in a similar survey conducted in the following year.[82] Bearing in mind the

SPD's increasing *responsiveness* to public opinion (Chapter 6), the willingness of the party's leaders to break with German foreign policy tradition (Chapter 5), and the SPD commitment to reduce unemployment (its main pledge in the 1998 federal election campaign), this issue was likely to reappear. Eastern enlargement itself nevertheless remained a clear objective for the German political elites, so Commission proposals for making the applicant states fit for entry into the EU were consistently supported. Both government and opposition, after agreeing with the states selected for the first wave of accession, backed the decision of the Luxembourg Council to launch negotiations with *first-wave* candidate countries on the basis of the 'acquis communitaire'.

As the SPD developed its *policy for government*, enlargement was, however, a subject that was almost as invisible as it had been in 1994. While the party's election programme strongly supported the 'eastward enlargement of the European Union' because it would 'heighten ... economic and political security',[83] the two paragraphs devoted to EU enlargement were to be found only in the third sub-section of Section 12 on European policy. Enlargement as a whole was not an electorally attractive issue for the SPD, as there was virtually no difference between the party's policies and those of the Federal Government over issues relating directly to the accession process. The subject was – furthermore – of little interest to the electorate when compared with domestic economic affairs. The SPD, showing *electoral pragmatism*, placed more stress on the areas of *issue-linkage* mentioned above: essentially the 'all-too-long postponed reforms in the areas of agricultural policy and structural policy', and 'more budgetary justice in the European Union'.[84] Having no comprehensive policy on institutional reform, which was in any case something too vague for the electorate, this area was generally ignored. Aside from the emphasis on *budgetary justice* by the party leadership (and the Chancellor Candidate, in particular), the only other European policy issue raised in the election campaign was that of *long transition periods for workers* from the first wave of CEE states once they had joined the EU.[85] The SPD was also *pragmatic* in terms of German interests, economic and geo-political, that clearly lay in eastern enlargement, so that – given the fulfilment of the Copenhagen Criteria and the implementation of the *acquis* – even the party's most election-oriented and domestic policy oriented figures were 'in principle for the enlargement of the EU'.[86]

11
Reforming for Accession: A New EU for a New Europe

Chapter 11 analyses the course of SPD policy on eastern enlargement after the party came to power in 1998. It will look at the construction of a more comprehensive policy on eastern enlargement, led by the Federal Government through an altered matrix of actors and structures (policy context), with policy implementation as a close consideration. In opposition, SPD European policy was a product of the institutional and national contexts, which were overwhelmingly domestic policy- and election-oriented, so that enlargement policy was neglected by the party leadership aside from the related issue of the EU budget. The party's EU policy experts had only formulated detailed policy proposals in the are of budgetary reform (Chapter 10), which was just one aspect of the upcoming *Agenda 2000* negotiations, due to be tackled under the German Council Presidency (January to June 1999). The SPD was forced to deal with the whole range of European issues in government, and – finally recognising the importance of these questions – the party leadership launched its European policy review in 2000.

Chapter 11 will begin by examining enlargement policy in practice, looking at the *conditions* attached to enlargement by the SPD and – at the same time – its efforts to push the process along as it adapted to the altered policy contexts in government. The chapter will then explore the approach of the SPD in government to the *reform the EU* with regard to its financial and institutional architecture, paying particular attention to policy positions and negotiations leading up to the Berlin Summit (March 1999) and the Nice Summit (December 2000). The chapter will end by setting out the results of the SPD's European policy review, and analysing the party's efforts to achieve its *social democratic vision* in practice through an EU constitutional settlement.

The conditions for enlargement

The SPD started off in government as it had finished in opposition, offering a more *pragmatic* appraisal of enlargment than the Kohl governments. The *dynamics* in SPD EU policy that were evident in opposition, were also observable in government: the new Government's style was more assertive than its predecessor with respect to material German interest (Chapter 5), while its policies were also *responsive* to public opinion and other key actors in the national context (Chapter 6). The party's new-found pragmatism manifested itself in a more 'realistic' style of discourse over the speed of enlargement: this, Chancellor Schröder argued, was more effective and 'more honest than always stating the desirable' such as 'illusory target dates'.[1] He stated that, for the 'great work' of enlargement, 'the economic pre-conditions' for the entry of applicant states 'must be taken more seriously', which would realistically 'take time'.[2] On this point, the SPD Minister of Europe in the Foreign Office, Günter Verheugen, was in full agreeement: while the 'government is moving with the same decisiveness on enlargment as the old one', there is 'a small difference ... a certain realism has come into play. The idea that European enlargment could be completed by the end of 2000, as Chancellor Kohl said in Poland, is totally unrealistic.'[3] In relation to enlargment, another early feature of Federal Government European policy as its continued insistence on keeping the reduction of German budgetary contributions at the centre of the agenda for the German Presidency of the Council. Though the SPD had no solid position on institutional reform, this was also as an 'objective pre-condition' for enlargement.[4]

The adjustment of SPD policy to the strictures of government was not a smooth process. The role of the party's European policy groups was now to *augment* rather than *initiate* policy (Chapter 3).[5] The relative influence of SPD ministers over enlargement policy was clearly different to EMU. The function of the SPD Finance Minister (in addition to the Chancellor and Foreign Minister) in the formation of German policy for the governance of the Euro-zone was integral. Enlargement, on the other hand, was much more at the centre of the Foreign Minister's remit – in this case, Joschka Fischer (Green) – under the general guidance of the Chancellor. The Greens saw enlargement more in terms of political stability and the 'overcoming of nationalism' than the SPD,[6] which was more concerned that the material conditions for enlargement were met. The culture of the Foreign Office, furthermore, was less characteristic of the *bottom-line* approach adopted by the key SPD ministries, Fischer, therefore, laid far less emphasis on the need for a reduction in Germany's net contribution at the upcoming budgetary negotiations than Schröder, and in this way helped soften the Chancellor's sometimes abrasive style. In the early months of the Red–Green Government, the European policy of Finance Minister Lafontaine was tailored to securing growth and employment targets to accompany EMU, and his successor, Hans Eichel, was happy to admit that the 'the leadership of the enlargement process lies indisputably with the foreign ministers'.[7]

On moving into opposition, divisions began to appear in Christian Democrat European policy – differences that had been simmering under the surface since as far back as the early 1990s. The initial policy statements of the new party chariman, Wolfgang Schäuble, were positive about enlargment. A new document written with Karl Lamers seemed to show a continuation of the style and substance of EU policy under Kohl. The Federal Government was warned, for example, to 'be conscious of the fact that, in the eyes of our neighbours, enlargement of the European Union will bring with it an extension of German influence', and to avoid 'talk of Germany finally achieving normality' (as Schröder had done).[8] The CDU soon came under pressure, however, from its Bavarian sister party to take a more oppositional approach, with particular reference to the EU budgetary negotiations in early 1999. The CSU was also prepared to voice its doubts about eastern enlargement itself, which should not occur 'against the will of the German People',[9] or 'on the back of the German tax-payer'.[10] The formulation of such opinion in the *Länder* was nevertheless countered by the CDU at the federal level with its strong pro-European tradition. Volker Rühe, for instance, argued that 'a fixed date for enlargement should be set as soon as possible and suggested that January 2003 would be realistic'.[11]

The relevance of the views of big business as a major component of the German economy had increased for the SPD in government. The positive benefits of trade with the CEE states looked at in Chapter 10 had continued. Trade between the European Union and all applicant countries had trebled between 1993 and 1999.[12] Germany enjoyed a significant slice of the pie: 44 per cent of EU exports to Poland, 55 per cent of exports to the Czech Republic and 45 per cent of exports to Hungary.[13] According to the German Foreign Office, exports to the ten CEE states increased by over 20 per cent in 2000 alone.[14] In a period of low economic growth, the importance of this boost to the German economy was not lost on the political elites. For many companies, investment in or trade with these countries had, therefore, already brought tangible results. With regard to enlargment, the German business federations considered it likely that the German economy 'would be particularly able to profit, because it has a suitable range of products to fulfil the needs of the accession countries. That goes especially for the strong export branches of machine building, electro-technology and vehicle prodcution.[15] The Federal Government was in tune with the priorities set out by German industry, since these would fit with German economic interests. The trade unions, on the other hand, were preoccupied by plans for an EU 'strategy for growth and employment' rather than EU enlargement at this point (Chapter 9), citing the 'fight against youth unemployment' as the 'number one theme'.[16]

For *Länder* politicians of all political hues, support for enlargement could not hide real concerns about its impact: this was particularly true in those regions located on Germany's eastern border, which feared a possible mass immigration of cheap labour from the east after the CEE states' accession. The position of the *Länder* mirrored the scepticism of public opinion. Figure 10.3 showed that that German support for EU enlargement averaged about a third of the population (with a similar proportion against) from 1998 to 2000 (Chapter 10). It also illustrated that support varied greatly from country to country during this period. This was still the case late in 2000 when over three quarters of respondents favoured the accession of Hungary and over three-fifths were for the entry of Poland.[17] According to a *Eurobarometer* survey early in 2001, the main reasons for negative attitudes to enlargement in Germany were: 'a fear of more unemployement' (69 per cent); 'more immigrants' (68 per cent); more costs for Germany (61 per cent); a 'negative impact on the Euro' (58 per cent); 'organised crime' (58 per cent); and, 'more drug-trafficking' (51 per cent).[18] It was up to the Government to address some of these points, if it wanted to calm people's fears.

While the SPD and its representatives in the Federal Government focused on the financial arrangements for the *Agenda 2000* negotiations (eventually agreed at the Berlin European Council, March 1999), there was clear evidence of a more *pragmatic* approach towards enlargement in general. A major figure in the SPD European policy groups highlighted this in the context of Poland's EU candidacy: 'Helmut Kohl promised that they would be able to join in 2000, which was completely impossible. We as a Red-Green Government have developed a two-phase model. First, the European Union must have the capacity for accessions. Second, the accession countries must show themselves capable of and ready for accession. These are two sides of the same coin. On this, we have struggled against many CDU politicians – this is what one can call a more pragmatic policy.'[19] In other words, the new Government concentrated more on the details of EU enlargement, prioritising the twin goals of internal and external reform. The Government adopted a *carrot and stick* approach to individual accession candidates: while intensifying bilateral contacts and promoting the case for enlargement at the EU level, it was also made crystal clear to applicant countries that there would be no *political rebate* (i.e. concessions) over the accession criteria. Yet within the framework of government, even the most domestic-oriented of SPD politicians had to recognise the importance of enlargement for German interests. One example of the increasing prioritisation of enlargement was the nomination of Günter Verheugen to the EU Commission. Soon after Verheugen's appointment as Commissioner for Enlargement in September 1999, an accession strategy for negotiations with six more candidate countries was set out – proof of SPD and German keenness to drive the enlargement process forward: the Commission reported that the 'the main elements of a European strategy' formulated 'at the initiative of Günter Verheugen' would be 'recommended to the Council which will meet in Helsinki next December'.[20]

A further factor that came into the equation was the continuing conflict in the former Yugoslavia. NATO action against Serbia between March and June 1999 demonstrated more than ever the urgent need to anchor political stability through political and economic integration along the lines of the EU model. The Kosovo conflict, therefore, was a further catalyst in the enlargement process. The Commission itself recognised that 'the crises in the Balkans region have created a new momentum in the enlargement process and have emphasised the essential contribution of European integration to peace and prosperity in Europe'.[21] The German and SPD approach to the conflict was to promote political and economic integration between the EU and the Balkans, 'to open a "European prospect" to Southeast Europe'.[22] Germany was to contribute €150 million a year to a Balkans Stability Pact set up – on the initiative of the Federal Government – as the basis of such a solution.

The *European context* of government policy was something quite new to the SPD, inexperienced as it was in dealings with other EU governments and the EU institutions. The party had, to make matters more complicated, come to power when Germany's bilateral relations inside the EU appeared to be in a state of flux. Gone was the solidity of the Franco-German tandem that had existed when Kohl and Mitterrand were in power. Germany had acquired new interests since unification which were not so compatible with French policy. 'Geo-political and cultural asymmetries' of interest had developed between the two countries, according to Pedersen, as 'enlargement towards the East would benefit the Germans disproportionately, whatever the intentions of the German Government'.[23] The French political elite was concerned that eastern enlargement would shift the EU's centre of gravity to central Europe, despite constant German efforts to keep them on side by involving them in the enlargement process (e.g. the *Weimar Triangle*). Tensions in Franco-German relations were, furthermore, exacerbated by the election of a government willing to assert German interests with more force on such sensitive issues as CAP reform. On the other hand, regular contacts were maintained with the governments of CEE states to promote the enlargement process and SPD contacts with its sister parties in those countries were intensified. The Chancellor,for instance, visited Poland just a week after taking office, but had already held six meetings with the Polish opposition leader, Leszek Miller, by the time he became Prime Minister of Poland in September 2001.

Domestic public opinion was an equally important battlegroud. The public were earlier shown to be quite sceptical about the benefits of the EU for Germany by the mid-1990s. The SPD had been more in touch with the popular mood than the Kohl Governments when in opposition, and the party carried this *responsive* approach into government. They did not want enlargement to suffer from the same unpopularity as Monetary Union. This is what Günter Verheugen meant when he argued: 'now that the issue at stake is EU enlargement', Germany 'shouldn't make the same mistake again and make all the important decisions over the people's heads'.[24] Although a furore was created by (mis)reported stories that he had called for a referendum on the issue, Verheugen had made the important point that EU governments in general were doing too little to convince their populations of the virtues of an eastern enlargement,[25] as illustrated by the public opinion polls cited above. The Federal Government, while distancing itself from the idea of a referendum and reaffirming enlargement as 'the central task of German foreign policy',[26] began to see the necessity of gaining public support for this policy. Chancellor Schröder made this clear at an SPD regional conference in Oberpfalz, a Bavarian district bordering the Czech Republic: 'When one is here, when one talks to representatives, then one notices that there is much concern about enlargement, for craftsmen as for workers – concerns to which the Federal Government will respond.'[27]

The two greatest fears of Germans with regard to EU enlargement were, in early 2001, the threat to jobs and the prospect of mass immigration.[28] Given the backlash in Austria over these issues, it was doubly important for the Government to gain popular consent, in order to avoid what some saw as a potential 'Haiderisation of European politics' in Germany.[29] The areas of eastern Germany closest to the border were in a delicate position since they were also the regions with the highest incidents of far-right violence against foreigners. The situation was not helped by the regular appearance of stories in the German media about the likely influx of millions of workers from the CEE states once they joined and freedom of movement was introduced. 'Die Welt' reported, under the headline 'Threat of mass migration in Euorpe', for instance, that 'Four to six million immigrants seeking work will come to Germany with the EU's eastward enlargement'.[30] Only later in this piece, did it appear that these figures were based on estimates of total migration from all ten CEE states over 15 years (by a date somewhere near 2025). A Commission report presented similar findings somewhat differently: it estimated annual migration to Germany of around 120,000 per year once the ten CEE states had joined.[31] The SPD supported a two-pronged approach: 'to respond in some way to the fears of the public, but also to effect a change in public opinion by convincing them of the benefits of eastern enlargement.'[32]

In December 2000, Chancellor Schröder announced that Germany would be seeking to ensure that transition periods for the free movement of workers from new Member States were in place before their accession. He started by stressing the benefits of enlargement – 'All prognoses see an increase in the present GDP growth rate ... of anything up to one per cent ... just in the last year Germany's trade with its Central and East European partners grew by 17%' – and went on to stress the need for dealing with 'the meaning of labour market and structural change' for workers, 'concerns which are to be taken particularly seriously by a social democratic Chancellor, because he feels personally obliged to these people'.[33] In other words, despite the increased importance of economic interests for the SPD in government, it still had to respond to the fears of its core supporters and the electorate as a whole. He went on to propose a 'five point programme' for transition periods of seven years, which allowed for 'the shortening of the transition period for individual accession countries' and the possibility of 'controlled access' during the transition period to cover 'skills shortages' in existing Member States', in addition to a parallel transition period for 'the freedom of services in sub-areas' like construction.[34] This stance was strongly supported by the party, including the SPD European policy groups. One MEP revealed that 'polls of the social democratic membership' showed that followers of the party were especially 'sceptical' about

EU enlargement in relation to the 'gap in wages' between Germany and the CEE states, because 'they fear that this will make companies move away and also put people on the job market who would do anything for just a few Deutschmarks'.[35]

Foreign Minister Fischer explained the Federal Government's position to the *Bundesrat*: citizens' fears 'must not be downplayed but also not dramatised. We want to take the people with us.[36] The idea of transition periods for the free movement of workers received a mixed reception from the Christian Democrat parties. The chair of the CDU/CSU parliamentary group, Friedrich Merz, rejected the proposals in general for the reason that workers from the CEE states would be needed in the German economy, while others – in particular, those from *Länder* governments bordering Poland or the Czech Republic, for example, Bavaria – welcomed the proposal. Merz's position was also the view of big business in Germany, which pointed out the need for immigrants to the country to maintain the ratio of workers to retired people, to support the pensions system. The country's trade unions, on the other hand, were a powerful force behind the transition periods in the first place, emphasising their importance in the area of 'services', and calling for 'legislation passed to ensure that operators from new EU Member States pay their employees who are working in Germany at German rates'.[37]

While the transition periods may have been necessary in terms of building up public support at a domestic level, they nevertheless threatened to impede eastern enlargement at the EU level. Although the Federal Government could count on the support of Austria on this issue, the agreement of transition periods with existing Member States was to prove more difficult. Spain, for instance, tried to link them to the continuation of Structural Funds for current recipients after enlargement. Perhaps more dangerous was the message it sent to accession states about the EU's intentions. Most believed that the fears were misplaced, and that the imposition of transition periods would only undermine public support for the EU in their countries.[38] A second problem was that it had the potential of increasing CEE states' demands of concessions in return, such as long transition periods for the purchase of land by foreigners.

The Commission soon came out in favour of these transition periods, thanks to the efforts of Commissioner Verheugen. In proposals released in April 2001, Verheugen explained that: because 'serious distortions to national labour markets could not be ruled out with any far-reaching certainty ... the Commission supported, in principle, the proposal of the German Chancellor to minimise the risks through an intelligent, flexible system of transition'.[39] The EU governments agreed to transition periods at the European Council in Gothenburg (June 2001). Germany was, thereby, successful in achieving a key policy objective both for the Federal Government and the SPD, easing the path to enlargement (in terms of the national network at least). Verheugen nevertheless, like the Federal Government and the SPD, still fully supported the eastward enlargement process, pressing to finish negotiations with *first wave* candidates in 2002.[40]

Reform of the European Union

The SPD, as a party of government, clearly supported the eastern enlargement of the EU and pursued it unambiguously in its dealings at the EU level, but at the same time had to carry the support of key domestic actors. The significance of public opinion for the SPD and the Federal government was illustrated by the issue of transition periods. The German *Länder* also played an important part in SPD policy in the two aspects of EU reform required for enlargement to take place – the reform of the financial and institutional architecture of the Union. While the CSU· Government in Bavaria was the *Land* with the loudest voice on European policy through the 1990s, reigning in the powers of the EU had become a growing concern for SPD *Länder* with the increasing penetration of EU politics into erstwhile domestic domains, for example, EU Competition Policy (Chapter 9).

The reform issues addressed were an integral part of the enlargement process, identified both by the *Copenhagen Criteria* and *Agenda 2000*. On coming to power, Verheugen had clarified the *linkage* between EU reform and the enlargement process. 'Its is clear that the Union must be reformed itself before it can be in any way capable of accession. Everyone knows that ... the two process run parallel.'[41] For the SPD members of the Federal Government, the primary goal at the beginning of the German Presidency was 'to find a satisfactory solution to the net contribution problem',[42] something leading members of the SPD (Gerhard Schröder, in particular) had emphasised in the run-in to the 1998 federal elections. In governmental terms, moreover, the EU budget was a central issue of the SPD as it fell more within the remit of the Finance Minister. At his first EU summit meeting, the European Council in Vienna (December 1998), the new Chancellor demanded *budgetary justice* for Germany in the upcoming financial negotiations. Even the SPD's European policy groups, while putting it in less demonstrative terms, did not 'find it improper at all that the Federal

Government ... wants to reduce its net contribution. It is just as fair as the British wanting to hold on to their budgetary rebate.'[43] This was certainly the position held by the German public. The Christian Democrat opposition parties, under the influence of Stoiber, pursued a 'competitive' European policy. They placed huge reductions in German contributions at the centre of their European policy, leading some to conclude (somewhat prematurely) that the Christian Democrats were 'thereby giving up Kohl's pro-European line'.[44] The reduction of German contributions threatened to be no easy task, however, since budgetary negotiations are viewed by Member States as a *zero-sum game*. It was a goal that was made even more difficult by the fact that Germany, holding the Council Presidency, was theoretically bound to moderation and neutrality. After initially promising to pursue Germany's budgetary interests 'brutally',[45] the Government therefore held back from a unilateral pursuit of this goal, preferring instead to shape the agenda towards a reduction of the financial burden for the largest net contributors as a whole (including the Netherlands and Sweden).

On the input side of the equation, the Federal Government set itself three objectives: to reduce German payments through a reform of CAP and Structural Funds and thereby abolish the British rebate (proposals almost identical to those of the *Schwerpunktkommission* in 1997). First, a reform of CAP was essential to prevent the EU budget from going through the roof on the accession of the large agricultural economies of central and eastern Europe. This is what Schröder meant when he said that 'those who advance the "Agenda" are the true allies of the accession countries'.[46] Although Germany received around 15 per cent of CAP subsidies itself, the scheme was inefficient and wasteful, and receipts lay well below German payments (for about a quarter of this policy).[47] The Federal Government proposed *co-financing* as a solution, a policy forwarded by SPD EU policy group as early as 1996, which might have saved Germany around €660 million each year.[48] It was nevertheless indicative of the inexperience and brashness of the Federal Government in its first few months in power that it so openly challenged a core interest of its closest EU partner – France – without prior consultation. The French government, in the event, rejected the proposals out of hand. Reform would now have to come from the reduction of subsidies along the lines of Commission proposals.

With regard to EU Structural Funds, Germany lined up with the other large net contributors in an attempt to keep the overall level of the Structural Funds down and to concentrate funding on poorer *Objective 1* areas (such as the new German *Länder*). Verheugen emphasised that: 'per capita distribution in target areas should be decided on the basis of regional rather than national prosperity'.[49] Within the Structural Funds, the Federal Government also sought the abolition of the Cohesion Fund once recipient states had joined in Single Currency. Like the *co-financing* idea, however, this had to be withdrawn well before the Berlin European Council (March 1999) due, in particular, to Spanish resistance. A further target for the Federal Government was ending the 'British rebate', costing Germany well over €500 million per year, but this was only feasible on the basis of substantial CAP reforms, which had not been achieved.

In the context of Germany's EU presidency and the crises that enveloped the EU, pursuing *hard* material interests would not have been an easy task. The plummeting of the newly formed Euro in the international currency markets was further tangible evidence for the Red–Green government of the interdependent nature of the EU, which the SPD had underestimated on coming to power. This helped to soften the edges of German policy, which was thereby more prepared to make compromises for the good of the EU and its relations with other Member States. The new budget finally hammered out at a 20-hour marathon session in Berlin was, therefore, a combination of small reductions of German net contributions along with small reforms to the EU's financial framework where possible. The changes made to CAP were unsatisfactory in the perspective of enlargement, since the cuts to intervention prices proposed by the Commission had been significantly watered down,[50] but spending had at least been frozen. While the Cohesion Fund had not been cut off from members of the Single Currency, the final level of Structural Funds – nearly €220 billion for the seven-year period – was about €25 billion less than the figure put forward by the Commission.[51] The funding the structurally poor regions was, furthermore, to be more heavily concentrated (in line with SPD, Federal Government and Commission goals), on regions comprising 42 per cent rather than 51 per cent of the EU population (by 2006), with about 70 per cent of these funds going to *Objective I* regions with GDP under 75 per cent of the EU average (including the eastern German *Länder*). Although the British rebate was retained, Germany was relieved to some extent: its share of payments for the Rebate would decrease to under 20 per cent. The Federal Government estimated that, overall, Germany would receive relief of approximately €715 million by 2006, reducing its proportion of net payments from about 0.6–0.4 per cent of GDP.[52]

Though more assertive over its own budgetary interests than previous governments, there was also a large degree of continuity in German policy. When it came to the crunch the new Government, in close co-ordination with the Commission, opted in favour of common European interests. The SPD had to recognise that its desired reform of CAP, for example, formulated in opposition, could not easily be implemented in the *European context* in government. Although there were no *veto players* in the SPD in this policy area, the French government fulfilled this role at the EU level. Alternative strategies, therefore, had to be sought for the time being. The German Presidency of the EU nevertheless secured funds to be set aside for applicant countries ('pre-accession instruments') and established mechanisms for the integration of of accession states into Community policies ('financial framework for EU-21')[53] – key steps towards incorporating the CEE states into the EU's financial architecture.

It has been mentioned earlier that the SPD had no real overarching conception of the EU's institutional architecture when it came into government. This was no different, however, from the position of the Christian Democrat parties during the previous governments, which – with the exception of the 1994 Schäuble-Lamers paper – were reluctant to spell out their view of a future EU institutional settlement for fear of being seen as too dominant by Germany's partners. The need for institutional reform to prepare for enlargement had been recognised in a protocol annexed to the Amsterdam Treaty, but there was little common ground between Member States over what the Unioin should eventually look like. Under the German Presidency of the Council, the Federal Government found it impossible to make any solid steps towards the reform of EU institutional structures. One innovation that went largely unnoticed at the time was the setting up of a committee to draw up a 'Charter of Fundamental Rights'. This was an idea promoted by Foreign Minister Fischer, but had been present in SPD policy for several years. While the Charter was to be non-building in the first instance, it was to become a central component of SPD policy in the near future.

The Helsinki European Council (December 1999) decided upon the remit for the IGC in 2000 on institutional reform: it would look at 'the size and composition of the Commission'; 'the weighting of votes in the Council'; 'the possible extension of qualified-majority voting in the Council'; and, 'other Treaty changes' that might be needed in connection with the Amsterdam Treaty.[54] The IGC was inaugurated in February 2000 under the Portuguese Council Presidency. In this context, Foreign Minister Fischer delivered a speech to the Humboldt University in May 2000 which, though supposedly made as a 'private person', marked an important turning point in German policy. It was a major step for a serving German minister to offer such a concrete vision for Europe outside the joint declarations of the Franco-German partnership. In the speech, Fischer outlined his concept of a European 'finality'.[55] He spoke of the need to meet the 'historic challenge' of eastern enlargement and 'integrate the new members without substantially denting the EU's capacity for action', to 'put into place the last brick in the building of European integration, namely political integration'.[56] While suggesting measures for a European Parliament and Commission with more powers and more directly linked to the electorate, he also argued for a 'constituent Treaty which lays down what is to be regulated at European level and what is still to be regulated at national level' based on a clear definition of subsidiarity.[57] He further stated that differentiation was 'inevitable' in an enlarged Union, and supported a non-exclusive 'avant-garde' of Member States that wished to press ahead, which would act as a 'centre of gravity' for further integration.[58] This would involve flexibility mechanisms similar to those outlined in the Schäuble-Lamers paper, though it was emphasised that the core would remain 'open'.

The SPD's European policy experts, on the other hand, without a position on a European finality, preferred to concentrate on achievable goals for the IGC: 'enhanced' or 'structured' co-operation, and the reform of the Commission and the Council.[59] They, more specifically, objected to Fischer's advocacy of a 'European core' because they saw European integration as a process without an end-model.[60] The SPD leadership nevertheless had to face the tensions between *deepening* and *widening* of the EU head-on in government. Without a long-term vision, it focused on the *pragmatic* aspects of institutional reform, supporting 'flexible integration' in the form of *structured co-operation* if it was not possible to extend QMV to any great degree. This could be an alternative way of widening the Union without diluting integration. Key SPD figures in the Federal Government and party presidium (including the Chancellor), however, supported Fischer's initiation of a 'European dialogue' (even if they were not in full agreement with some of his ideas),[61] and had no problems with his forthright approach, because they recognised that it was important to have an end goal in sight, not least to help win popular approval for the EU. They therefore set the party the task of coming up with a response to these policy challenges, so that by summer 2000 'this core Europe ... [was] being discussed long and hard' inside the party.[62]

The Federal Government sought the dual goals of 'legitimacy' and 'efficiency' with regard to the reform of the Commission and the Council.

For Germany, it was important that the number of Commissioners was reduced as far as possible to streamline the body. They wanted the Council to be reformed in two ways: first, through a re-weighting of votes, in order for population sizes to be better reflected in the number of votes allocated to each Member State;[63] and, second, through an extension of QMV in all areas but the most sensitive.[64] The position of the Federal Government was designed to create enough efficiency within the EU to enable enlargement and at the same time maintain or improve the quality of political integration.

Under the agreements reached at the European Council in Nice (December 2000), QMV became applicable in ten new articles,[65] but was not adopted in important areas for the Federal Government and the SPD such as 'taxation' and 'minimum requirements in social policy'.[66] Germany proposed either a re-weighting of votes more in line with populations or a 'double majority' system for the allocation of votes in the Council (a mixture of the existing system and a purely demographic procedure). The first option was significant because it challenged German parity with the UK, Italy and (significantly) France in the Council as it would give Germany more votes. This was in marked contrast to Kohl's previous assurances that 'Germany would not seek to break the current parity in voting weights which it holds with France and Britain'[67] – evidence enough of a more assertive policy. Germany nevertheless played a continuing role as the *advocate of the accession countries*. The Federal Government – along with Commission – ensured that prospective members were allocated votes fairly in accordance with their populations (relative to existing members), against the French Presidency's proposal that Poland would have fewer votes than Spain (though they had approximately equal populations). France's rejection of a single majority system more weighted towards demographic factors, however, resulted in a yet more cumbersome 'triple majority' system.[68] The process of *structured co-operation*, at least, was made easier after Nice, with the abolition of the veto mechanism for closer co-operation between Member states in *first pillar* policies.[69] The powers of the European Parliament were only moderately strengthened in parallel to the extension of QMV in the Council. After much wrangling, it was agreed that the Commission was to be comprised of a maximum of one Commissioner per Member State after 2005.

Although the institutional reforms agreed at Nice did not go far enough in several areas for the liking of the SPD, the Chancellor argued that 'the central goal was achieved: the European Union is capable of enlargement from 2003'.[70] The SPD in government had demonstrated its commitment to enlargement both by pressing for a 'fair treatment' of the CEE states at the IGC,[71] and by consulting regularly with its sister parties in those countries.[72] The postponement of the reform of the Commission was a disappointment, but a mechanism had at least been put in place for its eventual resolution. The party had to admit that 'the advances in the transition to qualified-majority voting in the Council are ... as a whole, too little ... especially in the areas of taxation, common foreign and security policy, social policy, structural funds and common trade policy'.[73] The reform of the Council had, with the allocation of votes to the candidate countries, nevertheless made the enlargement process seem much more real. Of further consolation were the changes that would make *structured co-operation* easier to initiate.

The Federal Government could also claim success with the establishment of a 'post-Nice process', despite the French government's attempt to distance itself from this proposal. It centred around the agreement of a further IGC with the purpose of creating a more lasting settlement between the EU institutions and the Member States. Acceptance of this was indispensable to the Federal Government, because of the demands of the *Länder* for a clearer division of competences and the need to present a less fuzzy picture of European integration to the population at large. It was also important to the coalition parties, who were committed to a more integrative form of institutional reform than had been agreed at Nice. Despite the atmosphere at the European Councils in Berlin and Nice, and the Federal government's insistence upon a reduction in budgetary payments and a relative increase in voting weight in the Council, German policy was still more inclined towards compromise than its partner states within the context of the preparations for enlargement: 'Even if some of the reform project could not be pushed through as we would have wished in Nice, the overall balance was positive. With the decision on institutional reform, the formal barriers to enlargement were overcome.'[74]

SPD enlargement policy: a new vision

The SPD's enlargement policy in government was composed of three different elements resulting from the *dynamics* described in the introduction: first, it was a more assertive policy (Chapter 5) placing greater emphasis on German interests; second, it was adjusted to fit better with the European policy context in government (Chapter 6); and, finally, it recognised the fundamental importance of enlargement and the fact that it needed to be sold more effectively to the key players in the domestic arena (Chapter 7). In all these dimensions, the party showed itself to be 'flexible' or 'pragmatic' in adapting to the realities of eastern enlargement. As a consequence, the SPD in government has pursued reform – both in the CEE states and the EU – and responded to the concerns of various domestic actors, attaching conditions to the enlargement process. At the same time, the party has represented deep German interests in eastern enlargement by promoting its positive aspects to domestic actors. These changes provided a *synthesis* of competing demands in the European policy environment.

The SPD members of the Government responded to public fears by insisting that the Copenhagen criteria would be fully applied, and interceded over specific concerns, for example, transition periods for the free movement of workers. Schröder also made clear to the SPD parliamentary group in 2001 that border controls at the new EU boundaries (after accession) must 'function from the start, otherwise the entire accession process will get into difficulties ... Germany will not tolerate a running down of control standards'.[75] They still believed, however, that 'the earlier the Central and East European reform states can be accepted into the European Union ... the better for us: first, politically, but also – if we do it right, and we shall do it right – economically',[76] so the benefits of eastern enlargement were promoted. This dual strategy was evidence on the Chancellor's 'Sommerreise' (summer holiday) to the eastern *Länder* and neighbouring CEE states in August 2001. On the first day of his ten-day tour, he actively 'canvassed for the eastern enlargement of the EU' in West Pomerania,[77] to overcome the 'mostly unfounded fears of Eastern Germans' by showing them 'the enormous opportunities and advantages of enlargement'.[78] Transition periods, on the other hand, were highlighted as a barrier to 'wage-and price-dumping'. In spite of the development of this positive strategy, the SPD still lacked a concrete long-term vision to underpin government policy for the institutional and financial reform of the European Union that could help win over public confidence for enlargement.

The Federal Government was satisfied that the process of accession would be led by the Commission, so that the negotiations would largely take care of themselves.[79] The German political elites, from the more sceptical to the most ardent pro-Europeans nevertheless accepted the fact that 'the EU is presently neither structurally nor financially in the position to cope with further members'.[80] After the conclusion of the Nice Summit, the SPD accelerated its European policy review to deal with these issues. The policy document, *Responsibility for Europe* was published in April 2001 as a draft motion for the party conference in November of that year. It provided a comprehensive set of EU policies that were passed with only a few minor amendments at the conference. Under the heading, 'Uniting Europe', the paper underlined the benefits of eastern enlargement in terms of employment: 'In Germany, as one of the most important economic partners of the Central and East European accession states, trade with central and eastern Europe already safeguards many jobs.'[81] The SPD sought to engage itself in eastern enlargement in a positive but realistic way, not wishing to endanger the 'quality' of European integration. Thus, the party set out policy goals to 'promote swift yet careful enlargement negotiations so that the most advanced countries could participate in the next elections to the European Parliament in 2004'; for 'seven year transition periods in especially sensitive areas like the free movement of workers and the freedom of services'; to formulate 'suitable solutions for the special problems of the border regions'; and, to implement 'comprehensive information and communication strategies incorporating discussion of the chances and challenges of enlargement'.[82] Other concerns of the public and the (easten) *Länder* addressed by the SPD included the proposal of 'a common border-guard service' for the EU borders,[83] to counter the specific fear of post-enlargement immigration. The SPD's 2002 *programme for government* contained a similar mixture of support for enlargement and conditions to make it acceptable.[84]

With respect to the division of competence demanded by the *Länder*, the SPD described the situation thus: 'Member States ... have in the course of this [European integration] process, lost the capacity for political design, although in many areas decisions would be better made on their level. On the other hand, the European Union does not yet exercise the competences needed for the realisation of its interests on the international plane or for the realisation of internal security.'[85] In other words, the party would seek a more exact division of competences, based on the subsidiarity principle for the 2003–04 IGC. They went on to identify areas that were of particular interest to the SPD and SPD-*Länder*: 'the Single Market competences and competition rules must not lead to an undermining of the circumstances in Member States ... for safeguarding state provision'; 'foreign and security policy, internal security and migration' were to be strengthended through further commu-nitisation; and, 'the areas of agricultural and structural policy' should be 'relocated on the national plane'.[86] Thus, the party set out a specific social democratic model for Europe integrating domestic and European policy within the context of *globalisation*.

A second medium-term objective was, as one interviewee central to the party's European policy stressed, a binding 'Social Charter of

Fundamental Rights which is enforceable and possible to push through'.[87] The *Responsibility for Europe* paper advocated the 'incorporation of the Charter of Fundamental Rights into the [EU] Treaties' as a 'further step in the direction of a European constitution'.[88] This was key to the SPD's new EU social democratic model, because the Charter would include social as well as political rights. The 53 Articles of the draft Charter released in September 2000 – in addition to covering rights like 'the protection of minorities' and 'cultural and religious diversity' – also contained a list of social provisions such as a 'worker's right to information and consultation' (Article 27) and to 'collective bargaining and action' (Article 28) in Chapter IV on 'Solidarity'.[89] Although many social rights were watered down, the fact that business interests rejected its 'mixture of social and economic demands as well as the numerous political goals'[90] was proof enough that, were it to become binding, it would not be without meaning. Professor Jürgen Meyer (SPD), the *Bundestag* representative on the convention that drafted the Charter, emphasised the point that with 'the incorporation of economic and social fundamental rights ... a counter-point to the American "hire and fire" principle is formulated'.[91] The Charter would, for the SPD, form the first part of a European constitution. The second element would be the 'long overdue division of competences between the different European institutions ... and between Brussels and the national capitals and regions',[92] outlined above. A third part would be the EU's financial framework.

The SPD's proposal for the return or at least the part-return of agricultural and structural policy to the national plane would mean great changes to the EU's system of financing, but prevent a large increase in the EU budget (and German payments) once enlargement took place. A report published by Dresdner Bank estimated that if the EU expanded to all the CEE applicant states plus Cyprus and Malta by 2005, and old Member States continued to receive current levels of funding, the Union would have to find an extra €44 billion for that year alone (a 38 per cent increase in the planned budget), under which circumstances Germany's net contribution to the EU budget would double to €21 billion.[93] Germany's Minister for Consumer Protection, Food and Agriculture, Renate Künast (Green), was convinced that the change in net contributions after enlargement would mean that the large beneficiaries from CAP 'will approach matters differently than in the 1999 negotiations on reform',[94] so that some sort of re-nationalisation could be possible.

Another aspect of the SPD's European policy paper was its long-term constitutional vision for the EU. Just as Fischer's speech to the Humboldt University the year before had marked a change in Federal

Government policy, the SPD model of a European 'finality' was the party's first public portrayal of constitutional *end-goals* (something the European policy groups had been averse to for many years).

Official SPD policy now called for deeper integration and democratisation of the EU through the following changes: greater 'transparency of decision-making on the European level through an extension of the Commission into a strong European executive ... the further strengthening of the European Parliament by means of an extension of co-decision-making and full budgetary sovereignty as well as the extension of the Council into a European chamber of states'.[95] All this would be enabled by a full extension of QMV in the Council. In choosing these final objectives, the SPD set out the basis of a *federal system* for the EU level, based (like the German system) on the decentralisation of power, with the Council acting as a more powerful model of the *Bundesrat*. Although this model attracted a lot of criticism, not least from other Member States such as the UK and France,[96] the party thought it crucial to establish a *dialogue* with the people – 'we must also discuss the questions that relate to the finality of Europe'[97] – to achieve popular backing for *deepening* and *widening*.

The SPD's policy of *conditionality* also manifested itself in Federal Government policy over the naming of official target dates for enlargement. Germany initially opposed the setting of these dates up until the European Council in Gothenburg (June 2001), due to concern that, if they were set, Poland might not make the first wave of countries. As it turned out, target dates were agreed for the end of negotiations with first-wave countries, leading Schröder to reiterate his wish for Poland 'to be among the first row of accession countries' whilst cautioning that 'there will be no political rebate' if the criteria were not fulfilled.[98] The Commission's evaluations of the accession candidates, with the exception of Bulgaria and Romania, however, were positive, the negotiations were closed and Member States agreed to a package for the admission of new members at the Copenhagen Council (December 2002). An accession treaty was signed in Athens (April 2003), which sanctioned the accession of the candidate countries on 1 May 2004, after the treaty had been ratified in all national parliaments. The formal acceptance of enlargement left the SPD and the Red–Green Government free to concentrate their full energies on the further reform of the EU. In the Government statement after the Copenhagen Summit, the Chancellor explained the benefits of enlargement and – at the same time – sought to assuage public fears about *free movement* and *border controls*, but the real focus of the statement was on the reform of the European Union.[99]

Although the agreements reached at Berlin (1999) and Nice (2000) had achieved minimum requirements for enlargement to take place, the arrangements were far from finalised. The SPD in government had to formulate a strategy, based on its new European policy concept, for the financial and institutional framework of the EU within the context of the debate over the future of the Union, the European Convention and the upcoming IGC on institutional reform. Here, the SPD was seeking to exert the third dimension of power (Chapter 1) – 'systemic power' – to alter the *rules of the game* at the EU level. The European Convention was a gathering of European, national and regional parliamentary and government representatives charged with the task of drawing up a European constitution. As explained above, the SPD was particularly interested to make its input felt in the Constitutional Convention. In this respect, Jürgen Meyer, the (SPD) *Bundestag* representative, was made speaker of the socialist group at the convention. The SPD in government firmly believed that 'deepening – the constitutional process – is the flip side of enlargement. Only both together makes any sense'.[100]

After the 2002 German election, Fischer took over as the German representative on the Convention, and he was particularly active in this period in promoting the German position through a renewal of the Franco-German motor. During the Convention, the Government (led by Fischer) took part in intensive negotiations with the French Government, to find a common vision for the EU. By November 2002, joint proposals had been published for the closer co-ordination of economic policy (explored in Chapter 9), a financial framework for the forthcoming budgetary negotiations, and the new EU institutional architecture, to mark the 40th anniversary of the Elysée Treaty on Franco-German co-operation. In the weeks and months leading up to the Franco-German agreement, the party and the Red–Green Government had given up the re-nationalisation of CAP and Structural Funds as realistic short- or medium-term goals, and instead concentrated on a stabilisation of the EU budget. Germany's high budgetary contribution was, once again, a big issue, but when push came to shove the Government was prepared to accept consolidation: according to Chancellor Schröder, Germany would 'remain the largest net donor out of solidarity ... but we must not be overwhelmed'.[101] The fact that Germany continued to foot most of the bill for the EU budget, could nevertheless act as leverage for the German positions in other areas of European policy. The central issue was still the level of CAP payments after enlargement.[102] The deal negotiated by the French and German governments meant that the EU agricultural budget was to rise at less than the expected rate of inflation after 2006 thanks to the phasing in of payments to the accession states over a ten-year period (i.e. involving no significant reforms to CAP itself), and was reluctantly supported by the Council. The Federal Government signed up to the deal to remove the threat of a ballooning net contribution and to gain France's final acceptance of the enlargement process. Here, the party in government showed *pragmatism* both in terms of German material interests and Germany's broader European interests. According to Schröder: 'This is a good day for Germany and a good one for enlargement.'[103]

The Franco-German proposals presented to the Constitutional Convention called for a 'better division of competences' based on the principle of subsidiarity and the charter of fundamental rights, to be entrenched within a European constitution; the European Council to elect a chair for a two-and-a-half year period, to 'lead the work of the European Council' and to 'represent the EU on the international level'; the election of the President of the Commission by the European Parliament; the automatic extension of co-decision rights in the Parliament with the broadening of QMV in the Council; the extension of QMV, particularly in the areas of Justice and Home Affairs and Common Foreign and Security Policy; and, the creation of a European Foreign Minister by merging the role of the Council High Representative and the Commissioner for External Affairs.[104] These proposals were more controversial in the parliamentary party and its European policy groups, which had – in line with official SPD policy – sought a strengthening of the Commission and the Commission Presidency rather than the French preference for a President of the Council (further bolstering the intergovernmental approach. Ultimately, the party had to accept the idea of a Council President, though the Commission retained the exclusive right of initiative in EU system of governance (against the wishes of those in favour a more intergovernmentalist solution). Despite these reservations, the SPD strongly advocated certain aspects of the Franco-German proposals – especially for the 'further development of European Foreign and Security Policy into a European security and defence union ... [and] the possibility of enhanced co-operation also in the framework of ESDP [European Security and Defence Policy]'.[105]

The European Convention presented its 'draft constitution' to the Council on 18 July 2003 incorporating the central ideas of the Franco-German paper: for example, on the Presidency of the Council, the EU Foreign Minister, greater co-decision rights for the European Parliament and its election of the Commission President.[106] The Charter of

Fundamental Rights was also integrated into the document.[107] The SPD therefore lent its strong support to the draft: 'even if not all of our wishes could be fulfilled by the constitution, it is nevertheless a great success that the rights of the European Parliament are strengthened, that ... the EU Foreign and Security Policy may develop further with the creation of a European foreign minister, and that the charter of fundamental rights is integrated into the constitution'.[108] German and SPD objectives for a division of competences were furthermore satisfied by the defining of areas of activity where the EU had either 'exclusive competence' or 'shared competence' with Member States.[109] The SPD and the German Government were prepared to put their full weight behind the *draft constitution*,[110] insisting that it be adopted wholesale by the Council in full at the Intergovernmental Conference starting under the Italian Presidency in late 2003. While Member States accepted the vast majority of the draft constitution at the IGC, the question of voting rights in the Council proved more difficult to resolve, as Poland and Spain – in particular – made clear their preference for the agreement reached at Nice. With the failure to reach a settlement at the Brussels Summit in December 2003, the Red–Green Government was not afraid to use its clout, threatening 'serious consequences' for the Poles if they refused to compromise, referring to their future receipts from the EU budget. More pertinently, the German Government again opened the prospect of the further integration of a European 'avant-garde' (a position first taken by Fischer, then repeated by the Chancellor and in the SPD European policy review) if the constitution was not accepted,[111] to achieve their model of the EU. Although this was not the SPD's preferred method of integration, the party kept this pathway open as a practical alternative to achieve its vision of a social democratic EU.

Conclusion

The European policy of the German Social Democrats has undergone significant change since 1990. SPD policy has become more assertive in pursuing specific German interests, but is more aware of common European Union interests (Chapter 5). The party's European policy has reflected the views of an increasingly broad range of domestic and European actors, but began to 'lead' opinion where it could in these policy relationships (Chapter 6). Whilst the SPD has become more keen to 'modernise' Germany to the realities of *economic globalisation*, it has constructed an EU social democratic model to offer its citizens *security in change* (Chapter 7). SPD policy has reflected the substantial developments in the policy environment in Germany, Europe and the world that have affected actors and structures in the SPD, Germany and Europe. Change brought about by German unification and the end of the Cold War, European integration and globalisation. This study will conclude by summarising what it reveals about SPD EU policy and German EU policy in general. For instance, what does it tell us about the role of 'pragmatism' in SPD policy? To what extent has SPD policy provided a synthesis of the views of various institutional, national and European actors and created a long-term and sustainable strategy? Finally, the conclusion investigates the prospects for future SPD and German EU policy within the shifting contexts of policy formation and implementation.

Pragmatism, synthesis and vision

The book began by looking at the theoretical foundations upon which this work was based, and emphasis was placed upon interpreting and understanding SPD European policy rather than establishing general

214 Europeans Policy of the German Social Democrats

rules by which policy could be explained and predicted (Chapter 1). This explains the space devoted to complex and changing policy contexts in Part II. While the course of public policy in the *observable* public domain provided the central focus, a significant proportion of the book dealt with the way SPD policy was formulated and pursued (below the surface) and its implications. The factors brought into the equation were not only those deriving from geopolitical, economic and psychological changes in Germany (Chapter 2), but also those stemming from historical and institutional circumstances (Chapter 1). To these were added the *input factors* looked at in Part II – the actors and structures that formed the *structured context* in which SPD policy existed. Part III analysed the main dynamics of SPD policy after 1990 that detail the development of party policy in the changing policy environment described above (Chapters 5 to 7). The main findings of the case studies on European Economic and Monetary Union and the eastern enlargement of the EU to central and eastern Europe were detailed in Chapters 8–11. SPD European policy by 2002 was characterised by *pragmatism, synthesis* and *vision*. This was a far cry from the party's European policy in the early- to mid-1990s, which was defined by the *loosely coupled anarchy* (a result of the pluralism which existed within the party).

The initial impetus for policy change came from the *climatic changes*, which – in turn – affected the policies of various actors within the institutional, national and European contexts. This is not to say that 1990 or any other date was a 'Stunde Null' (zero hour) for SPD European policy, but rather that a series of events and processes, starting with the fall of the Berlin Wall, marked the beginning of significant changes in the formulation and articulation of German interests. Some aspects of *climatic change* (i.e. European integration) nevertheless added weight to continuity in SPD policy and, after the party came to power, in German European policy. Common European interests became a counterweight to the party's more assertive representation of material German interests. The development of SPD policy since unification was, therefore, marked both by continuity and change.

The *realist* assessment of the impact of the *climatic change* saw unification and the opening-up of central and eastern Europe as a natural precursor to German dominance. This study has shown, however, that this is based on two false assumptions – that governments are unitary actors and that definable *national interests* are pursued in a *zero-sum game*. In reality, marked interdependence exists between states and interests have become complex and merged, and this is especially true in a highly integrated European Union. *Multilateralists* have pointed out that deep (economic and political) German interests continue to lie within the EU framework, and that this has led to the continued projection of *soft* power – *agenda-setting* and *systemic power*. The Red–Green Government's initial overuse of *direct* channels of power was illustrated by its failed attempts to massively reduce German payments to the EU budget. The party leaders in government soon recognised that an agreement had to be reached in the midst of the crises that arose in March 1999 and the need for an accord on financial reform to enable enlargement to take place.[1] The mixed use of these three forms of power was captured by the *pragmatic multilateralism* of SPD European policy by the end of its first term in power. In short, the SPD has been more assertive in pursuing key material interests viewed within the context of Germany's *Europeanised* interests.

The dynamism in SPD EU policy was captured by three types of change – generational, electoral-strategic and ideological. The changes in the positions adopted by the SPD leadership, according to the contexts in which they operated, was evidence of their 'pragmatism' or 'flexibility'. The new *generation* of party leaders that emerged in the 1990s took a more *pragmatic* approach to the pursuit of German interests that had been altered by *climatic change* (Chapter 5). The historical reasoning behind post-war German policy was less relevant and, as Chancellor Schröder recognised: 'my way of doing things makes me a bit freer'.[2] Their less constrained stance on European policy enabled them to interpret *climatic change* into a new style of German policy, ready to articulate material German interests (e.g. the *paymaster* position) and confident enough to sanction the use of German troops in Kosovo and Afghanistan and oppose US intervention in Iraq. After the strategic indecision of the 1980s, when the SPD largely played to its own supporters, the party became more *responsive* to public opinion (from the early 1990s). It then began to interact with a broader set of domestic interests as it moved towards government, and then European interests in order to pursue its goals more effectively in government (an *electoral-strategic dynamic* – Chapter 6). This resulted in the sometimes populist use of European policy by the party's leadership *Troika* in the mid-1990s. As the SPD moved towards becoming a *government in waiting* and finally gained power, it was still prepared to reflect material concerns, but also fundamental German interests in a healthy and integrated European Union. To pursue what the SPD leaders in office soon recognised to be *Europeanised* German interests, it was necessary to lead – not just follow – public opinion. The party therefore finally took an active role in promoting European policy, which uniquely featured as the first policy area in the SPD's 2002 programme for government.³ The third *dynamic* was *ideological change* (Chapter 7). The SPD was characterised by programmatic pluralism in the 1980s and early 1990s. After unification, the party focused on domestic economic issues to profile itself against the Government. By the late 1990s, European policy under Wieczorek-Zeul began to be *linked* to domestic issues more regularly, though most party leaders still saw the EU as a secondary concern. In government, while Lafontaine's ideas to promote growth and regulate the markets were unlikely to be achieved, Chancellor Schröder supported more modest *co-operative* steps, as illustrated by the Lisbon European Council in 2000. A more long-term social democratic model came with the integration of domestic and European policy into a *federal* concept that sought the entrenchment of specific social democratic goals within a European constitution.⁴ The new generation of SPD leaders acted as policy entrepreneurs (even if a lot of the time they were merely instruments of *climatic change*), articulating new German interests within the pressures and constraints of the policy contexts explored in Chapters 3 and 4.

The SPD's first term in office saw the transposition of the three European policy *dynamics* onto the governmental stage. The *generational change* manifested itself in a more assertive style of European policy. Maull makes the point that a 'new foreign policy style does not imply *per se* a new substance'.⁵ Yet the SPD leadership's clearer articulation of post-unity German interests and greater use of *direct* channels of power put issues on the agenda that may well have been avoided under *exaggerated multilateralism* (e.g. the discussion of a European *finality*). Germany under an SPD-led Government, therefore, became more 'normal' in the sense of Germany standing up for its interests as France or Britain stand up for theirs.⁶ Because the SPD leaders in the Federal Government have had a less historical conception of the European Union than their predecessors, they have been more willing to use *direct power* (which *realists* have stressed in relation to German policy) to supplement the still more frequent use of *agenda-setting power* (which *multilateralists* have emphasised). 'Die Welt' wrote of a 'change in paradigm in German foreign and European policy' in reference to the 2000 IGC on institutional reform.⁷ It noted that Germany, while behaving as a 'model European', also listed its own key interests even 'where it hurts other major European powers'.⁸

In government, the SPD increasingly took into account common European interests and the views of European actors given the interdependent reality of government and the advances in European integration. These influences were added to the broad range of domestic actors that were already a major policy component by 1998. Although the SPD was becoming more *responsive* to key actors, the relationship was an interactive one. Matthias Machnig has spoken of the 'two-way exchange of ideas and concepts' as a central pillar of party strategy.[9] The party's attempt to lead public opinion as well as respond to it was illustrated by its position on enlargement. Transition periods were secured for the free movement of workers, while the economic benefits of eastern enlargement were praised at the same time, in an effort to convince the electorate and other sceptical domestic actors (e.g. the *Länder*) of its advantages. In April 2000, an official from the SPD's European policy groups conceded that the party 'had not brought forward an externally effective policy strategy' in the past which could lead to a European policy dialogue.[10] This was to change a year later with the publication of the SPD's European policy review, even if the failure of Europe as a lead issue in the 2002 federal election manifesto illustrated the continued difficulties of engagement with the general public in this area.

Finally, even the most domestic-oriented of SPD leaders eventually underwent an *ideological change* that led to the prioritisation of European policy in the party within an integrated programme of domestic and European policy. This development heralded a *synthesis* of opinion between different groups in the party and of domestic and European policy into a social democratic *vision* for the EU.[11] The synthesis of European policy within the party began in the late 1990s when the SPD's European policy experts began to weave some of the demands of the leadership and German public opinion into the existing fabric of European policy. On the other hand, politicians like Schröder, who strongly represented these domestic demands, eventually accepted that traditional pro-European German policy was representative of what were fundamental German interests (both political and economic) in the EU. While Schröder had expressed views on the EU that challenged the style and content of German policy from the early 1990s (e.g. his speculation on the postponement of EMU), he nevertheless was flexible enough to adapt to the new surroundings of the Chancellor's Office. He came to recognise the importance of European policy for a German Chancellor, and personally pushed forward the party's European review process, to find a position that could reconcile Germany's domestic and European interests.[12] The views of the SPD *Länder*, despite their growing criticisms of the EU, were, therefore, also incorporated into the review (i.e. support for the division of competences), and it is striking to note the *on-message* stance of (then) Minister-President Clement, in contrast to the chaos of the SPD *Troika*'s European policy in the mid-1990s. In an article for the SPD magazine, '*Vorwärts*', Clement supported communitisation and re-nationalisation in the exact same areas outlined by the *Responsibility for Europe* paper a month earlier.[13]

The social democratic *vision* formulated in the European policy review was to feed into the SPD's piecemeal development of a new *Basic Programme*. The idea of presenting the European Union as an answer to globalisation was first put forward by Lafontaine in the late 1990s, but this was not taken to heart by the SPD as it focused on domestic issues for the 1998 elections, and Lafontaine's ideas were not sufficiently integrated into the domestic policy programme. The *Responsibility for Europe* paper, however, managed to *synthesise* domestic and European policy through a *federal* conception of the European Union, which would re-nationalise competences in areas that profited German interests (e.g. CAP and the EU Structural Funds) and communitise policy in areas that would best suit Germany's common European interests (e.g. foreign and security policy). One SPD EU policy expert emphasised the difference between Lafontaine's conception of an EU-level European social policy and current party aims to 'interpret' policies nationally that are 'coordinated on the European level'.[14]

German interests in Europe were now seen through a Kantian lens: European policy was deemed to be 'a policy of enlightened self-interest' within the context of a positive-sum game.[15] The aim was also to create a decentralised federal structure that resembled the existing political structures of the Federal Republic. While advocating both domestic and European economic modernisation, the SPD also proposed a social democratic EU which could act as a counterweight to the Anglo-Saxon capitalism: an alternative model 'which makes the attempt to combine economic stability with social security ... [and] is greater than that of the USA, in both a long and medium term perspective'.[16] On the domestic and European levels, the state was to provide *opportunity for all* and minimum social standards as new form of social justice in era characterised by 'individualisation', 'German unification', 'Europeanisation', 'globalisation' and the emergence of the 'new economy'.[17] Gerhard Schröder expressed it in the following way to the party conference in November 2001: 'the content of our conception of Europe not only deals with the market, but also with our quite specific political concepts that reflect our social democratic values, which we are fighting for in our national policy and likewise want to see realised in our European policy'.[18] The Constitutional Convention set up in 2002 and the IGC launched in 2003 presented the party with the opportunity to promote their socio-economic model on the EU plane. In this regard, the Franco-German proposals for a constitutional settlement in late 2002 played an important part in shaping the EU *draft constitution*. The focus on European policy, and the party's efforts to influence its policy environment, marked an attempt by the SPD to exert *systemic power* by altering the *rules of the game* on the EU level.

Future prospects

The effects of *climatic change* have been highlighted throughout this study. Yet changes to the policy environment continue to inform German European policy-making, limiting the strategic options for the SPD within the context of the Federal Government. This is the reasoning behind the party's efforts to respond to the continuing challenges posed by German unification, the end of the Cold War, increased European integration and economic *globalisation* through national and EU-level policies. *Climatic change* is an ongoing process, and though the events of the late 1980s and early 1990s represented a historic watershed, new challenges emerge that affect the foreign policy environment, such as the threat to international security post-*September 11*. While it is difficult to speculate on the future of SPD or German European policy, current *climatic* trends can open a window onto future developments.

The main trend that will impact upon European policy in Germany and the SPD in the medium-term is the poor state of the German economy. The low levels of growth and rising employment in 2002 were undoubtedly the major issue in the German elections, until the natural disaster of the floods in Eastern Germany and the looming US intervention in Iraq emerged in the final stage of the election campaign. This book has already explained how these problems and the policy solutions devised for these problems – that is, *Agenda 2010* – became the dominant political issue, but also encouraged the SPD to pursue its policy goals on the EU level. This development nevertheless has the potential to lead to the more assertive or pursuit of material German interests in the European arena. Two further trends that seem likely to extend their influence into the future are European integration and *globalisation*. Schröder's more pro-European stance after he had been in power for several months was a reflection of the importance of the European context in setting the parameters for German policy. Deeper EU integration should further entrench the positive-sum, multilateral perspective of German European policy-makers, which is an approach that is well suited to a more interdependent EU and Western world. In this sense, integration will continue to act as a counter-balance and *reality check* to other domestic pressures in the face of future economic and political challenges.

The SPD hopes to develop an enlarged Union with a federal system (based on subsidiarity) and a modern economy that maintains social and environmental standards in the face of *globalisation*. By 2001, for the SPD European policy groups, 'globalisation' had become 'the political guideline under which everything else is subsumed ... the European integration process is the answer of the old continent to the globalised world, to globalised relations – this is the instrument with which to push through social democratic values'.[19] In this sense European integration has seen both the *Europeanisation* of domestic policy and the *domestication* of European policy.[20] The *Responsibility for Europe* paper argued that: 'There is no alternative to further integration and Europeanisation.'[21]

Despite the European and global integration processes that should continue to increase the logic of common European interests for German Social Democrats, a fully sovereign Germany in a post-Cold War world led by a *pragmatic* generation of leaders is nevertheless likely to increasingly articulate its diplomatic weight in the European Union, moving closer towards the policy styles of other Member States like the UK and France, and taking on more responsibility for leading the way in Europe. This was already observable in the context of the negotiations on EU financial and institutional reform that took place in 1999 and 2000. Though the UK and France may well begin to look more to the strategic dimensions of power, with the penetration of international affairs into domestic politics, it is probable that Germany will begin to use the first dimension of *direct power* more – thus retreating further from *exaggerated multilateralism*.

While taking greater *responsibility for Europe*, the SPD-led Government has also attempted to take on a greater role in international affairs. This can be seen by the confidence of the Federal Government to commit to military involvement in Kosovo and Afghanistan and to take an active role in the resulting peace processes within the context of German foreign policy. It was furthermore decided in September 2001 that German troops would, for the first time, lead a NATO mission, a conflict prevention force in Macedonia. Chancellor Schröder spoke of this development in a government statement about the 'international operation against terrorism in Afghanistan': 'After the end of the Cold War, the recreation of the unity of the German state and the re-attainment of our full sovereignty, we have taken up a new form of international responsibility. A responsibility which reflects our role as an important European and transatlantic partner, but also our strong democracy and strong political economy at the heart of Europe.'[22] He further asserted that Germany's role as a 'secondary' player in international affairs was 'gone forever'.[23] The medium-term aim of SPD policy remains, however, to secure a common EU foreign and security policy to strengthen its hand in the international arena through multilateral means.[24] The need for Europe to speak with one voice was further illustrated to the party by the divisions of opinion in the EU over the Iraq conflict in 2003.

As mentioned in the previous section, the SPD's 2000–01 European policy review sought to synthesise the popular feeling articulated by the party leadership with the views of other key domestic actors like the German *Länder*, while at the same time representing the interests of the German economy (and the *social partners*) in a Single European market (which typified the approach of the party's European policy groups). This synthesis was a by-product of the *electoral-strategic change* that had taken place through the 1990s – the more effective networking of various interests and a greater appreciation of the *structured context* of European policy-making. Although the SPD had managed to integrate the different views on European policy within the party and the country, it was still crucial that their views could command a cross-party consensus, to allow the Federal Government freedom in pursuing its interests on the European stage. In a major policy statement on enlargement in February 2001, the Government acknowledged that such a 'cross-party consensus was and is the guarantee for a successful German European policy'.[25] The Christian Democratic Union saw the ideas presented by the SPD moving 'completely in the direction of ... the Union parties' and even the more sceptical Christian Social Union stated that Schröder's concepts (which had incorporated various *Länder* demands) 'on many points reflected old CSU positions'.[26] In fact, the CDU chairman of the *Bundestag* European Affairs' Committee, Friedbert Pflüger, commented – in relation to the SPD paper – that 'in its essential features, a European policy consensus was developing in Germany'.[27] The projection of a distinctly German, federal system onto the EU, entrenched through a constitutional settlement, could certainly form the basis of a new *grand strategy* for German European policy.

If the SPD had been relatively successful in selling its new grand strategy for German European policy to the German political elites, what were its chances for implementation on the EU-level? After 1999, the Federal Government pursued policies of *modernisation* and *social justice* on both the national and the European planes, and this gained added momentum in 2002 as a consequence of the economic problems referred to above. The European Union heads of government had, on the EU level, all signed up to the *modernisation* goals of improving Member States' positions in the new technologies sector and using *benchmarking* to improve all-round economic performance at the Lisbon Summit in 2000. Lisbon also saw members setting themselves an ambitious employment target: an increase of almost 15 per cent in ten years. In the pursuit of a social democratic model for the European Union, solid progress in the *social justice* dimension has not gone far beyond the national level, however, given the reluctance of – in particular – the UK and Spain to subscribe to these goals. Although the Constitutional Convention and the *draft* constitution incorporated central SPD goals (such as the inclusion of the Charter of Fundamental Rights), without Majority Voting in key areas these reforms will not go far enough. Closer co-ordination in EU Foreign and Security Policy and economic and social policy is seen as a critical goal by the German Social Democrats, so that the *structured co-operation* of a (non-exclusive) European *avant-garde* – might be the next *pragmatic* step.

Notes

Introduction

1. See P. Lösche and F. Walter, *Staatspartei, Volkspartei, Quotapartei* (Wissensch. BG Dst, 1992).
2. The 'Responsibility for Europe' document became integrated into the SPD interim report on a new party programme, passed at the Nürnberg party conference in November 2001: SPD Vorstand, *Leitantrag: Verantwortung für Europa* (30/04/01), www.spd.de
3. The term 'European policy' will be used to convey the meaning of 'European Union policy', much like the term 'Europapolitik' in Germany.
4. See G. Braunthal, *The West German Social Democrats, 1969–1982: profile of a party in power* (Bolder: Westview, 1983); Lösche and Walter (1992); S. Miller, *Kleine Geschichte der SPD* (Bonn: Dietz, 2002); F. Walter (Berlin: Alexander Fest, 2002).
5. While comprehensive accounts of SPD European policy were published in the 1960s–70s – see, for example, J. Bellers, *Reformpolitik und EWG-Strategie der SPD: die innen- und außenpolitischen Faktoren der europapolitischen Integrationswilligkeit einer Oppositionspartei (1957–63)* (Munich: tuduv, 1979); W. Paterson, *The SPD and European Integration* (Farnborough: Saxon House, 1973) – the only account of any great depth in the 1990s was M. Roth, *Die Europapolitik der SPD: Positionen, Probleme und Perspektiven zwischen Maastricht und Regierungskonferenz* (Frankfurt: Johann Wolfgang-Goethe Universität, 1996) (Roth soon became an SPD *Bundestag* member responsible for European policy).
6. The term 'federal' is used, as in the German sense, to denote both the national level of politics as well as the multi-level political system.
7. P. Katzenstein, *Policy and Politics in West Germany: the growth of a semi-sovereign state* (Philadelphia: Temple University Press, 1987).
8. European Commission, *Eurobarometer 40* (Brussels: December 1993), Brussels, p. 59.
9. Cited in 'German foreign minister at top of popularity poll', *BBC Monitoring Service*, www.bbc.co.uk
10. 'Net contribution' means the amount paid to the EU minus redistribution through various Community policies.
11. 'Hard' and 'soft' are used here to denote the difference between interests that are short-term and material and those that are long-term and strategic – see J. Anderson, *Hard Interests, Soft Power, and Germany's Changing Role in Europe*, in P. Katzenstein (ed.), *Tamed Power: Germany in Europe* (Cornell University Press, 1987), pp. 80–107.
12. Cited in 'Kosovo Krise: Union unterstützt Rot-Grün', *Die Welt* (27/03/99), www.welt.de
13. Cited in 'Out of Kohl's shadow', *The Financial Times* (27/03/99), www.ft.com

14. See K. Dyson and K. Goetz, *Germany, Europe and the Politics of Constraint* (Oxford: Oxford University Press, 2003).
15. A. Cole, 'National and partisan contexts of Europeanisation: the case of the French Socialists' (March 2001), *Journal of Common Market Studies 39 (1)*, pp. 15–36, p. 16.
16. The idea of a 'structured context' is set out in the 'strategic-relationship' approach to 'strategic learning' set out by C. Hay, 'Structure and agency' in D. Marsh and G. Stoker (eds), *Theory and Methods in Political Science* (Basingstoke: MacMillan, 1995), pp. 189–206.
17. The student radicalism of the 1960s is a history these SPD leaders share with a number of their Green coalition partners.
18. Engholm's tenure was not, however, long enough for him to have a major impact on policy.
19. The new generation of SPD leaders were referred to as the 'grandchildren' of Willy Brandt.
20. See K. Dyson and K. Featherstone, *The Road to Maastricht: negotiating economic and monetary union* (Oxford: Oxford University Press, 1999), pp. 16–17.
21. The SPD was not necessarily conscious of its more *normal* foreign policy, but – intentional or not – it was nevertheless a feature of their socialisation in a Federal Republic reintegrated into the international community.
22. Gerhard Schröder; cited in G. Hellmann, 'The sirens of power and German foreign policy: who is listening?' (August 1997), *German Politics 6 (2)*, pp. 29–57, p. 47.
23. See F. Unger, A. Wehr, K. Schönwälder, *New Democrats, New Labor, Neue Sozialdemokraten* (Berlin: Elefanten Press, 1998).
24. Bodo Hombach, an architect of the SPD's 'Neue Mitte' (New Centre) group stated: 'we wish to seek a consensus over the best solution. Government must listen to social participants.' Bodo Hombach, speaking at the LSE (28/04/99) (author's notes).

1 Grounding European Policy: Policy, Power and Parties

1. The level of West German exports at the time of unification – as a proportion of Gross Domestic Product – was approximately three times that of either the US or Japan.
2. 'Parapublic' was a term used by Katzenstein (1987) to denote the distinct form of semi-autonomous public institutions in Germany.
3. Katzenstein (1987).
4. H. P. Schwarz, *Geschichte der Bundesrepublik* (Wiesbaden: Deutsche Verlags-Anstalt, 1981).
5. Anderson (1997), pp. 80–107.
6. Ibid.
7. W. Paterson, 'Beyond semi-sovereignty: the new Germany in the new Europe' (August 1996), *German politics 5 (2)*, pp. 169–70.
8. The success of post-war West German diplomacy was marked, notably, by the return of the Saarland region to West Germany and the creation of the EC in 1957.

9. The concept of *Ostpolitik* was also heavily identified with Egon Bahr.
10. Despite the commitment to a gradual movement towards economic and Monetary Union made at the Hague Summit (December 1969), more tangible steps were taken towards the *widening* and *democratisation* of the Community between 1969 and 1974. Brandt was widely acknowledged to have finally persuaded Pompidou to allow British entry in 1973, and he also promoted elections for the European Parliament (first taking place in 1979).
11. Until the emergence of the Greens, potential coalition partners had only been located to the Right of the SPD.
12. See in particular, A. Baring (ed.), *Germany's New Position in Europe* (Oxford: Berg, 1994); and, G. Niedhard (ed.), *Deutschland in Europa* (Mannheim, Palatium, 1997).
13. C. Hacke, 'Die Bedeutung der nationale Interesses für die Aussenpolitik der Bundesrepublik', in Niedhard (1997), p. 26.
14. Ibid.
15. 'Twenty-hour talk marathon ends in compromise', *The Financial Times* (29/03/99), www.ft.com
16. European Commission, *Eurobarometer 49* (Brussels: Spring 1998).
17. Interests are not seen here as objective, absolute or indivisible, nor are they viewed as *always* resulting from 'relative gains' and a 'zero sum' perspective (although this may be true on many occasions) – an approach forwarded by the *realist* school.
18. See particularly J. Mearsheimer, 'Back to the future: instability in Europe after the Cold War' (1990), *International Security 15*, pp. 5–56; A. Markovits and S. Reich, 'Should Europe fear the Germans?' in Huelshoff *et al.* (eds) *From Bundesrepublik to Deutschland: German Politics after Unification* (Michigan: University of Michigan, 1991), pp. 271–90; T. Garton Ash, *Im Namens Europa: Deutschland und der geteilte Kontinent* (Munich: Hanser, 1993).
19. Markovits and Reich (1991).
20. The *realist* analysis is founded on the implicit belief in the homogeneity of a policy-forming elite and the indivisibility of interests, involving a clear hierarchy of policy objectives. It emphasises the dominance of inter-state relations and relegates domestic politics and international organisations to minor roles.
21. R. Keohane and J. Nye, 'Realism and complex interdependence', in M. Smith (ed.), *Perspectives on World Politics* (London: Croom Helm, 1981), pp. 121–30, p. 130.
22. See also W. Hanrieder, 'Dissolving international politics: reflections on the welfare state', in M. Smith (1981), pp. 132–45.
23. Keohane and Nye (1981), pp. 120–31.
24. W. Wallace, 'The sharing of sovereignty: the European paradox' (1999), *Political Studies 47 (3)*, pp. 503–21.
25. While this study tries to avoid falling into the *realist* trap of oversimplifying the complex and changing world of international relations (by analysing the multilayered contexts in which the SPD policy is formulated – Chapters 3 and 4), it nevertheless utilises an individual actor – the SPD – as the 'lens' of this study (see Figure I.1) as a practical means for delimiting the area of social construction covered.

26. See Paterson (August 1996); Hellman (August 1997), pp. 29–57; S. Bulmer, C. Jeffery and W. Paterson, 'Deutschlands europäische Diplomatie' in W. Weidenfeld (ed.), *Deutsche Europapolitik* (Bonn: Europa Union, 1998), pp. 11–102.
27. See Katzenstein (1997).
28. M. Kreile, 'Will Germany assume a leadership role in the European Union?', in B. Heurlin (ed.), *Germany in Europe in the Nineties* (London: MacMillan, 1996), pp. 123–51, p. 123.
29. The concept of state governments acting as 'gatekeepers' was used in S. Bulmer, 'Domestic politics and European Community policy-making' (1983a), *Journal of Common Market Studies 21 (4)*.
30. S. Bulmer, C. Jeffery, W. Paterson, *Germany's European Diplomacy: shaping the regional milieu* (Manchester: Manchester University Press, 2000).
31. S. Lukes, *Power: A Radical View* (London: Macmillan, 1974).
32. See R. Dahl, 'The concept of power' (1957), *Behavourial Science 2 (3)*, pp. 201–15.
33. Bulmer, Jeffery and Paterson (2000), p. 7.
34. P. Bachrach and M. Baratz, *Power and poverty: theory and practice* (Oxford: Oxford University Press, 1970).
35. C. Hay, *Political Analysis* (Basingstoke: Palgrave, 2002), pp. 174–8.
36. Lukes (1974), pp. 22–3.
37. Hay underlines the problem with this idea: that A gets B to do something that is not in B's genuine interests, which can only open the door to a normative evaluation of what those genuine interests are. Hay (2002), pp. 180–1.
38. See also Bulmer's third and fourth faces of power in S. Bulmer, 'Shaping the rules? The constitutive politics of the European Union and German power', in Katzenstein (1997), pp. 49–79, pp. 75–6.
39. See C. Hay, 'Divided by a common language: political theory and the concept of power' (1997), *Politics* 17 (1), pp. 45–52, p. 51; Bulmer, Jeffery and Paterson (2000), p. 7.
40. Bulmer (1997), pp. 72–6.
41. *Direct power* is similar to Bulmer's first face of power; Bulmer (1997), p. 73.
42. Bulmer, Jeffery and Paterson (2000), p. 7.
43. See Bulmer's third and fourth faces of power: Bulmer (1997), pp. 75–6.
44. Ibid.
45. The *Bundesrat* is the upper chamber of the German Parliament, comprising representatives of the regional governments.
46. The Maastricht Treaty (Treaty on European Union) agreed upon the principle of subsidiarity.
47. M. Duverger, *Political Parties: their organization and activity in the modern state* (1954) in P. Mair (ed.), *The West European Party System* (Oxford: Oxford University Press, 1990), pp. 37–45.
48. Kirchheimer, 'The catch-all party' (1966) in Mair (1990), pp. 50–60, p. 58.
49. Kircheimer (1990), pp. 58–9.
50. A. Panebianco, 'political parties: organisation and power' (Cambridge: Cambridge University Press, 1988).
51. P. Mair, *Party System Change: approaches and interpretations* (Oxford: Oxford University Press, 1997), p. 20.

52. G. Sani and G. Sartori, 'Polarization, fragmentation and competition in western democracies', in H. Daalder and P. Mair (eds), *Western European Party Systems: continuity and change* (London: Sage, 1983), pp. 307–40.
53. T. Saalfeld, 'Germany: Bundestag and interest groups in a parliamentary democracy', in P. Norton (ed.) *Parliaments and Pressure Groups in Western Europe* (London: Frank Cass, 1990), p. 43.
54. See M. Schmidt, 'West Germany: the policy of the middle way' (1987), *Journal of Public Policy (2)*, pp. 139–77.
55. Saalfeld (1990), p. 43
56. Panebianco (1988), p. 261.
57. A. Lijphart, 'Dimensions of ideology in European Party Systems' (1981) in Mair (1990), pp. 253–65.
58. See, for instance, Panebianco (1988); Daalder and Mair (1983); and Mair (1997).
59. H. Daalder, 'The comparative study of european parties and party systems: an overview' in Daalder and Mair (1983), p. 21.
60. Panebianco (1988), p. 273.
61. Ibid.
62. The weakening of *collective political identity* is highlighted by the significant decline in the membership of most political parties in Western Europe.
63. The SPD executive consists of the *Presidium* and the *Vorstand*.
64. The study focuses on those SPD members of the *Bundestag* on the all-party Committee for European Union Affairs.
65. Panebianco (1988), p. 44.
66. Mair (1997), p. 21.
67. See D. Hough, *The Fall and Rise of the PDS in Eastern Germany* (Birmingham: Birmingham University Press, 2002).
68. Panebianco (1988), p. 273.
69. Cited in Mair (1997), pp. 36–7.
70. See T. Meyer, 'Soziale Demokratie statt demokratischer Sozialismus. Alte SPD und neue Realität: Ketzereien eines bekennenden Sozialdemokraten', *Frankfurter Rundschau* (18/09/03), www.fr-aktuell.de
71. See Hay (1995); and, B. Jessop, 'Interpretive sociology and the dialectic of structure and agency' (1996), *Theory, Culture and Society* 13 (1), pp. 119–28.
72. *Pragmatic multilateralism*, thus, provides a bridge between *rational choice theory* – which sees 'individual actors as the basic unit of analysis' – and the 'new institutionalist' belief that history and institutions matter; see Hay (2002), pp. 7–13.
73. J. Dewey, *Creative Intelligence: essays in the pragmatic attitude* (New York: Holt and Company, 1917); D. Fott, *John Dewey: America's philosopher of democracy* (Oxford: Rowman and Littlefield, 1998).
74. Figures given in 'Survey on Germany', *The Financial Times* (01/06/99), p. VIII.
75. Gerhard Schröder, cited in *Die Süddeutsche Zeitung* (27/03/99), www.sueddeutsche.de
76. The main changes desired by the SPD at Berlin were a reform of the Common Agricultural Policy (CAP), and the abolition of the British rebate and the Cohesion Fund (Chapter 11).

2   A New Policy Environment

1. Joschka Fischer, 'Berlin's foreign policy' (2000), *Internationale Politik (Transatlantic Edition) (1)*, pp. 3–10, p. 4.
2. D. Marsh and M. Smith, 'Understanding policy networks: towards a dialectic approach' (March 2000), *Political Studies 48*, pp. 4–21, p. 8.
3. See Bulmer, S. *et al.*, 'Electricity and communications: fit for the European Union?', in K. Dyson and K. Goetz (eds), *Germany in Europe* (Oxford: Oxford University Press, 2003), pp. 251–69.
4. J. Anderson, *German unification and the Union of Europe* (Cambridge, Cambridge University Press, 1999), p. 23.
5. 'Togetherness: a balance sheet', *The Economist* (24/10/00), www.economist.com
6. Figures from German EU Presidency, *Deutschland und die Währungsunion* (June 1999), www.eu-praesidentschaft.de
7. OECD, *Economic Outlook no. 74* (December 2003), www.oecd.org, Annex Table 33.
8. Ibid.
9. 'Twenty-hour talk marathon ends in compromise', *The Financial Times* (27/03/99), www.ft.com
10. Gerhard Schröder, interview with 'Focus', 06/11/95, www.focus.de
11. Interview with SPD official in Government department (formerly responsible for European policy).
12. Cited in 'Kohl's mark on history', *BBC News Online* (03/10/00), www.bbc.co.uk
13. European Commission, *Eurobarometer 49* (Spring 1998).
14. The idea of a German *mission* to East Central Europe was famously suggested by Francois Mitterrand to Margaret Thatcher in January 1990; see S. Crawshaw, 'Germany looks East', *Prospect* (January 1997), www.prospect-magazine.co.uk
15. W. Paterson, 'From the Bonn to the Berlin Republic' (April 2000), *German Politics 9 (1)*, pp. 23–40, p. 35.
16. Figures taken from before the adoption of the Single Currency are calculated in Euros according to the fixed rate set after currency union in 1999.
17. Steve Crawshaw, *Prospect* (January 1997)
18. M. Zimmer, 'Return of the *Mittellage*' (April 1997), *German Politics 6 (1)*, pp. 23–38, p. 31.
19. See Mearsheimer (1990); Markovits and Reich (1991).
20. Crawshaw (January 1997).
21. Zimmer (April 1997), p. 24.
22. Ibid.
23. S. Eyre and M. Lodge, 'National tunes and a European melody? Competition Law reform in the UK and Germany' (March 2000), *Journal of European Public Policy 7 (1)*, pp. 63–79, p. 77.
24. Cole (March 2001), p. 16.
25. See the European Commission, *Final Report of the Committee of the Wise Men on the Regulation of the European Securities Markets* (February 2001), www.europa.eu.int
26. Eyre and Lodge (March 2000), p. 64.

27. See Pierson, 'The path to European integration' (1996), *Comparative Political Studies 29 (2)*, pp. 123–63.
28. M. G. Schmidt, 'Die Europäisierung der öffentlichen Aufgaben' (1999), *ZeS-Arbeitspapier (3)*, Bremen
29. 'Europe reinvented', *Financial Times* (15/01/01), www.ft.com
30. European Commission, *Impact and Effectiveness of the Single Market: special feature no. 6, January 1997* (06/01/97), www.europa.eu.int
31. H. Maull (ed.), 'Vier Monate rot-grüne Außenpolitik' (March 1999), *Trier Arbeitspapiere zur Internationalen Politik (1)*, p. 4.
32. Cole (March 2001), p. 24.
33. 'Policies on jobs under attack', *The Financial Times* (05/09/00), www.ft.com
34. 'Administrative fit' is associated with Bulmer's *fourth face of power* discussed in Chapter 1; Bulmer (1997), pp. 75–6.
35. The importance of state provision within the context of European integration was emphasised by interviewees from the SPD European policy groups, its Left-wing and the main body of the parliamentary party.
36. *State guarantees* give *Landesbanks* a higher credit rating, enabling them to borrow at a preferable rate.
37. This point was emphasised by an SPD politician specialising in European policy, May 2000, Berlin.
38. R. Ladrech, 'Europeanization and political parties: towards a framework for analysis' (2001), *Keele European Parties Research Unit Working Paper (7)*, www.keele.ac.uk
39. In this regard, German policy was supported by a European Court of Justice ruling in March 2001.
40. Pascal Lamy (EU trade Commissioner), *Harnessing globalization: do we need cosmopolitics* (speech at the LSE) (01/02/01), www.gobaldimension.net
41. OECD figures, cited in Oskar Lafontaine and Christa Müller, *Keine Angst vor Globalisierung* (Bonn: Dietz, 1998), p. 27.
42. World Trade Organisation (WTO), *International Trade Statistics 2000* (November 2000), www.wto.org, p. 8.
43. Thilo Sarrazin, *Der Euro: Chance oder Abenteuer?* (Bonn: Dietz, 1998), p. 48.
44. WTO (November 2000), p. 9.
45. 'Steadfast or stubborn', *The Economist* (11/04/01), www.economist.com
46. F. Scharpf, 'The German disease', *Prospect* (January 1998), www.prospect-magazine.co.uk
47. *The Financial Times* (19/03/01), www.globalarchive.ft.com
48. 'OECD attacks Germany on labour and aid policies', *The Financial Times* (07/03/01), www.ft.com
49. 'Berlin pledge to sell Telekom stake', *The Financial Times* (29/09/00), www.ft.com
50. *The Financial Times* (07/03/01), www.ft.com
51. Increasing US protection in a climate of lower growth and less buoyant equity markets was illustrated by the imposition of steel tariffs in 2002; J. Gray, 'Goodbye to globalization', *The Guardian* (27/02/01), www.guardian.co.uk
52. Lamy, LSE (01/02/01).
53. Lafontaine and Müller (1998), p. 340.

54. SPD Vorstand, *Leitantrag: Verantwortung für Europa* (30/04/01), www.spd.de
55. This point was emphasised in an interview with a top European official in the SPD European policy groups.
56. Interview with a top European official in the SPD European policy groups.
57. Gerhard Schröder, *Regierungserklärung von Bundeskanzler Schröder am 14. März 2003 vor dem Bundestag* (14/03/03), www.bundestag.de
58. A. Miskimmon and J. Sloam, 'A third way for social democratic foreign and security policy?' (2–4 September 2003), *Paper Presented to the UACES Annual Conference*, Newcastle.
59. Gerhard Schröder, 'Modernise or die', *The Guardian* (08/07/03), www. guardian.co.uk
60. SPD Vorstand, *Erneuerung und Zusammenhalt – Wir in Deutschland: Regierungsprogramm 2002–2006* (2002), www.spd.de, pp. 13, 15.

3   European Policy-making in the SPD

1. Interview with SPD official in Government department (formerly responsible for European policy); interview with official in the SPD European policy groups; interview with a top European official in the SPD European policy groups.
2. The changing nature of the institutional context is further illustrated by the very different operation of policy-making in office, where the party's EU policy groups have usually played a *reactive* role *vis-à-vis* Government policy, supplementing the roles of figures like Chancellor Schröder and Finance Minister Eichel.
3. The prime role of the party conference for the SPD is expressed by the party's organisational statute; SPD Vorstand, *Organisationsstatute* (June 2000), www.spd.de, Article 15 (1).
4. Jusos (SPD Young Socialist Group), *Neue Zeiten Denken* (Jusos federal congress, 2000), www.spd.de
5. Roth (1996), p. 8.
6. P. Lösche, 'Lose verkoppelte Anarchie: zur aktuellen Situation von Volksparteien am Beispiel der SPD' (October 1993), *Aus Politik und Geschichte* 43, p. 35.
7. J. Strasser, interview with *Der Spiegel 35* (1995), p. 30.
8. Sylvia notes a drop in the percentage of *blue-collar* SPD members from 55 per cent to 21 per cent and a rise in the proportion of *white-collar* workers and students from 21 per cent to 46 per cent between 1958 and 1982; S. Sylvia, 'Loosely coupled anarchy: the fragmentation of the left' in S. Padgett (ed.), *Parties and Party Systems in the New Germany* (Aldershot: Dartmouth, 1993), pp. 171–89, pp. 172–3.
9. A. Panebianco, from extracts in A. Ware, *Political Parties and Party Systems* (Oxford: Oxford University Press, 1997), p. 99.
10. Lösche (October 1993), p. 35.
11. See K. Lawson and P. Merkl (eds), *When Parties Fail* (Princeton University Press, 1988).
12. K. Blessing, 'Abschied von der Mitglieder Partei', in H. P. Bartels and M. Machnig (eds), *Der Rasende Tanker: Analysen und Konzepte zur Modernisierung der sozialdemokratischen Organisation* (Göttingen: Steidl, 2001), pp. 90–100.

13. U. Jun, 'Innerparteilichen Reformen im Vergleich: Der Versuch einer Modernisierung von SPD und Labour Party', in J. Borchert (ed.), *Das Sozialdemokratische Modell* (Opladen, Leske and Budrich, 1996), p. 220.
14. Björn Engholm, 'Foreword' to Karlheinz Blessing (ed.), *SPD 2000: die Modernisierung der SPD* (Bonn: SPD Vorstand, 1993), Bonn, p. 7.
15. Blessing (2001), pp. 91–2.
16. Blessing (2001), pp. 91–3.
17. M. Machnig, 'Vom Tanker zur Flotte', in H. P. Bartels and M. Machnig (eds), *Der Rasende Tanker: Analysen und Konzepte zur Modernisierung der sozialdemokratischen Organisation* (2001), pp. 101–17.
18. The defeat of Müntefering's measures in his home district of Western Westphalia in March 2001 illustrated the difficulty of effecting formal organisational change in the SPD.
19. W. Paterson, 'Political parties and the making of foreign policy' (1981), *Review of International Studies*, pp. 227–35, p. 232.
20. Ibid.
21. Cited in *Die Zeit* (17/02/99).
22. Maull (March 1999), p. 1.
23. M. Machnig, 'Die Kampa als SPD-Wahlkampfzentrale der Bundestagswahl '98' (1999), *Forschungsjournal Neue Soziale Bewegungen 3*, pp. 20–39.
24. The ineffectiveness of SPD opposition to Monetary Union appeared to be borne out by the failure of the campaign for the Baden-Württemberg regional elections, run on a strong anti-EMU message (Chapter 8).
25. J. Lindner, 'Europapolitik der SPD Bundestagsfraktion' (1996), *Perspektivends 4* (SPD *Bundestagsfraktion* newsletter), pp. 293–305, p. 295.
26. The party chairmen promoted from the *Länder* were Engholm (Schleswig-Holstein), Scharping (Rheinland-Pfalz) and Lafontaine (the Saarland).
27. F. Walter, *Vom Proletariat zum Neue Mitte* (Berlin: Alexander Fest, 2002), p. 251.
28. Interview with official in the SPD European policy groups.
29. Germany's row with the UK and France precipitated by Environment Minister, Jürgen Trittin (Green Party) over re-processing contracts for nuclear waste is a good example of the lack of co-ordination in the first few months in government.
30. The details here were clarified in interviews with the SPD European policy groups, 17 April 2001, Berlin.
31. P. Glotz, internet interview with the Jusos (02/03/99), www.jusos.de
32. Paterson (1981), p. 231.
33. Cole (March 2001), pp. 20–1.
34. Cole (March 2001), p. 21.
35. Cited in 'Schröder takes it easy', *The Financial Times* (27/04/00), www.ft.com
36. Bellers (1979), p. 94.
37. Heidi Simonis, cited in *Stern 2* (2000), p. 29.
38. Bulmer wrote similarly in 1983 that the 'low priority they [political parties in Germany] give to EC matters is consistent with the electorate's apparent apathy towards Community membership.' S. Bulmer, 'West German political parties and the European Community' (1983b), *Political Studies 31*, pp. 566–83, p. 578.
39. Lösche (October 1993), p. 40.

40. 'Gerhard Schröder fährt am Limit', *Die Welt* (26/07/00), www.welt
41. Ibid.
42. See 'Michael Steiner' (Charlemagne column), *The Economist* (13/10/01), p. 46.
43. Interview with SPD official in Government department (formerly responsible for European policy).
44. The SPD international section is headed by the International Secretary, an SPD official, directly subordinate to the General Secretary and the *federal leader of business*.
45. SPD, *Arbeitsplanung 2000/2001, Kommissionen: Europa* (June 2000), www.spd.de
46. Wieczorek-Zeul was a key figure in SPD European policy (European spokeswoman) through the 1990s up until she became the German Development Minister in 1998.
47. Heidemarie Wieczorek-Zeul, *Überlegungen zur Weiterentwicklung der Europäischen Union* [internal paper] (Koordinierungsstelle Europapolitik der SPD, 03/02/1995), p. 1.
48. Ibid.
49. Roth (1996), pp. 75–6.
50. Bulmer (1983b), p. 566.
51. Interview with of SPD member of the Bundestag.
52. Cited in SPD Vorstand, *Schwerpunktkommission protocol* (Archiv der sozialen Demokratie, 11/07/97).
53. Paterson (1981), p. 231.
54. Friedrich Ebert Stiftung, *Die Stiftung in Fakten und Zahlen* (2003), www.fes.de
55. Bellers (1979), p. 95.
56. Bellers (1979), p. 97.
57. The SPD's parliamentary Working Group for European Union Affairs was set up to complement the formation of the Bundestag Committee for European Union Affairs.
58. SPD Bundestagsfraktion, *Europapolitik der SPD-Bundestagsfraktion in der 14. Legislaturperiode, 1998–2002* (2003), www.spdfraktion.de
59. Ibid.
60. SPD Bundestagsfraktion, *Arbeitsgruppe Angelegenheiten der Europäischen Union* (2003), www.spdfraktion.de
61. 'Article 23 and 45, introduced by the Law amending the Basic Law of 21 December 1992' in J. Bila, U. Gehlen, H. Groos, B. Hasenjäger, *The Committee on the Affairs of the European Union of the German Bundestag* (Bonn: German Bundestag, July 1998), Annexure I.
62. 'Law on co-operation between the Federal Government and the German Bundestag in matters concerning the European Union of 12 March 1993' in Bila *et al.* (July 1998), Annexure II, Section 3.
63. Bellers (1979), p. 96.
64. Lindner (1996), p. 295.
65. Ibid.
66. Ibid.
67. The deputy chairs of the SPD *Fraktion* are key players in the parliamentary party's development of policy and strategy.
68. J. Raschke, 'Durch die Mitte an die Macht', *Der Spiegel* (06/11/95), pp. 64–70, p. 70.

69. Cited in *Der Spiegel* (04/03/91).
70. S. Padgett, 'The German Social Democratic Party: between old and new Left' in D. Bell and E. Shaw (eds), *Conflict and Cohesion in the West European Social Democratic Parties* (London: Pinter, 1994), pp. 10–30, p. 26.
71. SPD *Länder* have been especially keen to see a clearer division of competences after concern over the threat to German public provision posed by EU Competition Policy became clear in the late 1990s e.g. over the issues of regional *Landesbanks*.
72. Wolfgang Clement (SPD), then Minister-President of North Rhine-Westphalia, cited in *Financial Times Deutschland* (05/03/01), www.ftd.de
73. The role of the SPD Control Commission is to check that the activities of the party agree with the organisational statutes.
74. SPD Vorstand, *Organisationsstatute*, www.spd.de
75. Lösche (October 1993), p. 35.
76. Lösche (October 1993), p. 42.

4 Policy-making in a Wider Context

1. The SPD has been committed to representing a relatively wide range of interests under the broad banner of the *Volkspartei* (as stipulated by Article 21 of the *Basic Law*) in comparison to parties in other countries such as the UK.
2. Maull (March 1999).
3. See R. Dahl, *Pluralist Democracy in the United States: conflict and consent* (Chicago: Rand McNally, 1967).
4. Klaus Kinkel (FDP), *Plenarprotokoll 13/210* (Bonn: Deutscher Bundestag, 11/12/97), p. 19110.
5. Interviews with leading figures in the *Bundestag* European and Foreign Affairs Committees.
6. Cited in *Frankfurter Allgemeine Zeitung* (23/08/00).
7. 'Up for Grabs: Who is in Charge of Europe in the German Government', *Frankfurter Allgemeine Zeitung* (18/06/01), www.faz.com
8. After 1998, the post of European Minister in the Foreign Office was filled by three successive SPD politicians: Günter Verheugen, Christoph Zöpel and Hans-Martin Bury.
9. 'Up for grabs: who is in charge of Europe in the German Government', *Frankfurter Allgemeine Zeitung* (18/06/01), www.faz.com
10. Text of report by German news agency DPP; *BBC Monitoring service* (03/03/01), www.bbc.co.uk
11. C. Jeffery and W. Paterson, 'Germany and European integration: a shifting of tectonic plates', in H. Kitschelt and W. Streeck (eds), *Germany: beyond the stable state* (London: Frank Cass, 2004), pp. 59–75, p. 71.
12. Die Grünen Vorstand, *Bündnis 90/Die Grünen: 1998–2002. Vier Jahren für einen politischen Neuanfang* (1998), www.gruene.de
13. For example, state secretaries Günter Pleuger and Wolfgang Ischinger in the Foreign Office during the first term of the Red–Green Government, had taken the diplomatic route to office.
14. Article 79 (2) of the Basic Law; *Grundgesetz für die Bundesrepublik Deutschland* (Baden-Baden, nomos, 1999), p. 116.

15. Article 23 (2) and (3); *Grundgesetz für die Bundesrepublik Deutschland* (1999), p. 39.
16. Article 23 (4), *Grundgesetz für die Bundesrepublik Deutschland* (1999), pp. 39–40.
17. The Committee was established under the new Article 45 with reference to Article 23; *Grundgesetz für die Bundesrepublik Deutschland* (1999), p. 68.
18. Representatives from the Government (e.g. Foreign Minister Kinkel) and EU institutions (e.g. Commissioner for Employment and Social Affairs, Padraig Flynn) were regularly consulted by the European Affairs Committee.
19. Article 23 (5); *Grundgesetz für die Bundesrepublik Deutschland* (1999), pp. 40–1.
20. *Länder* participation in EU negotiations was a further source of information for the SPD when in opposition. The party, for instance, had a representative from the Rhineland-Palatinate government at the 1996–97 IGC.
21. See C. Jeffery, 'A giant with feet of clay? United Germany in the European Union', *Institute for German Studies Discussion Paper 95/6* (Birmingham: University of Birmingham, December 1995), pp. 28–32.
22. Article 79 (3) in combination with Article 20 further stated that the democratic principle defined in Article 38 cannot be violated even through amendments to the Basic Law, *Grundgesetz für die Bundesrepublik Deutschland* (1999), pp. 35–6, pp. 115–7.
23. Deutsche Bundesbank, *Opening Statement made by the President of the Deutsche Bundesbank, Prof. Dr. Hans Tietmeyer, before the Finance Committee and the Committee for European Union Affairs of the German Bundestag* (03/04/1998), www.bundesbank.de, pp. 2–3.
24. See D. Marsh, *The Bundesbank: the Bank that Rules Europe* (London, Mandarin, 1993).
25. Fritz Scharpf has argued that the federal system encourages negotiations between the Federal Government and the *Länder* that often result in *horse-trading* (a sub-optimal solution); F. Scharpf, 'The joint-decision trap: lessons from German federalism and European integration' (1988), *Public Administration 66*, pp. 239–78.
26. *Der Spiegel* (24/07/95), p. 23.
27. Ibid.
28. Walter (2002), pp. 251–2.
29. European Commission, *Eurobarometer 40* (December 1993), p. 59.
30. P. Lösche, 'Die SPD nach Mannheim: Stukturprobleme und aktuelle Entwicklungen' (February 1996), *Aus Politik und Geschichte 6*, pp. 20–8, p. 27.
31. See J. Sloam, 'Germany: President of the EU, keeper of the peace', *Institute for German Studies Working Paper 99/14* (Birmingham: University of Birmingham, 1999).
32. Ibid.
33. Labour interests are also represented in the SPD's Working Group for Workers' Affairs ('Arbeitsgemeinschaft für Arbeitnehmerfragen').
34. IG Metall, *Europapolitische Forderungen der IG Metall* (Frankfurt am Main: IG Metall Vorstand, 26–27 January 1999), p. 5.
35. Lindner (1996), p. 303.
36. *Frankfurter Rundschau* (27/05/97).
37. Scharping was party chairman, chair of the *Bundestagsfraktion* and, then, German Defence Minister between 1993 and 2002.

38. PES, *The PES in the EU Institutions* (June 2001), www.eurosocialists.org
39. Presseservice der SPD, *Gemeinsame Erklärung des Ersten Sekretärs der Sozialist Partei Frankreichs, Lionel Jospin, und der SPD Parteivorsitzender Oskar Lafontaine* (Bonn: 28/05/97), no. 215/97.
40. Jeffery and Paterson (2004), pp. 71–2.

5 The Next Generation

1. 'Der Advokat', *Die Zeit*, No. 45, 2000, www.zeit.de
2. Helmut Schmidt, *Globalisierung* (Berlin: Siedler, 1999), pp. 49–50.
3. On historical memory and German policy in the early 1990s, see T. Banchoff, 'German policy towards the European Union: the effects of historical memory' (April 1997), *German Politics 6 (1)*, pp. 60–76.
4. Interview with top European official in the SPD European policy groups.
5. Chancellor Kohl, speaking in the German Bundestag (02/12/92); cited in Banchoff (April 1997), p. 65.
6. SPD Vorstand, *Wahlkampf 1990: Argumente und Perspektive* (Bonn: October 1990).
7. K. Korte, 'Solutions for the decision dilemma: political styles of Germany's chancellors' (April 2000), *German Politics 9 (1)*, pp. 1–22, p. 2.
8. Chancellor Kohl, opening a *Bundestag* debate on Europe, cited in 'Kohl tries to allay fears about Germany', *The Financial Times* (13/12/96).
9. Gerhard Schröder, interview with *The Financial Times* (17/03/97).
10. E. Noelle-Neumann (ed.), *Allensbacher Jahrbuch der Demoskopie 10, 1993–7*, (Munich: Saur, 1997), p. 1155.
11. Interview with SPD MEP, 11 March 2000, Bonn.
12. See Walter (2002), pp. 181–213.
13. Walter (2002), p. 193.
14. Paterson (April 2000), p. 38.
15. Chancellor Schröder, *Financial Times* (10/11/00), www.ft.com
16. Paterson (April 2000), p. 33.
17. *Der Spiegel* (28/03/94), p. 52.
18. Data taken from the European Audit Office and presented in 'Geld Zurück', *Der Spiegel* (28/03/94), p. 55.
19. Die SPD im Deutschen Bundestag, *Forderungen an die deutsche EG-Ratspräsidentschaft* (Bonn: 11/01/88).
20. *Der Spiegel* (28/03/94), p. 52.
21. The *Republikaner* was Germany's most successful Far Right party at the time.
22. Private letter from Detlev Samland MEP to Oskar Lafontaine (then, Minister-President of the Saarland) (Archiv der Sozialdemokratie, 13/05/94).
23. Interview with SPD MEP.
24. Interview with SPD official in Government department (formerly responsible for European policy).
25. Ibid.
26. Theo Waigel, interview with *Bild am Sonntag* (26/07/97), www.bild.de
27. Chancellor Schroeder, interview with *The Financial Times* (04/12/98), www.ft.com
28. The co-financing plan meant a partial re-nationalisation of CAP by which Member States would part-finance EU agricultural subsidies.

29. *Stern 9* (1999).
30. Ibid.
31. The German EU presidency was beset by the weak beginning of the Euro in the currency markets, the resignation of the Commission, and the Kosovo conflict.
32. SPD Vorstand, *Leitantrag: Verantwortung für Europa* (30/04/01), www.spd.de
33. See SPD Vorstand, *Jahrbuch der SPD 1991–2* (Foreign, European and Security Policy – Die SPD im Deutschen Bundestag), (Bonn: 1992), pp. 127–8.
34. Cited in *Der Spiegel* (27/05/91), p. 32.
35. Interview with Member of *Bundestag* Foreign Affairs Committee, March 2000, Berlin.
36. Björn Engholm, Interview with *Der Spiegel* (25/03/91), p. 24.
37. SPD, *Reformen für Deutschland – Regierungsprogramm 1994–1998* (Bonn: SPD Vorstand, 1994), p. 34.
38. See Jeffery and Paterson (2004), pp. 71–2.
39. Cited in *Die Süddeutsche Zeitung* (12/05/99).
40. SPD Vorstand, *Erneuerung und Zusammenhalt – Wir in Deutschland: Regierungsprogramm 2002–2006* (2002), www.spd.de, p. 12.
41. SPD and Bündnis 90/Die Grünen, *Erneuerung – Gerechtigkeit – Nachaltigkeit* (2002), www.spd.de
42. Cited in *Die Welt* (12/09/02), www.welt.de
43. SPD, *Europamanifest der SPD* (November 2003), www.spd.de, p. 6.
44. 'Mit Gewehr, aber ohne Kompass', *Die Zeit 38* (2002), www.zeit.de
45. Cited in Noelle-Neumann, 'Europe: ready or not, here it comes', *Frankfurter Allgemeine Zeitung* (18/05/01), www.faz.com
46. Chancellor Schröder, cited in 'Foreign policy: getting over the Iraq episode', *The Financial Times* (25/11/03).

6   Winning Elections and Strategic Change

1. Hay (1995), p. 190.
2. See Lösche (October 1993).
3. H. Kitschelt, *The Transformation of European Social Democracy* (Cambridge: Cambridge University Press, 1994), p. 39.
4. Ibid.
5. S. Padgett and W. Paterson, 'The rise and fall of the West German Left' (March–April, 1991), *New Left Review 186*, pp. 46–77, p. 57.
6. Lösche (October 1993), p. 36.
7. Rudolf Scharping, cited in *Der Spiegel* (04/10/93), p. 21.
8. Interview with SPD MEP, March, Bonn.
9. See A. Downs, *An Economic Theory of Democracy* (New York: Harper & Row, 1957).
10. Machnig (August 2002), www.spd.de
11. Ibid.
12. M. Machnig, *On the Way to a Network Party* (November 2000), www.spd.de
13. H. Schwarz, 'Europe's central power' (Spring 2000), *Internationale Politik (1)* (Transatlantic Edition), pp. 45–50, p. 46.

14. SPD General Secretary, Franz Müntefering has given his forthright support to the idea of referenda – see, for example, 'Wie dumm ist das Volk', *Der Spiegel* (05/04/2001), www.spiegel.de
15. See Bartels and Machnig (2001), pp. 9–13.
16. Korte (April 2000), p. 15.
17. J. Blondel; cited in G. Braunthal, *The West German Social Democrats, 1969–1982: profile of a party in power* (Bolder: Westview, 1982), p. 61.
18. Bodo Hombach, *The Politics of the New Centre* (Oxford: Blackwell, 2000), pp. xxxi–xxxii.
19. Olaf Scholz, *Gerechtigkeit und Solidarische Mitte im 21. Jahrhundert* (2003), www.spd.de, p. 11.
20. T. Meyer, 'Basic values, communication and party organisation' in R. Cuperus and J. Kandel (eds), *European Social Democracy: transformation in progress* (Amsterdam: Wiardi Beckman Stichting/Friedrich Ebert Stiftung, 1998), pp. 257–62, p. 259.
21. Franz Müntefering, 'Die Kraft der Gemeinschaft', *Vorwärts* (09/2000), www.vorwaerts.de
22. T. Meyer, 'From Godesberg to the *Neue Mitte*: the new social democracy in Germany' in G. Kelly (ed.), *The New European Left* (London: Fabian Society, 1999).
23. Opposition to Monetary Union was largely a consequence of the loss of the Deutschmark and the notion that the convergence criteria were forcing government austerity measures.
24. Noelle-Neumann, 'Europe: ready or not, here it comes', *Frankfurter Allgemeine Zeitung* (18/05/01), www.faz.com
25. SPD Bundestagsfraktion, *Vermerk für Heidemarie Wieczorek-Zeul MdB – Europapolitische Themen* (Bonn: Koordinierungsstelle für Europafragen, 14/07/93), p. 1.
26. Ibid.
27. SPD Bundestagsfraktion (14/07/93), pp. 1–2.
28. This was pointed out in interviews with SPD MEPs: February 2000, Soest; February 2000, Cologne.
29. Walter (2002), p. 223.
30. For a review of this campaign see N. Reinhardt, 'A turning point in the German EMU debate: the Baden-Württemberg regional election of March 1996' (April 1997), *German Politics 6 (1)*, pp. 77–99.
31. Gerhard Schröder, 'Postscript', Hombach (2000), pp. 151–6, p. 155.
32. See T. Blair and G. Schröder, 'Europe: the third way/die Neue Mitte' in Hombach (2000), pp. 157–77.
33. See Paterson and Sloam (2004).
34. Bartels *et al.*, 'Heute für Reformen Kämpfen: Was die gewonnene Bundestagswahl für die nächste sozialdemokratische Generation bedeutet' (September 2002), *Berliner Republik*, www.b-republik.de
35. Gerhard Schröder, *Mut zur Wahrheit – Wille zum Wandel* (speech of the SPD chairman to the party confernce) (Bochum, 17/11/03), www.spd.de
36. Detlev Samland, 'So weit weg, so wichtig' (2000), *Der Berliner Republik (1)*, pp. 6–8, p. 7.
37. Interview with a leading politician in the SPD's European policy community.

38. 'Schröder keeps friends at home but loses others further afield', *Financial Times* (13/09/00), www.ft.com
39. Chancellor Schröder, *Plenarprotokoll 14/144* (Drucksache, 14/3723: 19/01/01), www.bundestag.de
40. Interview with a top European official in the SPD European policy groups.
41. SPD Vorstand, *Erneuerung und Zusammenhalt – Wir in Deutschland: Regierungsprogramm 2002–2006* (July 2002), www.spd.de, pp. 12–18.
42. SPD Vorstand, *Leitantrag: Verantwortung für Europa* (30/04/01), www.spd.de
43. SPD, *400 Engagierte Denken sich 5000 Wahlkampf-Ideen aus* (November 2003), www.eurokampa.de
44. ZDF, 'Wer interessiert für Europa', *Politbarometer* (broadcast) (24/05/04), www.zdf.de
45. Ibid.

7 A Change of Heart

1. SPD Vorstand, *Erneuerung und Zusammenhalt – Wir in Deutschland: Regierungsprogramm 2002–2006* (July 2002), www.spd.de
2. SPD Vorstand, *Leitantrag: Verantwortung für Europa* (30/04/01), www.spd.de
3. See Ware (1996), p. 320.
4. Grundwertekommission beim SPD Parteivorstand, *Dritte Wege – Neue Mitte: sozialdemokratischer Markierungen für Reformpolitik im Zeitalter Globalisierung* (Berlin: SPD Vorstand, September 1999), p. 8.
5. Hombach (2000), p. xxxii.
6. Padgett and Paterson (March–April 1991), p. 60.
7. Walter (2002), p. 221.
8. SPD, *Basic Policy Programme of the Social Democratic Party of Germany* (20/12/89), www.spd.de, Section I.
9. Padgett and Paterson (March–April 1991), p. 56.
10. In other words, the party establishment prioritised low inflation and limited public spending, as advocated by the *Bundesbank*.
11. Cited in Sylvia (1993), p. 106.
12. Cited in SPD Vorstand, *Wahlkampf '90: Argumente und Perspektive* (Bonn: October 1990), p. 18.
13. Noelle-Neumann (1997), p. 868.
14. R. Inglehart, 'From class-based to value-based politics'; Mair (1990), pp. 266–84, p. 277.
15. Unger *et al.* (1998), p. 170.
16. T. Blair, 'Third way, phase two' (March 2000), *Prospect*, www.prospect-magazine.co.uk
17. Hombach (2000), p. xxxv.
18. 'Schröder shifts his party to Blair's way of thinking', *The Guardian* (20/10/00), www.guardian.co.uk
19. Hombach (28/04/99).
20. The *Youngsters* represent a group of relatively young SPD members of the *Bundestag* – also known as the 'Netwerk' group – who contributed the 'Youngster Papier' to the 'Grundsatzdebatte' (debate over basic principles) launched in 2000.

21. Hans-Martin Bury, the (then) 34 year old Minister of State in the Chancellor's Office, cited in 'Keine Gerechtigkeitsmaschine' (1999), *Vorwärts (11)*, www.vorwaerts.de

22. In the German economy, large institutional investors have maintained significant holdings in other German companies.

23. SPD Vorstand, *Leitantrag: Verantwortung für Europa* (30/04/01), www.spd.de

24. Chancellor Schröder, *Regierungserklärung von Bundeskanzler Schröder am 14. März 2003 vor dem Deutschen Bundestag* (Deutscher Bundestag, 14/03/03), www.bundestag.de, pp. 2, 12, 14.

25. SPD Vorstand, *Erneuerung und Zusammenhalt – Wir in Deutschland: Regierungsprogramm 2002–2006* (July 2002), www.spd.de

26. Wolfgang Clement, *Rede des stellvertretenden SPD-Parteivorsitzenden, Bundesminister Wolfgang Clement, auf dem Parteitag der Sozialdemokratischen Partei Deutschlands in Bochum am 17. November 2003* (SPD Vorstand, 17/11/03), www.spd.de, p. 3. In real terms, €7 billion were released for a 'communal investment programme' and €8 billion for private house building; see Gerhard Schröder (14/03/03), www.spd.de

27. Opposition to *Agenda 2010* included an attempt by the Left and workers' wings of the party to gather enough signatures of SPD members to force a vote at the 2003 party conference on a new platform for 'growth' and 'employment'. These efforts nevertheless collapsed, when it was realised that the 67,000 necessary signatures would not be collected.

28. Olaf Scholz (16/07/03), www.spd.de

29. Scholz (16/07/03), www.spd.de, pp. 5, 7.

30. See Sigmar Gabriel, *Die Akkus nicht entladen und den Kompass nicht wegwerfen* (23/08/03), www.spd.de; and, Heidemarie Wieczorek-Zeul, *Was ist das Ziel der Debatte?* (09/09/03), www.spd.de

31. SPD, *Basic Policy Programme of the Social Democratic Party of Germany* (20/12/89), www.spd.de, Section II (2).

32. Oskar Lafontaine, *Speech to the Mannheim party conference* (Bonn: Presseservice der SPD, November 1995).

33. SPD, *Basic Policy Programme of the Social Democratic Party of Germany* (20/12/89), www.spd.de

34. SPD, *Der Neue Weg: ökologisch, sozial, wirtschaftlich stark – Regierungsprogramm, 1990–1994* (Bonn: SPD Vorstand, 1990), p. 22.

35. SPD, *Reformen für Deutschland – Regierungsprogramm 1994–1998* (Bonn: SPD Vorstand, 1994), pp. 72–4.

36. Lafontaine (November 1995).

37. Lafontaine and Müller (1998), p. 108.

38. Interview with leading Left-wing SPD member of the *Bundestag*.

39. Lafontaine and Müller (1998), pp. 12, 19.

40. SPD Vorstand, *Arbeit, Innovation und Gerechtigkeit – Regierungsprogramm 1998–2002* (1998), www.spd.de, pp. 43–4.

41. Klaus Hänsch, cited in Michael Roth (1996), p. 3.

42. 'SPD urges financial curbs', *The Financial Times* (03/12/97), www.ft.com

43. Oskar Lafontaine, 'Globalization and international co-operation' and Gerhard Schröder, 'German economic policy from a European and global perspective' in D. Dettke (ed.), *The Challenge of Globalization for Germany's Social Democracy* (Oxford: Berghan, 1998), pp. 1–7, pp. 11–17.

44. Despite reasonable levels of support in the party for the need to alter the ECB remit to allow for a more growth-oriented policy, Lafontaine's position was inopportune given the apparent fragility of the newly launched Euro in the currency markets.
45. European Council, *Cologne European Council Presidency Conclusions* (Press Release No. 150/9, 04/06/99), www.eu-praesidentschaft.com
46. Blair and Schröder (2000), pp. 157–77, pp. 163–3, pp. 176–7.
47. Blair and Schröder (2000), p. 164.
48. Blair and Schröder (2000), pp. 173–5.
49. Interview with a leading politician in the SPD's European policy community.
50. SPD Vorstand, *Leitantrag: Verantwortung für Europa* (30/04/01), www.spd.de
51. Interview with a top European official in the SPD European policy groups.
52. See, for example, Gerhard Schröder's speech to the 5th PES Congress (07/05/01), www.pes-congress.de
53. SPD Vorstand, *Leitantrag: Verantwortung für Europa* (30/04/01), www.spd.de

8 EMU in Opposition: Consensus, Conflict and Conditionality

1. European Commission, *From Rome to Maastricht: a brief history of EMU* (August 2000), www.europa.eu.int
2. Anderson (1999), p. 6.
3. Dyson and Featherstone (1999), p. 307.
4. President Mitterrand cited in 'Warum das neue Geld die deutsch-französischen Verhältnisse schon seit zehn Jahren prägt', *Die Zeit* (07/05/98), www.zeit.de
5. Dyson and Featherstone (1999), pp. 256–452.
6. See Dyson and Featherstone (1999), pp. 289–93.
7. See Committee of the Study of Economic and Monetary Union, *Report on Economic and Monetary Union in the European Community* (Luxembourg: European Commission, 1989).
8. Dyson and Featherstone (1999), p. 306.
9. European Commission, *Treaty Establishing the European Community* (TEC) (as of October 2001), www.europa.eu.int, Articles 107 and 108 (ex Articles 106 and 107).
10. Dinan (1999), pp. 140–1.
11. Although the Maastricht Treaty eventually included four criteria, very similar to those laid down by the *Bundesbank* – an inflation rate of no more than 1.5 per cent above the average of the three lowest rates in the Union; a budgetary deficit of 3 per cent or less of GDP and a debt ratio of 60 per cent or less; the observance of ERM rates of currency parity; and, an interest rate not more than 2 per cent above that of the three lowest rates – Article 104 (ex Article 104c) of the TEC nevertheless defined the deficit and debt criteria only as 'reference values' and stated that countries need merely be 'approaching the reference value at a satisfactory pace'; European Commission ('TEC') (October 2001), Article 121 (ex Article 109j), Article 104 (ex Article 104c).
12. European Commission, *White Paper on growth, competitiveness, and employment: The challenges and ways forward into the 21st century* (05/12/93), www.europa.eu.int

13. Tensions between Kohl and Pöhl contributed to the latter's resignation in 1991, four years before the end of his full term.
14. Dyson and Featherstone (1999), p. 14.
15. Noelle-Neumann (1997), p. 1177.
16. IG Metall (26–7 January 1999), p. 5.
17. Interview with a SPD MEP.
18. See *Das Bild* (10/12/91).
19. European Commission, *Eurobarometer 40* (December 1993), pp. 55, 59.
20. Interview with SPD official in Government department (formerly responsible for European policy).
21. SPD (Arbeitsgruppe Europäische Gemeinschaft – internal paper), *Positionspapier* (Archiv der Sozialdemokratie, September 1990).
22. Ibid.
23. Die SPD im Deutschen *Bundestag, Europapolitik – Positionen und Initiativen der SPD Bundesfraktion* (Ausgabe 1/92) (Bonn: SPD Bundestagsfraktion: 31/01/92), p. 5.
24. SPD (internal paper), *Vermerk: Maastricht Beschlüße, Risiken EWU und Verhältnis EWU–EPU* (Archiv der Sozialdemokratie, for presentation to the sitting of the SPD Presidium on 9 March 1992), p. 3.
25. SPD (Archiv der Sozialdemokratie, September 1990).
26. Ibid; see also SPD, *Basic Policy Programme of the Social Democratic Party of Germany* (20/12/89), www.spd.de
27. Die SPD im Deutschen Bundestag (31/01/92), p. 7.
28. Die SPD im Deutschen Bundestag (31/01/92), p. 8.
29. Article 23 (2), (3), Grundgesetz für die Bundesrepublik Deutschland (1999), p. 39.
30. Oskar Lafontaine, interview with *Die Berliner Zeitung* (06/03/92).
31. Sozialdemokratischer Pressedienst (Parlemantarisch-Politischer Pressedienst), *Bulletin No. 46* (Bonn: SPD Vorstand, 06/03/92), pp. 1, 3.
32. Interview with leading Left-wing SPD member of the *Bundestag*.
33. SPD (09/03/92), p. 4.
34. Presseservice der SPD, *Bulletin No. 811/92* (Bonn: SPD Vorstand, 02/11/92).
35. Norbert Wieczorek MdB, 'Die Währungsunion als Mittel zur Verbesserung der internationalen Währungsordnung' in Christa Randzio-Plath (ed.), *Wenn der Euro kommt* (1994), pp. 123–35, p. 125.
36. Deutscher Bundestag, *Antrag der Fraktion der SPD* (Bonn: Drucksache, 12/3366, 07/10/92).
37. Deutscher Bundestag, *Entschließungsantrag der CDU/CSU, SPD, FDP zu dem Gesetzentwurf der Bundesregierung* (Bonn: Drucksache, 12/3905, 02/12/92), p. 2.
38. Dinan (1999), p. 465.
39. SPD, *Reformen für Deutschland – Regierungsprogramm 1994–1998* (Bonn: SPD Vorstand, 1994), p. 33.
40. SPD Bundestagsfraktion, *Forderungen zur Zukunft der Europapolitik der Bundesregierung*, (Bonn: Deutscher Bundestag – Drucksache, 12/6106, 10/11/93), p. 2.
41. Rudolf Scharping, interview with *Der Spiegel* (28/06/93), p. 24.
42. DGB deputy chair, Ursula Engelen-Kefer, cited in 'Bundestag, Europa, Zusammenfassung', *Vorwärts* (07/12/95).

242 *Notes*

43. The Schäuble-Lamers paper was co-authored by Wolfgang Schäuble, head of the CDU *Bundestagsfraktion*, and Karl Lamers, CDU European policy spokesman.
44. The Federal Government distanced itself from the Schäuble-Lamers paper after complaints from its EU partners.
45. Chancellor Kohl cited in 'Kohl links his political fate to a united Europe', *The Financial Times* (23/11/96).
46. Roth (1996), p. 53.
47. Roth (1996), p. 74.
48. 'SPD accused on monetary union stance', *The Financial Times* (31/10/95)
49. Ibid.
50. Reinhardt (April 1997), p. 82.
51. See Roth (1996), p. 54.
52. Ibid.
53. Gerhard Schröder, interview with Der Spiegel (25/12/95), p. 25.
54. Cited in *Presseservice der SPD* (12/12/95).
55. Interview with SPD MEP.
56. Roth (1996), pp. 54–5.
57. Norbert Wieczorek, *Plenarprotokoll 13/144* (Bonn: Deutscher Bundestag, 22/06/95), p. 3559.
58. Wieczorek, *Plenarprotokoll 13/144* (22/06/95), p. 3560.
59. Helmut Schmidt, 'Der zweite Anlauf, die letzte Chance', *Die Zeit* (05/04/96).
60. Gerhard Schröder, cited in *Der Spiegel*, 25/12/95, p. 25.
61. Monika Wulff-Mathies, cited in 'Die Genossen auf Wahlfang', *Focus* (06/11/95), www.focus.de
62. Heidi Simonis, cited in Bonn *General Anzeiger* (01/11/95).
63. Wieczorek, *Plenarprotokoll 13/144* (22/06/95), pp. 3559–60.
64. Detlev von Larcher, cited in 'Die Genossen auf Wahlfang', *Focus* (06/11/95), www.focus.de
65. Cited in *The Financial Times* (31/10/95).
66. 'Die Genossen auf Wahlfang', *Focus* (06/11/95), www.focus.de
67. Ibid.
68. Cited in Sarrazin (1998), p. 88.
69. Gerhard Schröder, cited in Roth (1996), p. 54.
70. Figures cited in Anderson (1999), p. 47.
71. Ibid.
72. Reinhardt (April 1997), p. 83.
73. Deutscher Bundestag, *Große Anfrage der SPD zur Wirtschafts- und Währungsunion* (Bonn: Drucksache, 13/2638, 05/10/95).
74. Lösche (February 1996), p. 26.
75. Roth (1996), p. 54.
76. Cited in Roth (1996), p. 57.
77. Cited in *Handelsblatt* (16/11/95).
78. SPD, 'Europapolitische Anträge' (Mannheim Party conference) (Bonn: SPD Vorstand, 16/11/95), p. 6.
79. Cited in *Handelsblatt* (16/11/95).
80. Cited in Reinhardt (April 1997), pp. 86–7.

81. Reinhardt (April 1997), p. 77.
82. SPD Vorstand, *Jahrbuch der SPD, 1995–6* (Schwerpunktkommission – Europapolitik) (Bonn: 1996), p. 105.

9 Governing the Euro-Zone

1. See 'Triumph of the little man', *The Financial Times* (18/11/95).
2. Oskar Lafontaine, interview with *Die Woche* (13/6/97).
3. Ibid.
4. See Presseservice der SPD (600/95), *Forderungen an den EU-Gipfel und die Konferenz zur Überprüfung des Maastricht-Vertrages* (15/12/95).
5. SPD Vorstand, *Jahrbuch der SPD, 1995–6* (Schwerpunktkommission – Europapolitik) (1996), p. 105.
6. SPD Vorstand, *Jahrbuch der SPD, 1995–6* (SPD Bundestagsfraktion: Europa auf eine solide Grundlage zu stellen) (1996), p. 223; Presseservice der SPD (uncorrected protocol), *Rede des SPD Fraktionsvorsitzenden Rudolf Scharping in der Europa-Debatte der Deutschen Bundestag an 12. Dezember 1996* (12/12/96), p. 2.
7. Cited in 'SPD falls in behind Kohl to support single currency', *The Financial Times* (23/12/96).
8. Cited in 'EMU requires political union says Tietmeyer', *The Financial Times* (04/11/95).
9. Ibid.
10. DGB, *Bericht zur gewerkschafts- und gesellschafts politische Lage* (March 1998), www.dgb.de, p. 9.
11. See Presseservice der SPD (408/94), *Gemeinsame Erklärung des Vorsitzenden der SPD, Rudolf Scharping, und des Ersten Sekretärs der Sozialistischen Partei Frankreichs, Michel Rocard* (Bonn: 06/06/94).
12. Deutscher Bundestag, *Antrag der Fraktion der SPD* (Bonn: Drucksache, 13/4002, 07/03/96), p. 2.
13. Ibid.
14. Deutscher Bundestag, *Antrag der Fraktion der SPD* (07/03/96), p. 3.
15. Interview with SPD official in Government department (formerly responsible for European policy).
16. Deutscher Bundestag, *Antrag der Fraktion der SPD* (07/03/96), p. 3.
17. Rudolf Scharping, Oskar Lafontaine and Jürgen Meyer, 'Keine Ratifizierung ohne aktive Beschäftigungspolitik', *Die Woche im Parlament* (13/12/96).
18. Oskar Lafontaine, *EU und NATO sind Eckpfeiler für friedliche Zukunft Europas* (Bonn: Presseservice der SPD 502/96, 06/11/96).
19. European Commission, *Treaty of Amsterdam amending the Treaty on European Union, the Treaties establishing the European Communities and certain Related Acts*, www.europa.eu.int, Articles 1 and 136–45.
20. *Frankfurter Rundschau* (27/05/96).
21. Foreign Minister Kinkel, cited in 'Germans drop objections to jobs chapter in EU treaty', *The Financial Times* (12/06/97).
22. TEC, www.europa.eu.int, Article 140,
23. Heidemarie Wieczorek-Zeul, letter to Foreign Secretary Kinkel (Archiv der Sozialdemokratie, 29/05/97).
24. *Frankfurter Allgemeine Zeitung* (15/09/97).

25. Hans Tietmeyer, cited in 'Bundestag, Europa, Zusammenfassung', *Vorwärts* (December 1995).

25. Hans Tietmeyer, cited in 'Bundestag, Europa, Zusammenfassung', *Vorwärts* (December 1995).
26. European Commission, *The Euro: Explanatory Notes* (February 1998), www.europa.eu.int

25. Hans Tietmeyer, cited in 'Bundestag, Europa, Zusammenfassung', *Vorwärts* (December 1995).
26. European Commission, *The Euro: Explanatory Notes* (February 1998), www.europa.eu.int
27. EMU was widely blamed for social security cuts and austerity measures in France, which had led to the rioting of French workers in Paris (December 1995).
28. ERM II consisted of exchange rate bands of 15 per cent.
29. Presseservice der SPD 515/95, *Wir brauchen eine Wirtschafts- und Währungsunion* (Bonn: 31/10/95).
30. SPD Vorstand, *Jahrbuch der SPD, 1995–6* (SPD Bundesfraktion: Europa auf eine solide Grundlage zu stellen) (1996), p. 224.
31. Deutscher Bundestag, *Antrag der Fraktion der SPD* (proposals for the European Council in Dublin on 13–14 December 1996 for the revision of the Maastricht Treaty) (Bonn: Drucksache, 13/6495, 11/12/96), p. 7.
32. The political interpretation of the convergence criteria was stated in Article 104 of the TEC (Chapter 8).
33. Verheugen, cited in 'SPD falls in behind Kohl to support single currency', *The Financial Times* (23/12/96).
34. Heidemarie Wieczorek-Zeul, *Plenarprotokoll 13/175* (Bonn: Deutscher Bundestag, 15/05/97), p. 15703.
35. Gerhard Schröder, interview with *The Financial Times* (17/03/97).
36. The *monetarist* view saw EMU itself as the best way of 'forcing ... adjustments', Sarrazin (1998), p. 78.
37. Gerhard Schröder, interview with *Focus* (06/11/95), www.focus.de
38. Ibid.
39. Cited in 'Kohl's calm ruffled by euro-sceptic noises', *The Financial Times* (09/09/97), www.ft.com
40. Chancellor Kohl, *Plenarprotokoll 13/185* (Bonn: Deutscher Bundestag, 27/06/97), p. 16736.
41. Doubts over the timetable for Monetary Union were shared to a large extent not only by the *Bundesbank*, but also by respected economists such as Herbert Hax, chair of the government's 'council of economic advisors'.
42. In his attempt to sell off German gold reserves, Finance Minister Waigel lost out in a fierce battle with the *Bundesbank*.
43. Wieczorek-Zeul (15/05/97), p. 15703.
44. Scharping, *Plenarprotokoll 13/175* (Bonn: Deutscher Bundestag, 15/05/97), p. 15717.
45. SPD *Vorstand, Reformen für Europa: Zwischenbericht der Schwerpunktkommission Europapolitk* (26/05/97), www.spd.de
46. Ibid.
47. Lafontaine and Müller (1998), pp. 95–7.
48. SPD *Vorstand* (26/05/97), www.spd.de
49. Heidemarie Wieczorek-Zeul, *Sozialdemokratische Politik in Europa* (21/10/97), www.spd.de
50. SPD, *Arbeit, Innovation und Gerechtigkeit – Regierungsprogramm 1998–2002* (1998), www.spd.de
51. Cited in 'SPD calls for EMU criteria on jobs', *The Financial Times* (23/09/97), www.ft.com

52. J. Goetschy, *The European Employment Strategy: Genesis and Development*, (European Commission, July 1999), www.europa.eu.int; see also European Commission, *Proposals of Employment Guidelines for Member States Employment Policies for 1998* (Brussels: 1997).

53. Goetschy (July 1999), www.europa.eu.int

54. Heidemarie Wieczorek-Zeul, *Plenarprotokoll 13/203* (Bonn: Deutscher Bundestag, 13/11/97), p. 18279. The unions in Germany also welcomed the commitment to national action plans, but regretted the lack of 'quantitative employment policy goals' and formalised 'consultations between employers and workers'; DGB, (March 1998), www.dgb.de, pp. 7–8.

55. 'Bundesbank to rule on EMU', *BBC News Online* (27/03/98), www.bbc.co.uk

56. 'SPD Chief warns on EMU', *The Financial Times* (26/03/98), www.ft.com

57. Interview with SPD official in Government department (formerly responsible for European policy).

58. Deutsche Bundesbank, *Opening Statement made by the President of the Deutsche Bundesbank, Prof. Dr. Hans Tietmeyer, before the Finance Committee and the Committee for European Union Affairs of the German Bundestag* (03/04/1998), www.bundesbank.de, pp. 1, 8–9. Both countries still recorded a public debt of over 120 per cent of GDP (twice the level of the criterion) at the start of the 1998; European Commission, *Report on Convergence, 1998* (Brussels, 1998), p. 142.

59. Deutsche Bundesbank (03/04/1998), p. 1.

60. Klaus Hänsch, cited in *Frankfurter Rundschau* (06/03/98).

61. Cited in 'SPD Chief warns over EMU', *The Financial Times* (26/03/98), www.ft.com

62. Internal letter from Wieczorek-Zeul to Rudolf Scharping, marked *Betr.: Gespräch am 12. Dezember über Vorhaben, Projekte, und Veranstaltungen der Fraktion 1998* (Bonn, 08/12/97), pp. 1–2.

63. Oskar Lafontaine, interview with *Die Woche* (13/06/97).

64. SPD, *Arbeit, Innovation und Gerechtigkeit – Regierungsprogramm 1998–2002* (1998), www.spd.de, '12. Neue Verantwortung für das geeinte Deutschland in Europa und in der Welt'.

65. Ibid.

66. SPD, *Arbeitsplanung 2000/2001, Kommissionen: Europa* (June 2000), www.spd.de

67. 'TEC', Article 108 (ex Article 107), www.europa.eu.int

68. Cited in 'As the Euro is born, Germany strikes a different tone', *The Wall Street Journal* (04/01/99), p. 4.

69. Cited in 'Red Oskar steals Wim's ball with crunch tackle', *The European* (19–25/10/98), p. 8.

70. Ibid.

71. EU Commissioner for Economic and Monetary Affairs, Yves-Thibault de Silguy, cited in *Die Süddeutsche Zeitung* (17/02/99).

72. Lafontaine, 'Morgenmagazin', 'ARD TV' (06:10, 08/01/99); SPD Vorstand, *SPD Fernseh-/ Funkspiegel Inland* (Berlin, 08/01/99).

73. Lafontaine, *Die Woche* (13/06/97).

74. Interview with SPD member of the Bundestag.

75. Interview with *Der Spiegel (1)* (1999), p. 42.

76. Schröder had pledged to reduce unemployment to under 3.5 million by the end of his first term in office.
77. The connection between Lafontaine's position on the Euro and market confidence was shown by the large gains made by the Euro in the currency markets on the news of his resignation as Finance Minister and party leader on 11 March 1999.
78. Interview with an SPD MEP.
79. Financial affairs are agreed by Finance Ministers through the ECOFIN Council at the EU level.
80. 'Germans discontented with the euro', *The Financial Times* (03/09/00), www.ft.com
81. BDI, *Prioritäten für die deutsche EU-Ratspräsidentschaft im 1. Halbjahr 1999* (Cologne: December 1998).
82. IG Metall (26–27/01/99), pp. 5–6.
83. Christa Randzio-Plath (SPD MEP and chair of the European Parliament Monetary Committee), 'Aktionsplan Europa', *Vorwärts* (December 1998), www.vorwaerts.de
84. See 'Spannungen um europäischen Beschäftigungspakt', *Die Welt* (04/06/99), www.welt.de
85. See European Commission, *Cologne European Council Presidency Conclusions* (04/06/99), www.europa.eu.int
86. Ibid.
87. Cited in 'Strings attached', *The Financial Times* (13/02/01), www.ft.com
88. Blair and Schröder (2000), p. 163.
89. Blair and Schröder (2000), pp. 164, 167.
90. Cited in 'EU-Kommission erhöht Druck im Landesbanken-Streit', *Financial Times Deutschland* (26/01/01), www.ftd.de
91. 10 per cent of German exports went to the US in 1999 (2 per cent above that for the Euro-zone as a whole), whilst many German 'companies have substantial investments in the American economy'; 'Running out of steam', *The Economist* (05/07/01), www.economist.com
92. 'Schröder weighs into battle over Mannesmann', *The Financial Times* (20/11/99), www.ft.com
93. 'Brussels and Berlin set to clash on take-overs', *The Financial Times* (24/06/02), www.ft.com
94. Interview with official in the SPD European policy groups.
95. Ibid.
96. SPD Vorstand, *Leitantrag: Sicherheit im Wandel*, (20/03/01), www.spd.de; SPD Vorstand, *Leitantrag: Verantwortung für Europa* (30/04/01), www.spd.de
97. SPD Vorstand, *Leitantrag: Verantwortung für Europa* (30/04/01), www.spd.de
98. Ibid.
99. European Council, *Lisbon European Council: Presidency Conclusions* (24/03/00), www.europa.eu.int
100. Interview with a top European official in the SPD European policy groups.
101. See 'Business and central bank warn Berlin over pact', *The Financial Times* (18/11/03), www.ft.com
102. SPD and Bündnis 90/Die Grünen, *Erneuerung – Gerechtigkeit – Nachaltigkeit* (2002), www.spd.de
103. Hans Eichel, 'The stability pact is not a blunt instrument', *The Financial Times* (17/11/03), p. 19.

104. Deutscher Bundestag (14/03/03), pp. 7–8.
105. Bundeskanzleramt, *Deutschland und Frankreich: Gemeinsam für mehr Wachstum in Europa* (18/09/03), www.bundeskanzler.de; see also 'Call for EU funds to boost growth', *The Financial Times* (18/11/03), p. 10.
106. Ibid.
107. SPD Vorstand, *Erneuerung und Zusammenhalt – Wir in Deutschland: Regierungsprogramm 2002–2006* (July 2002), www.spd.de, pp. 15–16.
108. German Foreign Office, *Beitrag von Joschka Fischer und Dominique de Villepin zur Arbeit des Europäischen Konvents über die Stärkung der wirtschaftspolitischen Zusammenarbeit* (December 2002), www.auswaertiges-amt.de
109. Ibid.
110. Gerhard Schröder, *Rede des SPD-Parteivorsitzenden, Bundeskanzler Gerhard Schröder, auf dem Europadelegiertenkonferenz der Sozialdemokratischen Partei Deutschlands in Bochum am. 16. November 2003* (16/11/03), www.spd.de, p. 6.

10 Eastern Enlargement of the EU

1. European Commission, *Enlargement: From cooperation to accession* (2003), www.europa.eu.int
2. Interview with a leading politician in the SPD's European policy community.
3. Helmut Kohl, 'Kulturgemeinschaft Europa. Die Zukunft des Kontinents' (31/10/91) in Banchoff (April 1997), p. 66.
4. See Dinan (1999), pp. 184–5.
5. Deutscher Bundestag, *Antrag der SPD und der Gruppe Bündnis 90/ Die Grünen* (Bonn, Drucksache 12/2559, 06/05/92), p. 1.
6. German Embassy, *Speech by Chancellor Helmut Kohl on the occasion of his acceptance of the "Vision for Europe" prize awarded by Luxembourg's Edmond Israel Foundation* (17/09/97), www.german-embassy.org.uk
7. See, for example, Rudolf Scharping, *Die deutsche-polnische Beziehungen* (Bonn: Presseservice der SPD 335/94, 11/05/94), pp. 3–4.
8. German Foreign Office, *Transformationsförderungen und regionale Stabilisierung* (August 2001), www.auswaertiges-amt.de
9. A key function of the Goethe Institute is to promote German language and culture abroad.
10. See German Foreign Office, *Die Bilateralen Beziehungen zwischen Polen und Deutschland* (March 2001), www.auswaertiges-amt.de; German Foreign Office, *Die Bilateralen Beziehungen zwischen Ungarn und Deutschland'* (July 2000), www.auswaertiges-amt.de; German Foreign Office, *Die Bilateralen Beziehungen zwischen Deutschland und der Tschechischen Republik* (March 2001), www.auswaertiges-amt.de
11. SPD, *Basic Policy Programme of the Social Democratic Party of Germany* (20/12/89), www.spd.de
12. Dinan (1999), p. 134.
13. Hans-Jochen Vogel, *Das Europäische Haus: Perspektiven europäischer Entwicklung* (Bonn: SPD Bundestagsfraktion, 13/10/89), p. 2.
14. Vogel (13/10/89), p. 5.
15. European Commission, *Enlargement: the Europe Agreements* (2003), www.europa.eu.int
16. Commission President Delors was 'exasperated' by the positions of Member States like France and Spain, which had ensured the maintenance of

'numerous protectionist hurdles ... in sensitive areas like coal, steel and textiles'; M. Dauderstädt, *The EC and Eastern Europe: the Light is fading in the Lighthouse* (Bonn: Friedrich Ebert Stiftung, 1993), p. 3. This liberalisation of trade came to benefit the EU more than the CEE states.

17. Björn Engholm, *Zum Maastricht-Gipfel am 29 October 1991* (Bonn: SPD Bundesfraktion, Wochenendtext no. 25), p. 23.

18. German Foreign Office, *Transformationsförderungen und regionale Stabilisierung* (August 2001).

19. The PHARE programme was soon extended from Poland and Hungary to most of the other CEE states. Overall expenditure was to average €621 million per year over the 1990–98 budgetary period; J. Pinder, *The European Union: a very short introduction* (Oxford: Oxford University Press, 2001), p. 129.

20. Dauderstädt (1993), p. 2.

21. SPD Vorstand, *Jahrbuch der SPD, 1988–90* (1990), p. C82

22. Die SPD im Deutschen Bundestag, *Europapolitik – Positionen und Initiativen der SPD Bundesfraktion* (31/01/92), p. 16.

23. Vogel (13/10/89), p. 3.

24. Cited in Banchoff (April 1997), p. 63.

25. Between 1987 and 1992 the number of asylum seekers entering Germany jumped from approximately 57,000 to a highpoint of around 458,000 each year; Interior Ministry, *Zuwanderung von Ausländern* (May 2002), www. bund.bmi.de

26. Dauderstädt and Lippert (1996), www.fes.de

27. Heidemarie Wieczorek-Zeul, *Plenarprotokoll 12/108* (Bonn: Deutscher Bundestag, 25/09/92), p. 9223.

28. Dauderstädt and Lippert (1996), www.fes.de

29. Deutscher Bundestag, *Erweiterung der Europäischen Union – Antwort der Bundesregierung auf die Grosse Anfrage der Abgeordneten Peter Hintze ... und der Fraktion der CDU/CSU* (Berlin: Drucksache, 14/5232, 07/02/01), p. 85.

30. German trade surpluses *vis-à-vis* the accession candidates had begun to decline by the end of the 1990s; figures from Deutscher Bundestag (07/02/01), pp. 83–5.

31. Heidemarie Wieczorek-Zeul, *Überlegungen zur Weiterentwicklung der Europäischen Union* (internal paper) (Bonn: Koordinierungsstelle Europapolitik der SPD, 02/02/95), p. 5.

32. European Commission, *Eurobarometer 42* (Brussels: Spring 1995), pp. 49–50. A *Forsa* poll reported in the same year that 58 per cent of Germans supported the acceptance of the *Visegrad* states into the EU, with only 30 per cent against, cited in *Die Woche* (20/06/95).

33. Emnid poll conducted for *Der Spiegel* (05/12/94), p. 47.

34. Cited in European Commission, *Enlargement: Accession criteria* (August 2001), www.europa.eu.int

35. Ibid.

36. Ibid.

37. The focus on a *deepening* as opposed to a *widening* of the EU was also demonstrated by the fact that this very quote was only listed at point 17 on a *Bundestagsfraktion* European policy document; SPD Bundestagsfraktion (10/11/93), p. 4.

38. SPD, *Reformen für Deutschland – Regierungsprogramm 1994–1998* (1994), p. 33.
39. Interview with central figure in the SPD *Bundestagsfraktion* in the 1990s who was heavily involved in the *Bundestag* committees, May 2000, Berlin.
40. SPD Bundestagsfraktion, *SPD European Policy Guidelines* (Bonn: Koordinierungsstelle für Europafragen, 26/05/94).
41. Dinan (1999), p. 192.
42. Apart from the assessment of candidates' readiness for accession, the Commission's evaluation was also useful for helping to target the resources of the PHARE programme.
43. W. Weidenfeld (ed.), *A New Ostpolitik – Strategies for a United Europe* (Gütersloh: Bertelsmann, 1997), pp. 83–4.
44. Weidenfeld (1997), p. 84.
45. Wolfgang Schäuble, interview with *Der Spiegel* (27/03/95).
46. See SPD Vorstand, *Antrag: EU 1 – Wir brauchen Europa* (Europäische Anträge, angenommen am 16. November 1995 auf dem Parteitag in Mannheim) (Bonn: November 1995), p. 5.
47. Heidemarie Wieczorek-Zeul, *Plenarprotokoll 13/96* (Bonn: Deutscher Bundestag, 15/03/96), p. 8567.
48. Heidemarie Wieczorek-Zeul (02/02/95), pp. 1–2.
49. Roth (1996), p. 122.
50. SPD Vorstand (16/11/95), pp. 7–8.
51. SPD Vorstand, *Leitsätze zur weiteren Finanzierung der Europäischen Union* (Bonn: 16/10/96), p. 4.
52. 'A nice welcome for new members', *The Economist* (07/12/00), www.economist.com
53. France profits greatly from financial redistribution under CAP due to its large number of small-scale farmers.
54. Roth (1996), p. 124.
55. European Commission, *TEC* (2001), www.europa.eu.int, Articles 128 and 129, 135 and 141 respectively.
56. These decisions on the size of the Commission were stated in the protocol attached to the Treaty of Amsterdam; European Commission, *Treaty of Amsterdam amending the Treaty on European Union, the Treaties establishing the European Communities and certain Related Acts* (2001), www.europa.eu.int
57. Deutscher Bundestag, *Anfrage der Abgeordneten Winfried Mante, Heidemarie Wieczorek-Zeul ... und der Fraktion der SPD* (Bonn: Drucksache, 13/5255, 08/07/96), p. 1.
58. *Das Handelsblatt* (24/09/97).
59. For a good overview of *Agenda 2000*, see European Commission, *Agenda 2000: For a stronger and wider Union* (2001), www.europa.eu.int
60. Dinan (1999), p. 193.
61. European Commission, '*Agenda 2000: For a stronger and wider Union*', *European Commission* (2001), www.europa.eu.int
62. Ibid.
63. *Objective 1* status was to be allocated to regions with a GDP per capita less than 75 per cent of the EU average. The plan was to concentrate funds on areas amounting to 35–40 per cent of the EU's population rather than the existing 51 per cent; European Commission, *Agenda 2000: For a stronger and wider Union* (2001), www.europa.eu.int

64. Cited in Deutscher Bundestag, *Kurzprotokoll der 63. Sitzung des Auschusses für die Angelegenheiten der Europäischen Union* (Bonn: 13:00, 29/10/97), p. 30.
65. The remaining CEE applicant states had a GDP per capita of only 28.9 per cent of the EU average; figures cited in 'A nice welcome for new members', *The Economist* (07/12/00), www.economist.com
66. Klaus Kinkel, cited in Deutscher Bundestag (29/10/97), Bonn, p. 31.
67. Cited in Deutscher Bundestag (29/10/97), p. 36.
68. Wieczorek, cited in Deutscher Bundestag (29/10/97), p. 36.
69. The European Parliament would enjoy co-decision in areas voted on under QMV in the Council; SPD *Vorstand, Reformen für Europa: Zwischenbericht der Schwerpunktkommission Europapolitk* (26/05/97), www.spd.de
70. C. Jeffery and S. Collins, 'The German *Länder* and EU enlargement: between apple pie and issue linkage', *German Politics 7 (2)* (August 1998), pp. 86–101, p. 96.
71. Gerhard Schröder, 'Nicht die deutsche Wirtschaft überfordern', interview with *Focus* (06/11/95), www.focus.de
72. Germany was a close second behind the Netherlands in its concerns for the costs of enlargement (another large budgetary contributor); European Commission, *Eurobarometer 48* (Brussels: Spring 1997), p. 51; European Commission (Spring 1998), p. 61.
73. Theo Waigel, interview with *Bild am Sonntag* (26/07/97), www.bild.de
74. Zwischenbericht der Schwerpunktkommission Europa (26/05/97), www.spd.de
75. SPD Vorstand, *Protokoll des Presidiums am 28/07/97* (internal document) Bonn, p. 4.
76. SPD Vorstand, *SPD Präsidium: Osterweiterung der EU als eine Chance*, (15/07/97), Bonn: Presseservice der SPD, 293/97.
77. Ibid.
78. European Commission, *For a Stronger and Wider Union* (Agenda 2000, Volume I, 15/07/97), www.europa.eu.int, Communication of the Commission, DOC 97/6
79. SPD Vorstand, (15/07/97).
80. SPD Vorstand, *Reformen für Europa: Zwischenbericht der Schwerpunktkommission Europapolitk* (26/05/97), www.spd.de
81. SPD Vorstand, (15/07/97).
82. European Commission (Spring 1997), p. 51 and (Spring 1998), p. 61.
83. SPD, *Arbeit, Innovation und Gerechtigkeit – Regierungsprogramm 1998–2002* (1998), www.spd.de
84. Ibid.
85. Gerhard Schröder, interview 'Europamagazin', 'ARD TV' (13:20, 12/09/98); SPD Vorstand, *SPD Fernseh-/Funkspiegel Inland I* (Berlin, 14/09/98), p. 45.
86. Ibid.

11 Reforming for Accession: A New EU for a New Europe

1. Here, Schröder referred to the early accession dates named by Kohl, interview with *The Financial Times* (03/12/98), www.ft.com

Notes 251

2. Cited in 'SURVEY – GERMANY: integration drive set to continue', *The Financial Times* (10/11/98) www.ft.com
3. Günter Verheugen, 'Information am Morgen', 'DLF radio' (7:20, 28/10/98); SPD Vorstand, *Fernseh-/Funkspiegel 1* (Berlin: Presse und Informationsamt der Bunderegierung, 28/10/98).
4. Chancellor Schröder, interview with *The Financial Times* (03/12/98), www.ft.com
5. SPD, *Arbeitsplanung 2000/2001, Kommissionen: Europa* (2001), www.spd.de
6. See Bündnis 90/Die Grünen, *1998–2002. Vier Jahre für einen politischen Neuanfang* (1998), www.gruene.de
7. Hans Eichel, interview with *Die Welt* (04/05/01), www.welt.de
8. Wolfgang Schäuble and Karl Lamers, *Reflections on European Policy II: the Future Course of European Integration* (03/05/99), www.cdu.de
9. Stoiber, cited in 'Rühe wants date set for EU enlargement', *Frankfurter Allgemeine Zeitung* (18/09/00), www.faz.com
10. Michael Glos, head of the CSU group in the Bavarian parliament, cited in 'Union warnt Regierung vor Risiken der Osterweiterung', *Die Welt* (17/09/99), www.welt.de
11. 'Rühe wants date set for EU enlargement', *Frankfurter Allgemeine Zeitung* (18/09/00), www.faz.com
12. Figures in German Foreign Office, *Die Erweiterung der Europäischen Union* (2001), www.auswärtiges-amt.de
13. Figures calculated from German Foregin Office, *Die Erwiterung der Europäischen Union* (2001), www.auswärtiges-amt.de; and Deutscher Bundestag (07/02/01), p. 84.
14. German Foreign Office, *Die Erweiterung der Europäischen Union* (2001), www.auswärtiges-amt.de
15. Ibid.
16. Dieter Schulte (chairman of the DGB), taken from his contribution to DGB, *Deutsche EU-Ratspräsidentschaft–Was Prominente erwarten* (1998), www.dgb.de
17. Ibid.
18. Christian Holz, 'Highlights Germany' in European Commission, *Eurobarometer 2001 – Special Edition: National Highlights* (Spring 2001), www.europa.eu.int
19. Interveiw with a leading politican in the SPD's European policy community, May 2000, Berlin.
20. European *Commission, Enlargement: Regular Report from the Commission on Progress towards Accession by Each of the Candidate Countries* (13/10/99), www.europa.eu.int
21. Ibid.
22. Heidemarie Wieczorek-Zeul, cited in 'Germany to Contribute DM1.2bn to Stability Pact for Southeastern Europe', *BBC Monitoring Service* (27/03/00), www.bbc.co.uk
23. T. Pedersen, *Germany, France and the Integration of Europe* (London: Pinter, 1998), pp. 188–9.
24. Cited in 'They Said, He Said', *Frankfurter Allgemeine Zeitung* (08/09/00), www.faz.com
25. See 'EU-Osterweiterung: Sind die Gremien Europas ausreichend legitimiert oder muss das Volk die letzte Entscheidung treffen?', *Der Tagesspiegel* (05/09/00), www.tagesspiegel.de

26. Chancellor Schröder, cited in 'Germany Quashes Idea of Poll on EU Newcomers', *International Herald Tribune* (05/09/00), www.iht.com
27. German Federal Government, *Rede von Bundeskanzler Gerhard Schröder anlässlich der Regionalkonferenz Oberpfalz 2000 am 18.12.2000 in Weiden*, www.bundesregierung.de
28. Christian Holz (Spring 2001), www.europa.eu.int
29. Angelika Volle (German Council on Foreign Relations), cited in 'Reasons of state', *The Economist* (17/05/01), www.economist.com
30. 'Europa droht eine Völkerwanderung', *Die Welt am Sonntag* (22/04/01), www.welt.de
31. European Commission, *The Economic Impact of Enlargement* (June 2001), www.europa.eu.int, pp. 37, 42.
32. Interview with leading SPD politician in the party's European policy groups, May 2000, Berlin.
33. German Federal Government, *Rede von Bundeskanzler Gerhard Schröder anlässlich der Regionalkonferenz Oberpfalz 2000 am 18.12.2000 in Weiden*, www.bundesregierung.de
34. Ibid.
35. Interview with a SPD MEP, February 2000, Soest.
36. Cited in a report from German news agency 'DPP' in *BBC monitoring service* (09/03/01), www.bbc.co.uk
37. Interview with leading Left-wing SPD member of the *Bundestag*, May 2000, Berlin.
38. Polish Foreign Minister, Vladimir Bartoshefsky, cited in 'European foreign ministers squabble over free movement of labor', *Frankfurter Allgemeine Zeitung* (06/05/01), www.faz.com
39. Günter Verheugen, *Die Erweiterung der Europäischen Union – Strategien für die Bewältigung der erweiterungsbedingten Herausforderungen* (03/04/01), www. europa.eu.int
40. See for instance, 'Verheugen gives Poles hope for EU aspirations', *Frankfurter Allgemeine Zeitung* (31/10/00), www.faz.com
41. Verheugen, 'Mittagsecho', 'WDR TV'; SPD Vorstand, *SPD Fernseh-Hörfunkspeigel Inland I* (Berlin: 04/01/99).
42. Günter Verheugen, 'Germany and the EU Council Presidency', *ZEI Discussion Paper* (1999), Bonn, p. 8.
43. Detlev Samland MEP, 'Bonn am Rohr', 'WDR TV'; SPD Vorstand, *SPD Fernseh-Hörfunkspeigel Inland I* (Berlin: 04/01/99).
44. *Stern* (04/03/99).
45. Cited in 'Vom Dressman zum Staatsmann', *Die Zeit No. 14* (1999), www. zeit.de
46. In an interview with *Der Spiegel (1)* (1999), p. 43.
47. Calculated from figures published in European Commission, *Allocation of 2000 EU operating expenditure by Member States* (September 2001), www. europa.eu.int, p. 34.
48. Figures calculated from 'Europas Viererbande kämpft um weniger Geld', *Die Welt* (26/03/99), www.welt.de
49. Verheugen (1999), p. 8
50. See Sloam (1999), pp. 8–12.

51. Figures cited in *Die Süddeutsche Zeitung* (27/03/99).

52. See German Foreign Office, *Bilanz der deutschen Präsidentschaft* (July 1999), www.auswärtiges-amt.de

53. European Council, *Berlin European Council – Presidency Conclusions* (Press Release No. 100/1/199, 25/03/99), www.europa.eu.int

54. Michael Barnier, *Adapting the Institutions to Make a Success of Enlargement*, (Brussels: European Commission, May 2000), p. 2.

55. Joschkar Fischer, *Vom Staatenbund zur Föderation – Gedanken über die Finalität der europäischen Integration* (12/05/00), www.auswärtiges-amt.de

56. Ibid.

57. Ibid.

58. Ibid.

59. Interview with SPD official in Government department (formerly responsible for European policy), June 2000, Berlin.

60. SPD views on Fischer's speech were confirmed in several interviews held in Berlin shortly after the event.

61. Fischer's speech sparked a debate across Europe, which soon included contributions from President Chirac (speaking at the German *Bundestag* in June 2000) and Prime Minister Blair (October 2000, Warsaw).

62. Interview with SPD official in Government department (formerly responsible for European policy), June 2000, Berlin.

63. If voting in the Council was not to better reflect population sizes, the EU faced the possibility of a minority of the EU population being able to impose its will upon the majority once enlargement had taken place.

64. One of the few areas in which Germany did not wish see the extension of QMV was immigration and asylum – see Chancellor Schröder's interview with *Der Spiegel* (04/12/00), www.spiegel.de

65. TEC Articles 13, 18, 65, 100, 123, 133, 157, 159, 279 and 181a; see European Commission, 'Treaty of Nice', *Official Journal of the European Communities* (2000), www.europa.eu.int

66. TEC Articles 93 and 137, respectively; for details of the agreements reached at Nice, see European Commission, '*Qualified Majority Voting: General Overview*', www.europa.eu.int

67. Reported in 'Kohl tries to allay fears about Germany', *The Financial Times* (13/12/96), www.ft.com

68. The Nice agreement meant that a motion required a qualified majority of slightly re-weighted Council votes, the support of 62 per cent of the EU population and a simple majority of Member States to be passed from January 2005.

69. The minimum number of Member States need to participate in *structured co-operation* would remain at eight after enlargement.

70. Gerhard Schröder, *Plenarprotokoll 14/144* (19/01/01), Deutscher Bundestag, www.bundestag.de

71. Ibid.

72. The party, for example, held a three-day conference in Berlin with CEE states' social democratic/socialist parties on the subject of EU institutional reform in February 2000, just prior to the start of the IGC.

73. SPD Bundestagsfraktion deputy chair, Joachim Poß *Plenarprotokoll 14/144* (19/01/01), www.bundestag.de
74. SPD Bundestagsfraktion, *Europapolitik der SPD-Bundestagsfraktion in der 14. Legislaturperiode 1998–2002: eine Bilanz* (2002), www.spdfraktion. de, p. 5.
75. Cited in 'Freizügigkeit erst nach sieben Jahren', *Financial Times Deutschland* (04/04/01), www.ftd.de
76. German Federal Government, *Rede von Bundeskanzler Gerhard Schröder anlässlich der Regionalkonferenz Oberpfalz 2000 am 18.12.2000 in Weiden*, www.bundesregierung.de
77. A further €1.1 billion was made available to help the border regions make eastern enlargement 'less painful' on the occasion of Schröder's visit; 'Auf seiner Sommerreise durch Ostdeutschland warb Gerhard Schröder für die EU-Osterweiterung', *Vorwärts* (September 2001), www.vorwaerts.de
78. Gerhard Schröder, cited in 'Auf seiner Sommerreise durch Ostdeutschland warb Gerhard Schröder für die EU-Osterweiterung', *Vorwärts* (September 2001), www.vorwaerts.de
79. For the SPD, the appointment of Verheugen as Commissioner for Enlargement was particularly important, after which the Federal Government and SPD could keep a closer reign on negotiations.
80. Helmut Schmidt, in conversation with Edmund Stoiber, in 'Begrenzt Europas Macht', *Die Zeit no. 7* (2001), www.zeit.de
81. SPD Vorstand, *Leitantrag: Verantwortung für Europa* (30/04/01), www.spd.de
82. Ibid.
83. See 'Schröder leads calls for union-wide police force', *European Voice* (03/05/01), www.european-voice.com
84. SPD Vorstand, *Erneuerung und Zusammenhalt – Wir in Deutschland: Regierungsprogramm 2002–2006* (July 2002), www.spd.de
85. SPD Vorstand, *Leitantrag: Verantwortung für Europa* (30/04/01), www.spd.de
86. Ibid.
87. Interview with a leading politician in the SPD's European policy community, May 2000, Berlin.
88. SPD Vorstand, *Leitantrag: Verantwortung für Europa* (30/04/01), www.spd.de
89. European Commission, *The Charter of Fundamental Rights of the European Union* (December 2001), www.europa.eu.int
90. Dieter Hundt, President of the BDA, cited in 'Arbeitgeber warnen vor 'Inflation der Grundrechte', *Tagesspiegel* (19/09/00), www.tagesspiegel.de
91. Jürgen Meyer, 'Modell für eine europäische Verfassungsgebung?', *Frankfurter Allgemeine Zeitung* (25/09/00), www.faz.com
92. Ibid.
93. Dresdner Bank, *Herausforderung EU-Erweiterung* (May 2001), Dresdner Bank, www.economic-research.dresdner-bank.de
94. Cited in 'Germany wants EU to cut agricultural expenses', *Frankfurter Allgemeine Zeitung* (24/05/01), www.faz.com
95. SPD Vorstand, *Leitantrag: Verantwotung für Europa* (30/04/01), www.spd.de
96. The UK and France balked at the relative loss of power for national governments that the SPD's proposed institutional model would bring.
97. Gerhard Schröder, *Plenarprotokoll 14/176* (21/06/01), Berlin: Deutscher Bundestag, p. 17213.

98. Cited in 'Endstation Osterweiterung', *Der Spiegel* (16/06/01), www.spiegel.de
99. Federal Chancellor's Office, *Regierungserklärung von Bundeskanzler Schröder zu den Ergebnissen des Europäischen Rates in Kopenhagen* (19/12/02), www.bundeskanzler.de
100. Gerhard Schröder (16/11/03), www.spd.de, p. 4.
101. Federal Chancellor's Office, *Schröder: Die Europäischer Union muss handlungsfähig bleiben!* (05/11/03), www.bundeskanzler.de
102. See 'Copenhagen has many obstacles to overcome in push for enlargement', *European Voice* (27/06/02), www.european-voice.com
103. Chancellor Schröder, cited in 'EU leaders reluctantly back farming deal', *The Financial Times* (25/10/02), www.ft.com
104. Europäischer Konvent, *Beitrag, der von den Mitgliedern des Konvents Herrn Dominique de Villepin und Herrn Joschka Fischer übermittelt wurde* (16/01/03), www.europa.eu.int, CONV 489/03.
105. Angelica Schwall-Düren, *Rede zur 40. Jahrestag des Elysée-Vertrages am 16. Januar im Deutschen Bundestag* (16/01/03), www.spdfraktion.de
106. European Convention, *Draft Treaty for establishing a Constitution for Europe* (18/06/03), www.european-convention.eu.int, CONV 850/03.
107. Ibid.
108. Angelica Schwall-Düren, *Rede im Bundestag* (2003), www.spdfaktion.de, p. 3.
109. Ibid.
110. See the SPD manifesto for the European elections in 2004; SPD, *Europamanifest der SPD* (16/11/04), www.spd.de
111. Joschka Fischer, cited in 'Paris and Berlin 'may drive EU integration', *The Financial Times* (17/11/03), www.fit.com

Conclusion

1. After the European Council in Berlin, Schröder argued that the 'Union must not end at Germany's eastern borders … There must be no policy of cool egoism'; Gerhard Schröder, cited in 'Kosovo-Krise: Union unterstützt Rot-Grün', *Die Welt* (27/03/99), p. 3.
2. Interview with *Der Spiegel (1)* (January 1999), p. 42.
3. See SPD Vorstand, *Erneuerung und Zusammenhalt – Wir in Deutschland: Regierungsprogramm 2002–2006* (July 2002), www.spd.de
4. SPD Vorstand, *Leitantrag: Verantwortung für Europa* (30/04/01), www.spd.de
5. Maull (March 1999), p. 2.
6. Interview with central figure in the SPD *Bundestagsfraktion* in the 1990s and heavily involved in the *Bundestag* committees, May 2000, Berlin.
7. 'Deutsche Interesse', *Die Welt* (05/12/00), www.welt.de
8. Ibid.
9. Matthias Machnig, 'Organisation ist Politik', *Berliner Republik (2)* (2001), www.b-republik.de
10. Interview with official in SPD European policy groups, May 2000, Berlin.
11. SPD Vorstand, *Leitantrag: Verantwortung für Europa* (30/04/01), www.spd.de
12. Lafontaine, on the other hand, found it difficult to adjust his strong views to the rigours of a stability-oriented ECB, a Single Market with a liberalisation agenda, and Member States who rejected demand-side economics.

13. See Wolfgang Clement, 'EU: Wer macht eigentlich was?', *Vorwärts* (June 2001), www.vorwaerts.de

14. Interview with politician in SPD European policy groups, April 2000, Berlin.

15. Chancellor Schröder, cited in 'Kernsätze: Außenpolitische Positionen des Bundeskanzlers', *Berliner Republik (1)* (2000), p. 15; for a discussion of philosophical underpinnings of the sharing of sovereignty in the Euro-zone see K. Dyson, *The Politics of the Euro-Zone* (Oxford: Oxford University Press, 2000), pp. 93–9.

16. Gerhard Schröder, Interview with *Die Berliner Zeitung*, (02/06/00), p. 5.

17. SPD Vorstand, *Leitantrag: Verantwortung für Europa* (30/04/01), www.spd.de

18. SPD, *Rede Gerhard Schröder zum Themenbereich: Außen- und Sicherheitspolitik* (21/11/01), (party conference in Nuremberg), www.spd-parteitag.de

19. Interview with a top European official in the SPD European policy groups.

20. The advance of the European polity is the reason why many key figures of the party have emphasised that the SPD should *Europeanise* its programmatic debate. See Wolfgang Thierse, *Die Sozialdemokratie muss dem Mainstream widerstehen* (12/09/03), www.spd.de

21. SPD Vorstand, *Leitantrag: Verantwortung für Europa* (30/04/01), www.spd.de

22. Federal Government, *Regierungserklärung von Bundeskanzler Schröder zur aktuellen Lage nach Beginn der Operation gegen internationalen Terrorismus in Afghanistan* (11/10/01), www.bundesregierung.de

23. Ibid.

24. As argued in the party's 2001 EU policy paper, SPD Vorstand, *Leitantrag: Verantwortung für Europa* (30/04/01), www.spd.de

25. Deutscher Bundestag (07/02/01), p. 2.

26. Friedbert Pflüger (CDU) and Reinhold Bockelt (CSU, Bavarian Minister for Europe), respectively, cited in 'Opposition unterstützt Schröders EU-Pläne', *Die Welt* (02/05/01), www.welt.de

27. Cited in 'Opposition conservative union divided over chancellor's EU proposals', *BBC Monitoring* (07/05/01), www.bbc.co.uk

Select Bibliography

General interest

Bachrach, P. and M. Baratz, *Power and Poverty: theory and practice* (Oxford: Oxford University Press, 1970)

Dahl, R., 'The Concept of Power' (1957), *Behavioural Science* 2 (3), pp. 201–15

Dahl, R., *Pluralist Democracy in the United States: conflict and consent* (Chicago: Rand McNally, 1967)

Dewey, J., *Creative Intelligence: essays in the pragmatic attitude* (New York: Holt and Co., 1917)

Fott, D., *John Dewey: America's Philosopher of Democracy* (Oxford: Rowman and Littlefield, 1998)

Downs, A., *An Economic Theory of Democracy* (New York: Harper & Row, 1957)

Frankel, J., *The Making of Foreign Policy* (Oxford: Oxford University Press, 1967)

Guzzini, S., 'Structural Power: The limits of neorealist power analysis' (1993), *International Organization 47 (3)*, pp. 443–78

Hay, C., 'Structure and agency', in D. Marsh and G. Stoker (eds), *Theory and Methods in Political Science* (Basingstoke: MacMillan, 1995), pp. 189–206

Hay, C., 'Divided by a Common Language: Political Theory and the Concept of Power' (1997), *Politics 17 (1)*, pp. 45–52

Hay, C., *Political Analysis* (Basingstoke: Palgrave, 2002)

Jessop, B., 'Interpretive sociology and the dialectic of structure and agency' (1996), *Theory, Culture and Society 13 (1)*, pp. 119–28.

Keohane, R. O. *et al.* (eds), *After the Cold War* (Cambridge: Harvard, 1993)

Lukes, S., *Power: a radical view* (London: Macmillan, 1974)

Marsh, D. and M. Smith, 'Understanding policy networks: towards a dialectic approach' (March 2000), *Political Studies 48*, pp. 4–21

Mearsheimer, J., 'Back to the future: instability in Europe after the Cold War' (1990), *International Security 15*, pp. 5–56

Schmidt, H., *Globalisierung* (Berlin: Siedler, 1999)

Smith, M. (eds), *Perspectives on World Politics* (London: Croom Helm, 1981)

Wendt, A., 'Anarchy is what states make of it: the social construction of power politics' (1992), *International Organization 46 (2)*, pp. 391–425

On international relations and the European Union

Bulmer, S., 'Domestic politics and European community Policy-Making' (1983a), *Journal of Common Market Studies 21 (4)*

Dauderstädt, M. and B. Lippert, *No Integration without Differentiation: On the strategy for a scaled eastern enlargement of the European Union* (London: Friedrich Ebert Stiftung, 1996)

Deutsche Bundesbank, *Opening Statement made by the President of the Deutsche Bundesbank, Prof. Dr. Hans Tietmeyer, before the Finance Committee and the*

258   *Select Bibliography*

Committee for European Union Affairs of the German Bundestag (03/04/1998), www.bundesbank.de

Dinan, D., *Ever Closer Union: an introduction to European integration* 2nd edition (London: Macmillan, 1999)

Dyson, K. and K. Featherstone, *The Road to Maastricht: negotiating economic and monetary union* (Oxford: Oxford University Press, 1999)

Dyson, K., *The Politics of the Euro-Zone* (Oxford: Oxford University Press, 2000)

European Commission, *Eurobarometer (34–59)* (Brussels: 1990–2001), www. europa. eu.int

European Commission, *'Proposals of Employment Guidelines for Member States Employment* policies for 1998' (1997), www.europa.eu.int

European Commission, *Agenda 2000: For a stronger and wider Union* (July 1997), www.europa.eu.int

European Commission, *Treaty of Amsterdam amending the Treaty on European Union, the Treaties establishing the European Communities and certain Related Acts* (2001), www.europa.eu.int

European Commission, *Treaty Establishing the European Community* (2001), www.europa.eu.int

European Commission, *The Economic Impact of Enlargement* (June 2001), www.europa.eu.int

European Commission, *The Charter of Fundamental Rights of the European Union* (December 2001), www.europa.eu.int

European Convention, *Beitrag, der von den Mitgliedern des Konvents Herrn Dominique de Villepin und Herrn Joschka Fischer übermittelt wurde* (16/01/03), www.europa.eu.int, CONV 489/03

European Convention, *Draft Treaty for establishing a Constitution for Europe* (18/06/03), www.european-convention.eu.int, CONV 850/03

European Council, *Berlin European Council – Presidency Conclusions* (Press Release 100/1/99, 25/03/99), www.europa.eu.int

European Council, *Cologne European Council – Presidency Conclusions* (Press Release 150/9, 04/06/99), www.europa.eu.int

European Council, *Lisbon European Council: Presidency Conclusions* (24/03/00), www.europa.eu.int

Eyre, S. and M. Lodge, 'National tunes and a European melody? Competition law reform in the UK and Germany' (March 2000), *Journal of European Public Policy 7 (1)*, pp. 63–79

German Federal Government, *Regierungserklärung von Bundeskanzler Schröder zur aktuellen Lage nach Beginn der Operation gegen internationalen Terrorismus in Afghanistan* (11/10/01), www.bundesregierung.de

Padoa-Schioppa, T. (eds), *Efficiency, Stability and Equity* (Luxembourg: Office for Official Publications of the European Communities, 1987)

Rosamond, B., *Theories of European Integration* (London: MacMillan, 2000)

Sarrazin, T., *Der Euro: Chance oder Abenteuer?* (Bonn: Dietz, 1998)

Schmidt, M. G., 'Die Europäisierung der öffentlichen Aufgaben' (1999), *ZeS-Arbeitspapier (3)*, Bremen

Wallace, W., 'The sharing of sovereignty: the European paradox' (1999), *Political Studies 47 (3)*, pp. 503–21

On political parties

Cole, A., 'National and partisan contexts of Europeanisation: the case of the French Socialists' (2001), *Journal of Common Market Studies 39 (1)*, pp. 15–36

Daalder, H. and P. Mair, *Western European Party Systems: Continuity and Change* (London: Sage, 1983)

Gaffney, J. (eds), *Political Parties and the European Union* (London: Routledge, 1996)

Ladrech, R., 'Europeanization and political parties: towards a framework for analysis' (2001), *Keele European Parties Research Unit Working Paper (7)*, www.keele.ac.uk

Lawson, K. and P. Merkl (eds) *When Parties Fail* (Princeton University Press, 1988)

Mair, P. (eds), *The West European Party System* (Oxford: Oxford University Press, 1990)

Mair, P., *Party System Change: approaches and interpretations* (Oxford: Oxford University Press, 1997)

Panebianco, A., *Political Parties: Organisation and Power* (Cambridge: Cambridge University Press, 1988)

Paterson, W., 'Political Parties and the Making of Foreign Policy' (1981), *Review of International Studies*, pp. 227–35

Sani, G. and G. Sartori, 'Polarization, fragmentation and competition in Western democracies', in H. Daalder and P. Mair, *Western European Party Systems: Continuity and Change* (London: Sage, 1983) pp. 307–40

Ware, A., *Political Parties and Party Systems* (Oxford: Oxford University Press, 1997)

On Germany and German European policy

Anderson, J., *German Unification and the Union of Europe* (Cambridge: Cambridge University Press, 1999)

Banchoff, T., 'German policy towards the European Union: the effects of historical memory' (April 1997), *German Politics 6 (1)*, pp. 60–76

Bulmer, S, 'West German political parties and the European Community' (1983b), *Political Studies 31*, pp. 566–83

Bulmer, S., C. Jeffery and W. Paterson, *Germany's European Diplomacy: shaping the regional milieu* (Manchester: Manchester University Press, 2000)

Bundesverband der Deutschen Industrie (BDI), *Prioritäten für die deutsche EU-Ratspräsidentschaft im 1. Halbjahr 1999* (December 1998), www.bdi.de

Conradt, D. *et al.* (eds), *Germany's New Politics* (Oxford: Berghan, 1995)

Deutsche Bundesbank, 'Recent developments in Germany's financial relations with the European Union', *Bundesbank Monthly Report* (July 1999), www. bundesbank.de

Deutsche Gewerkschaftsbund (DGB), *Bericht zur gewerkschafts- und gesellschafts politische Lage (Bundesausschußbericht* (March 1998), www.dgb.de

Dyson, K. and K. Goetz (eds), *Germany, Europe and the Politics of Constraint* (Oxford: Oxford University Press, 2003)

Fischer, J., 'Berlin's Foreign Policy' (Spring 2000), *Internationale Politik (1)* Transatlantic Edition), pp. 3–10

Fischer, J., *Vom Staatenbund zur Föderation – Gedanken über die Finalität der europäischen Integration* (12/05/00), www.auswärtiges-amt.de

Garton Ash, T., *Im Namens Europa: Deutschland und der geteilte Kontinent* (Munich: Hanser, 1993)

German Foreign Office, *Bilanz der deutschen Präsidentschaft – Kurzfassung* (July 2001), www.auswaertiges-amt.de

Grundgesetz für die Bundesrepublik Deutschland (Baden-Baden: Nomos, 1999)

Hacke, C., 'Die Bedeutung der nationale Interesses für die Aussenpolitik der Bundesrepublik', in G. Niedhard (eds), *Deutschland in Europa* (Mannheim: Palatium, 1997)

Hellmann, G., 'The sirens of power and German Foreign policy: who is listening?' (August 1997), *German Politics 6 (2)*, pp. 29–57

Heurlin, B. (eds), *Germany in Europe in the Nineties* (London: MacMillan, 1996)

Holz, C., *Higlights Germany, Eurobarometer 2001 – Special Edition: National Highlights* (European Commission, Spring 2001), www.europa.eu.int

Hrbeck, R., *Deutschland und Europa*, Bonn: Europa Union, 1972)

Huelshoff et al. (eds), *From Bundesrepublik to Deutschland: German Politics after Unification* (Michigan: University of Michigan, 1991)

IG Metall, *Europapolitische Forderungen der IG Metall* (Frankfurt am Main: IG Metall Vorstand, 26–27 January 1999)

Jeffery, C., 'A giant with feet of clay? United Germany in the European Union', *Institute for German Studies Discussion Paper 95/6* (Birmingham: University of Birmingham, December 1995)

Jeffery, C. and S. Collins, 'The German Länder and EU enlargement: between apple pie and issue linkage' (August 1998), *German Politics 7 (2)*, pp. 86–101

Jeffery, C. and W. Paterson, 'Germany and European Integration: a shifting of tectonic plates', in H. Kitschelt and W. Streeck (eds), *Germany: Beyond the Stable State* (London: Frank Cass, 2004), pp. 59–75

Katzenstein, P. J., *Policy and Politics in West Germany: the growth of a semi-sovereign state* (Philadelphia: Temple university press, 1987)

Katzenstein, P. J. (eds), *Tamed Power: Germany in Europe* (Cornell University Press, 1997)

Kitschelt, H. and W. Streeck (eds), *Germany: beyond the stable state* (London: Frank Cass, 2004)

Korte, K., 'Solutions for the decision dilemma: political styles of Germany's Chancellors' (April 2000), *German Politics 9 (1)*, pp. 1–22

Marsh, D., *The Bundesbank: the Bank that Rules Europe* (London: Mandarin, 1993)

Noelle-Neumann, E. (eds), *Allensbacher Jahrbuch der Demoskopie 10, 1993–7*, (Munich: Saur, 1997)

Paterson, W., 'Beyond semi-sovereignty: the new Germany in the New Europe' (August 1996), *German Politics 5 (2)*, pp. 167–84

Paterson, W., 'From the Bonn to the Berlin Republic' (April 2000), *German Politics 9 (1)*, pp. 23–40

Pedersen, T., *Germany France and the Integration of Europe* (London: Pinter, 1998)

Reinhardt, N., 'A turning point in the German EMU debate: the Baden-Württemberg regional election of March 1996' (April 1997), *German Politics 6 (1)*, pp. 77–99

Saalfeld, T., 'Germany: Bundestag and interest groups in a Parliamentary democracy', in P. Norton (eds), *Parliaments and Pressure Groups in Western Europe* (London: Frank Cass, 1990)

Scharpf, F., 'The joint-decision trap: lessons from German federalism and European integration' (1988), *Public Administration 66*, pp. 239–78.

Scharpf, F., 'The German disease' (January 1998), *Prospect*, www.prospectmagazine.co.uk

Schäuble, W. and Lamers, K., *Reflections on European Policy II: the future course of European integration* (03/05/99), www.cdu.de

Schmidt, M. G., 'West Germany: the policy of the middle way' (1987), *Journal of Public Policy 7 (2)*, pp. 139–77

Schwarz, H. P., *Geschichte der Bundesrepublik* (Wiesbanden: Deutsche Verlags-Anstalt, 1981)

Schwarz, H. P., 'Europe's central power' (Spring 2000), *Internationale Politik (1)* (Transatlantic edition), pp. 45–50

Sloam, J., 'Germany: President of the EU, Keeper of the Peace', *Institute for German Studies Working Paper 99/14* (Birmingham: University of Birmingham, 1999)

Weidenfeld, W. (ed.) *Deutsche Europapolitik* (Bonn: Europa Union, 1998)

Weidenfeld, W. (ed.) *A New Ostpolitik – Strategies for a United Europe* (Gütersloh: Bertelsmann, 1997)

ZDF, 'Wer interessiert für Europa', *Politbarometer* (broadcast) (24/05/04), www.zdf.de

Zimmer, M., 'Return of the Mittellage' (April 1997), *German Politics 6 (1)*, pp. 23–38

On social democracy, the German Social Democrats and SPD EU policy

Arend, P., *Die innerparteilichen Entwicklung der SPD, 1966–1975* (Bonn: Oldenbourg, 1975)

Bartels, H. P. and M. Machnig (eds), *Der Rasende Tanker: Analysen und Konzepte zur Modernisierung der sozialdemokratischen Organisation* (Göttingen: Steidl, 2001)

Bartels, H. P. et al., 'Heute für Reformen Kämpfen: Was die gewonnene Bundestagswahl für die nächste sozialdemokratische Generation bedeutet' (September 2002), *Berliner Republik*, www.b-republik.de

Bellers, J., *Reformpolitik und EWG-Strategie der SPD: die innen- und außenpolitischen Faktoren der europapolitischen Integrationswilligkeit einer Oppositionspartei (1957–63)* (Munich: tuduv, 1979)

Blair, T. and G. Schröder, 'Europe: the Third Way/die Neue Mitte', in B. Hombach *The Politics of the New Centre* (Oxford: Blackwell, 2000), pp. 157–77

Blair, T., 'Third Way, phase two' (March 2000), *Prospect*, www.prospectmagazine.co.uk

Blessing, K. (eds), *SPD 2000: die Modernisierung der SPD* (Bonn: SPD Vorstand, 1993)

Borchert, J. (eds), *Das Sozialdemokratische Modell* (Opladen: Leske & Budrich, 1996)

Braunthal, G., *The West German Social Democrats, 1969–1982: profile of a party in power* (Bolder: Westview, 1983)

262   Select Bibliography

Clement, W., 'EU: Wer macht eigentlich was?' (June 2001), *Vorwärts*, www.vorwaerts.de

Clement, W., *Rede des stellvertretenden SPD-Parteivorsitzenden, Bundesminister Wolfgang Clement, auf dem Parteitag der Sozialdemokratischen Partei Deutschlands in Bochum am 17. November 2003* (17/11/03), www.spd.de

Dettke, D., (eds), *The Challenge of Globalization for Germany's Social Democracy* (Oxford: Berghan, 1998)

Featherstone, K., *Socialist Parties and European Integration* (Manchester: Manchester University Press, 1988)

Federal Chancellor's Office, *Regierungserklärung von Bundeskanzler Schröder zu den Ergebnissen des Europäischen Rates in Kopenhagen* (19/12/02), www.bundeskanzler.de

Federal Chancellor's Office, *Schröder: Die Europäischer Union muss handlungsfähig bleiben!* (05/11/03), www.bundeskanzler.de

Gabriel, S., *Die Akkus nicht entladen und den Kompass nicht wegwerfen* (23/08/03), www.spd.de

Giddens, A., *The Third Way: the renewal of social democracy* (Cambridge: Polity Press, 1998)

Giddens, A., *'The Third Way and its Critics* (Cambridge: Polity Press, 2000)

Hombach, B., *The Politics of the New Centre* (Oxford: Blackwell, 2000)

Kitschelt, H., *The Transformation of European Social Democracy* (Cambridge: Cambridge University Press, 1994)

Lafontaine, O., *Speech to the Mannheim party conference, November 1995* (Bonn: Presseservice der SPD, November 1995)

Lafontaine, O. and C. Müller, Christa, *Keine Angst vor Globalisierung* (Bonn: Dietz, 1998)

Lindner, J., 'Europapolitik der SPD Bundestagsfraktion' (1996), *Perspektivends (4)*, pp. 293–305

Lodge, J., *The European Policy of the SPD* (London: Sage, 1976)

Lösche, P., 'Lose verkoppelte Anarchie: zur aktuellen Situation von Volksparteien am Beispiel der SPD' (October 1993), *Aus Politik und Geschichte (43)*

Lösche, P., 'Die SPD nach Mannheim: Stukturprobleme und aktuelle Entwicklungen' (February 1996), *Aus Politik und Geschichte (6)*, pp. 20–28

Lösche, P. and Walter, F., *Staatspartei, Volkspartei, Quotapartei* (Wissensch. BG, Dst., 1992)

Machnig, M, 'Die Kampa als SPD-Wahlkampfzentrale der Bundestagswahl '98' (1999), *Forschungsjournal Neue Soziale Bewegungen 3*, pp. 20–39

Machnig, M., *Auf dem Weg zur Netzwerkpartei* (November 2000), www.spd.de

Machnig, M., 'Organisation ist Politik' (2001), *Berliner Republik (2)*, www.b-republik.de

Maull, H. (eds), 'Vier Monate rot-grüne Außenpolitik' (March 1999), *Trier Arbeitspapiere zur Internationalen Politik (1)*

Meyer, T., 'Soziale Demokratie statt demokratischer Sozialismus. Alte SPD und neue Realität: Ketzereien eines bekennenden Sozialdemokraten', *Frankfurter Rundschau* (18/09/03), www.fr-aktuell.de

Miller, S., *Kleine Geschichte der SPD* (Bonn: Dietz, 2002)

Miskimmon, A. and J. Sloam, 'A third way for social democratic foreign and security policy?' (2–4 September 2003), *Paper Presented to the UACES Annual Conference*, Newcastle

Padgett, S., *The German Social Democratic Party: between old and new Left*, in
D.S. Bell and E. Shaw (eds) *Conflict and Cohesion in the West European Social
Democratic Parties* (London: Pinter, 1994), pp. 10–30
Padgett, S. and W. Paterson, 'The rise and fall of the West German Left'
(March–April 1991), *New Left Review (186)*, pp. 46–77
Paterson, W., 'Back to the future: 1968 and the Red–Green Government', in
M. Butler and R. Evans, *The Challenge of German Culture* (London: Palgrave,
2000), pp. 199–212
Paterson, W., *The SPD and European Integration* (Farnborough: Saxon House, 1973)
Paterson, W. and J. Sloam, 'Gerhard Schröder and the Unlikely Victory of the
German Social Democrats', in D. Conradt *et al.* (eds) *Germany's New Politics*
(Oxford: Berghan, 2004)
Randzio-Plath, C, 'Aktionsplan Europa' (December 1998), *Vorwärts*, www.spd.de
Roslowsky, D., *West Germany's Foreign Policy: the impact of the Social Democrats and
the Greens* (London: Greenwood, 1987)
Roth, M., *Die Europapolitik der SPD: Positionen, Probleme und Perspektiven zwischen
Maastricht und Regierungskonferenz* (Frankfurt: Johann Wolfgang-Goethe
Universität, 1996)
Samland, D., 'So weit weg, so wichtig' (2000), *Der Berliner Republik (1)*, pp. 6–8
Scharping, R., *Europäische Perspektiven in den Neunzigen Jahren* (Bonn, Presseservice
der SPD 231/94, 05/04/94)
Scholz, O., *Gerechtigkeit und Solidarische Mitte im 21. Jahrhundert* (2003), www.spd.de
Schröder, G., *Speech to the 5th PES Congress* (07/05/01), www.pes-congress.de
Schröder, G., *Rede Gerhard Schröder zum Themenbereich: Außen- und
Sicherheitspolitik* (21/11/01), www.spd-parteitag.de
Schröder, G., *Rede des SPD-Parteivorsitzenden, Bundeskanzler Gerhard Schröder, auf
dem Europadelegiertenkonferenz der Sozialdemokratischen Partei Deutschlands in
Bochum am. 16. November 2003* (16/11/03), www.spd.de
Schröder, G., 'Regierungserklärung von Bundeskanzler Schröder am 14. März
2003 vor dem Deutschen Bundestag' (Deutscher Bundestag, 14/03/03),
www.bundestag.de
Schwall-Düren, A, *Rede zur 40. Jahrestag des Elysée-Vertrages am 16. Januar im
Deutschen Bundestag* (16/01/03), www.spdfraktion.de
Schwall-Düren, A., *Rede im Bundestag* (2003), www.spdfraktion.de
Sloam, J., 'Responsibility for Europe: the EU policy of the German Social
Democrats since 1990' (2003), *German Politics 12 (1)*, pp. 59–78
Sylvia, S. J., 'Loosely coupled anarchy: the fragmentation of the Left', in S. Padgett
(eds), *Parties and Party Systems in the New Germany* (Aldershot: Dartmouth,
1993), pp. 171–89
Thierse, W., *Die Sozialdemokratie muss dem Mainstream widerstehen* (12/09/03),
www.spd.de
Unger, F., A. Wehr and K. Schönwälder, *New Democrats, New Labor, Neue
Sozialdemokraten* (Bonn: Elefanten Press, 1998)
Vogel, H.-J., *Das Europäische Haus: Perspektiven europäischer Entwicklung* (Bonn,
SPD Bundestagsfraktion, 13/10/1989)
Verheugen, G., 'Germany and the EU Council Presidency' (1999), *ZEI Discussion
Paper*, Bonn
Verheugen, G., *Die Erweiterung der Europäischen Union – Strategien für die Bewältigung
der erweiterungsbedingten Herausforderungen* (03/04/01), www.europa.eu.int

Walter, F., *Vom Proletariat zum Neue Mitte* (Berlin: Alexander Fest, 2002)
Wieczorek-Zeul, H., *Sozialdemokratische Politik in Europa* (21/10/97), www.spd.de
Wieczorek-Zeul, H., *Was ist das Ziel der Debatte?* (09/09/03), www.spd.de

Party documents

Bündnis 90/Die Grünen Vorstand, *Bündnis 90/Die Grünen: 1998–2002. Vier Jahren für einen politischen Neuanfang* (1998), www.gruene.de
SPD Grundwertekommission, *Dritte Wege – Neue Mitte: sozialdemokratischer Markierungen für Reformpolitick im Zeitalter Globalisierung* (Berlin: SPD Parteivorstand, September 1999)
SPD Bundestagsfraktion, *Europapolitik der SPD-Bundestagsfraktion in der 14. Legislaturperiode 1998–2002: eine Bilanz* (2002), www.spdfraktion.de.
SPD Vorstand, *Basic Policy Programme of the Social Democratic Party of Germany* (20/12/89), www.spd.de
SPD Vorstand, *Der Neue Weg: ökologisch, sozial, wirtschaftlich stark – Regierungsprogramm, 1990–1994* (Bonn: 1990)
SPD Vorstand, *Jahrbuch der SPD, 1988–90* (Bonn: 1990)
SPD Vorstand, *Jahrbuch der SPD 1991–2* (Bonn: 1992)
SPD Vorstand, *Reformen für Deutschland – Regierungsprogramm 1994–1998* (Bonn: 1994)
SPD Vorstand, *Jahrbuch der SPD 1995–6* (Bonn: 1996)
SPD Vorstand, *Reformen für Europa: Zwischenbericht der Schwerpunktkommission Europapolitk* (26/05/97), www.spd.de
SPD Vorstand, *Arbeit, Innovation und Gerechtigkeit – Regierungsprogramm 1998–2002* (1998), www.spd.de
SPD Vorstand, *Leitantrag: Sicherheit im Wandel* (20/03/01), www.spd.de
SPD Vorstand, *Leitantrag: Verantwortung für Europa* (30/04/01), www.spd.de
SPD Vorstand, *Rede Gerhard Schröder zum Themenbereich: Außen- und Sicherheitspolitik* (21/11/01) (party conference in Nuremberg), www.spd-parteitag.de
SPD Vorstand, *Erneuerung und Zusammenhalt – Wir in Deutschland: Regierungsprogramm 2002–2006* (2002), www.spd.de
SPD and Bündnis 90/Die Grünen, *Erneuerung – Gerechtigkeit – Nachaltigkeit* (coalition agreement) (2002), www.spd.de
SPD Vorstand, *Europamanifest der SPD* (November 2003), www.spd.de

Index